"*Post-Christian* is a provocative overvie\ ping post face. As the sea of faith tempoi fidence to debate ideas, raise children, and build institutions. Gene Veith explains the problems of constructing our own worlds, exalting barrenness, and building society without community. Some leaders say we'll survive by secularizing the church, but this book shows a better way: pray and work for a new reformation."

Marvin Olasky, Editor in Chief, *World* magazine

No one has taught me how to think like a Christian more than Gene Veith. *Post-Christian* just may be the magnum opus of a writer and thinker who has already contributed a body of work of immeasurable worth to the church. This book is a library in miniature for the Christian who wants to navigate the post-Christian world biblically, thoughtfully, and faithfully. It should be on the shelf in every Christian home.

Karen Swallow Prior, author, *On Reading Well* and *Fierce Convictions: The Extraordinary Life of Hannah More: Poet, Reformer, Abolitionist*

"Gene Veith's *Post-Christian* is a logical, cogent, sensible, no-spin, facts-based, unapologetic analysis of the zeitgeist in Western culture. Which is to say, it's not very politically correct. But that's a good thing! In this posttruth, reality-denying cultural moment, we need the grounded sanity this book provides. Highly informative and well-researched, *Post-Christian* is a treasure trove of wisdom and a valuable resource for the church's revitalization."

Brett McCracken, Senior Editor, The Gospel Coalition; author, *Uncomfortable: The Awkward and Essential Challenge of Christian Community*

"In the barrage of books attempting to make sense of our particular cultural moment, few authors exhibit the range of thought and clarity of mind that is on display in *Post-Christian*. Gene Veith is a competent guide through the maze of exhausted ideas that characterize late modernity. Science, technology, sex, politics, religion—nothing has escaped the corrosive effects of the attempt to abandon Christianity. This is, however, not a book of despair but of hope. As Veith reminds us, the truths of the Christian faith continually reassert themselves, for they are rooted in reality itself."

Mark T. Mitchell, Dean of Academic Affairs, Patrick Henry College

POST-CHRISTIAN

POST-CHRISTIAN

A Guide to Contemporary
Thought and Culture

Gene Edward Veith Jr.

WHEATON, ILLINOIS

Post-Christian: A Guide to Contemporary Thought and Culture

Copyright © 2020 by Gene Edward Veith Jr.

Published by Crossway
          1300 Crescent Street
          Wheaton, Illinois 60187

Cover design: Tim Green, Faceout Studios

Cover image: Getty Images #530189514. iStock #1003543236

First printing 2020

Printed in the United States of America

Unless otherwise indicated, Scripture quotations are from the ESV® Bible (The Holy Bible, English Standard Version®), copyright © 2001 by Crossway, a publishing ministry of Good News Publishers. Used by permission. All rights reserved.

Scripture quotations marked KJV are from the *King James Version* of the Bible.

Scripture references marked RSV are from *The Revised Standard Version*. Copyright ©1946, 1952, 1971, 1973 by the Division of Christian Education of the National Council of the Churches of Christ in the U.S.A.

Trade paperback ISBN: 978-1-4335-6578-6
ePub ISBN: 978-1-4335-6581-6
PDF ISBN: 978-1-4335-6579-3
Mobipocket ISBN: 978-1-4335-6580-9

Library of Congress Cataloging-in-Publication Data

Names: Veith, Gene Edward, Jr., 1951- author.
Title: Post Christian : a guide to contemporary thought and culture / Gene Edward Veith Jr.
Description: Wheaton : Crossway, 2020. | Includes bibliographical references and index.
Identifiers: LCCN 2019023077 (print) | LCCN 2019023078 (ebook) | ISBN 9781433565786 (trade
    paperback) | ISBN 9781433565793 (pdf) | ISBN 9781433565809 (mobi) | ISBN 9781433565816 (epub)
Subjects: LCSH: Christianity and culture.
Classification: LCC BR115.C8 V369 2020 (print) | LCC BR115.C8 (ebook) | DDC 261–dc23
LC record available at https://lccn.loc.gov/2019023077
LC ebook record available at https://lccn.loc.gov/2019023078

Crossway is a publishing ministry of Good News Publishers.

VP		30	29	28	27	26	25	24	23	22	21	20
15	14	13	12	11	10	9	8	7	6	5	4	3	2	1

To my grandchildren
Anastasia, Dorothea, Elizabeth, Evangeline, Hannah, John,
Lucy, Margaret, Mary, Michael, Samuel, and Thomas

Take but degree away, untune that string,
And, hark, what discord follows. . . .
Then everything includes itself in power,
Power into will, will into appetite;
And appetite, an universal wolf,
So doubly seconded with will and power,
Must make perforce an universal prey
And last eat up himself.

William Shakespeare (1601)
Troilus and Cressida,
Act 1. Scene 3. Lines 109–10, 122–27

Contents

Acknowledgments

This book is the product of many years of observing contemporary culture. Many people helped me to do so, more than I can mention here. I had long thought that I should update *Postmodern Times*.[1] My former student Jordan Sillars helped me with some research toward that end. Marlin Detweiler, who used *Postmodern Times* as part of his online *Veritas* curriculum, forced the issue, and his need for a new edition was a catalyst for this project. I soon realized that too much had happened since 1994 and that the previous book needed not an update but a sequel.

My *Cranach* blog, named after the Reformation artist and vocation exemplar Lucas Cranach, made me have to pay close attention to cultural developments. Thanks to Patheos for hosting me (https://www.patheos.com/blogs/geneveith/). Readers of my blog will notice certain themes and topics that we discussed online showing up in this book. I appreciate the commenters on my blog who helped me think through some of these issues.

Above all, I want to thank my wife, Jackie, for encouraging me to take on this project, though it interrupted our already busy retirement.

1. Gene Edward Veith Jr., *Postmodern Times: A Christian Guide to Contemporary Thought and Culture* (Wheaton, IL: Crossway, 1994).

Introduction

After Postmodernism

On September 11, 2001, when the World Trade Center in New York City collapsed, I thought that postmodernism was over. I was wrong.

I had written a book entitled *Postmodern Times: A Christian Guide to Contemporary Thought and Culture*, which came out in 1994.[1] I had drawn on Thomas Oden's milestones for the phases of Western thinking. The premodern era, he said, the age in which both classicism and Christianity were dominant, came to an end on July 14, 1789, with the fall of the Bastille: the French Revolution enthroned the Goddess of Reason in Notre Dame Cathedral, ushering in the Age of Modernism, with its trust in science, progress, and social engineering. That era, in turn, came to an end two hundred years later, on November 9, 1989, with the fall of the Berlin Wall. Communism was the ultimate expression of modernist ideology, but it led not to liberation and the elimination of all our problems, as promised, but to tyranny, economic collapse, and mass murder. The collapse of the Soviet Union and its empire, according to Oden, marked the beginning of the postmodern era.[2]

Oden saw postmodernism in a different light than I did. He saw it as a reversion to the sensibility of the premodern times, marking the

---

1. Gene Edward Veith, *Postmodern Times: A Christian Guide to Contemporary Thought and Culture* (Wheaton, IL: Crossway, 1994).
2. Thomas C. Oden, *Two Worlds: Notes on the Death of Modernity in America and Russia* (Downers Grove, IL: InterVarsity Press, 1992). See also Oden's book *After Modernity—What?* (Grand Rapids, MI: Zondervan, 1990).

end of theological liberalism and making possible a return to Christian orthodoxy. Oden wrote from the perspective of a mainline theologian, and, indeed, the collapse of modernistic, rationalistic liberal theology has been one of the great contributions of postmodern thought, though other kinds of liberal theology would rise up in its place. I, however, wrote from the perspective of an academic in the humanities, in which postmodernism had to do with moral, cultural, and intellectual relativism. This worldview, which Oden called "hypermodernism," was manifesting itself not just in the academic world but in popular culture, the arts, literature, politics, and religion.

But immediately after the 9/11 terrorist attacks, I thought I was witnessing another of Oden's milestones, a building's demolition that marked the end of an era and the beginning of something new. Postmodernists believe that reality is a *construction*—of the mind, the will, the culture—rather than an objective truth. But those planes flying into those skyscrapers, taking everyone by surprise, were no mental constructions. Nor were the deaths of nearly three thousand victims. Nor was the heroism of the firefighters, police, medics, and ordinary people caught up in the horrors of that day. This was all objectively *real*.

And as the dust was still settling, I was hearing on television, reading in the press, and listening to conversations that were distinctly *non*-postmodern. In considering the terrorists, their background, and their ideology, no one sounded like a relativist. What the terrorists did was *evil*, people were saying, and what the first responders did who ran into the buildings as they were collapsing to rescue people was *good*. It sounded as if not all cultures are equally valid after all. Maybe not all religions are equally beneficent. Meanwhile, the notoriously jaded and cynical New York arts scene was proclaiming "the end of irony"—that signature quality of postmodern expressions—and promising works of sincerity and human values.

Above all, in the aftermath of 9/11, there was a palpable sense of transcendence. The tribalism encouraged by postmodernism gave way to a deep experience of national unity. And even notable secularist journalists were saying to the families of victims, "God bless you," and "You are in our prayers."

But after the shock faded, so did the moral clarity. Moral, cultural, intellectual, and religious relativism surged back. But there was a difference.

Before, all religions, in elite opinion, were considered to be equally good. Afterward, all religions were considered to be equally bad. Terrorism began to be defined not as a moral transgression but as what you get when a group of people believe that "they have the only truth" and that "theirs is the only valid religion." The terrorists were Islamic "fundamentalists," so not Islam but fundamentalism was to blame, with Christian "fundamentalists" being considered, in many circles, as no better. Religious pluralism used to mean that different beliefs and traditions were allowed to exist side by side. But with the interfaith services that became ubiquitous after 9/11 and the reaction against every kind of fundamentalism, pluralism became something more like polytheism. You must accept all of these deities and religious traditions, but you are not allowed to believe in one of them only. Alternatively, you could reject all of those organized religions. Modernist atheists argued that God does not exist because anything supernatural has no place in their scientific, materialist worldview. Postmodernist atheists argued that God is simply a cultural construction. But the New Atheists launched *moral* criticisms of God, arguing that religion—particularly the Christian religion—is to blame for the world's problems. Many more Americans held on, in the postmodernist way, to their own private, interior, personal religions, constructing their own theologies and claiming to be "spiritual, but not religious."

The brief, shining moment of national unity was also shattered. Thirsting for retaliation, America went to war, only to find that the American ideals of democracy, liberty, and human rights might not be so universal after all, at least in societies that lack our classical and Christian infrastructure. The political divisions that go back to the Vietnam War reasserted themselves. So did the moral equivalence that is a corollary of relativism: Is our attacking the Taliban any different from Al Qaeda attacking us?

Postmodernism did not end with the fall of the World Trade Center. Rather, it hardened, becoming more political and less playful, more dogmatic and less tolerant. As we have moved deeper into the twenty-first century and new issues and new developments have come to the fore, postmodernism has mutated, taking on new forms and adapting to new conditions.

After Postmodernism, What?

In 1994, when *Postmodern Times* was published, the technological medium I discussed was television. I said some things about computers and how they could be interconnected to form a kind of "cyberspace."[3] The Internet was just starting to get off the ground when I was writing my book, but it was nothing like the all-pervasive information universe that it has become, with its social media and fake news. I knew something big was coming, referring to the "as yet unimagined electronic technology" on the horizon.[4] I did imagine the advent of virtual reality technology. I said, "The much-heralded union of computers, television, and video games will enable us to put on a helmet that will create the illusion that we are in the middle of a computer-generated world."[5] I then turned this, as yet unrealized, technology into a metaphor for the postmodernist worldview:

> According to the postmodernists, all reality is virtual reality. We are all wearing helmets that project our own separate little worlds. We can experience these worlds and lose ourselves in them, but they are not real, nor is one person's world exactly the same as someone else's. We are not creating our own reality, however. Rather, we accept a reality made by someone else. Just as the corporations that manufacture the virtual reality technology program the fantasy, the so-called objective world that we experience is actually programmed by large, impersonal social institutions. Despite our heroics in fantasy land, zapping space aliens and freeing the holographic princess, we are only playing a game. We are actually passive and at the mercy of our programmers.[6]

Contemporary culture has changed from what it was in 1994, with new issues to consider and new ways of thinking to understand. But

---

3. Veith, *Postmodern Times*, 82.
4. Veith, *Postmodern Times*, 204.
5. Veith, *Postmodern Times*, 61.
6. Veith, *Postmodern Times*, 61.

many of these changes are developments from earlier trends and consequences of what came before.

Postmodern Times discussed the sexual revolution in terms of extramarital sex; now the issues are homosexuality, pornography, and sex robots. In the 1990s we were deconstructing literature; in the twenty-first century we are deconstructing marriage. In the 1990s we were constructing ideas; in the twenty-first century we are constructing the human body. In the 1990s we had feminism; in the twenty-first century we have transgenderism. In the 1990s we were urged to embrace multiculturalism; in the twenty-first century we are warned about committing cultural appropriation. Pluralism has given way to identity politics. Relativism has given way to speech codes. Humanism has given way to transhumanism, the union of human beings and machines.

Not all of the new movements and developments are exaggerations of postmodernism, though many of them are. Hardcore postmodernists had denied the existence of the self, insisting that our experience of individual consciousness is itself a cultural construction. But today the self is back in vogue, along with its related values of autonomy and identity, to the point that we are hearing things like, "I was born in the wrong body"—a distinction between the soul and body that sounds almost Platonic, though today it accounts for transgenderism. Postmodernism used to be cynical and ironic. Today, emotion and sincerity are prized. Realism in art and fiction is back in fashion, sort of. According to one critic, irony has given way to the aesthetics of "trance," the zoned-out concentration of someone playing a video game or immersed in social media.[7]

These new developments and fashions mean, some are saying, that postmodernism is dead. So what shall we call whatever is taking its place? We must "embrace post-Postmodernism," says one scholar, "and pray for a better name."[8] Proposed alternatives include metamodernism, transpostmodernism, postmillennialism, altermodernism,

---

7. Alan Kirby, "The Death of Postmodernism and Beyond," *Philosophy Now* 58 (November/December 2006), accessed June 10, 2019, https://philosophynow.org/issues/58/The_Death_of_Postmodernism_And_Beyond.

8. Tom Turner, *City as Landscape: A Post Post-modern View of Design and Planning* (London: Taylor & Francis, 1995), 10.

cosmodernism, digimodernism, performatism, pseudomodern, postdigital, posthumanism.[9] These proposed terms refer to different movements, though they are mostly variations and extensions of postmodernism, with some twists.

This book is not an update but a sequel to *Postmodern Times*, offering a new "Christian guide to contemporary thought and culture." My approach will not be to trace down all of these oddly named movements, many of which are highly transitory and have already faded from history. Rather, I will look at our times as being post-Christian, what we are left with when we try to abandon the Christian worldview. Modernism, with its scientific materialism and trust in evolutionary progress, is post-Christian. So is postmodernism, which accurately recognizes the failures and weaknesses of modernism, but which has turned to alternative but equally non-Christian ways of approaching life. We still have modernists around today, as well as postmodernists and digimodernists, posthumanists, and the rest. They are all post-Christians.

The problem with that term, *post-Christian*, is that it implies that Christianity is somehow over. It is not. In fact, the various alternatives throw the superiority—and the truth—of Christianity in high relief. And some of the most cutting-edge observers are heralding the emergence of something completely different: the postsecular.

The Universal Wolf

Our contemporary secularist thought and culture are not nearly as formidable as they may seem. Post-Christian ways of thinking and living are running into dead ends and fatal contradictions.

William Shakespeare in 1601 wrote about the course of social, moral, and spiritual disorder in words that read like a prophecy of our own times:

> Take but degree away, untune that string,
> And, hark, what discord follows. . . .
> Then everything includes itself in power,

---

9. See the catalog of alternatives in "Post-postmodernism," Wikipedia, accessed June 10, 2019, https://en.wikipedia.org/wiki/Post-postmodernism. See also Alison Gibbons, "Postmodernism Is Dead: What Comes Next?," *Times* Literary Supplement, June 12, 2017.

Power into will, will into appetite;
And appetite, an universal wolf,
So doubly seconded with will and power,
Must make perforce an universal prey
And last eat up himself.[10]

The lines are from Shakespeare's strangely neglected tragedy *Troilus and Cressida*, a twisted rendition of the Trojan War. They are part of a larger speech by the wise and crafty Ulysses lamenting the disorder displayed by *both* the Greeks *and* the Trojans. *Degree* here means not just social hierarchy but, as the editor of the modern edition, Virgil K. Whitaker, explains, "the cosmic order" of God's creation—his moral, social, and natural laws.[11] We are used to thinking of the Trojan War in terms of Homeric heroism and the virtues of classical civilization, but Shakespeare focuses instead on the characters' pride, unbridled passions, and discord. Similarly, we may look to Shakespeare's own times as representing the pinnacle of Western art and literature. But, clearly, Shakespeare has his own society in mind as he, a Christian poet, fiercely criticizes the rampant sinfulness of his age.

Post-Christians of every variety reject *degree*, as we hear in common statements such as "life has no meaning," "the universe is absurd," "there are no absolutes." But what makes these lines from Shakespeare so uncanny, so startlingly relevant to our own times four centuries later, is that they zero in on the three major preoccupations of contemporary thought and culture: power, will, and appetite.

For both post-Marxists on the left and Nietzscheans on the right, all institutions, all governments, all art, all moral beliefs, and all religions are nothing more than *a mask for power*. All of culture—the family, social institutions, philosophical systems—is nothing more than one group exercising power over another group (men over women, whites over racial minorities, heterosexuals over homosexuals, humans over animals, etc.). Thus, every dimension of life is politicized and critiqued as part of a system of oppression. The only way to resist this

---

10. Shakespeare, *Troilus and Cressida*, act 1, scene 3, lines 109–10, 122–27. Quoted from *The History of Troilus and Cressida*, ed. Virgil K. Whitaker, in *William Shakespeare: The Complete Works* (New York: Penguin, 1969), 986.

11. See Whitaker's introduction to the play, 978–79. He observes that this cosmic order and the disastrous consequences of violating it are continual themes in Shakespeare.

oppression is to be *transgressive* and to seize power for your own group, which will include exercising oppression against your enemies (silencing them, marginalizing them, and otherwise punishing them).

Nietzsche stressed not just power but the "will to power," so the human will also has a central role today. Those who believe in abortion call themselves "pro-choice." *Whatever the woman chooses is right for her.* If she *chooses* to have the baby, then the child has value. If she *chooses* not to have the baby, then the child is nothing more than a growth in her womb that can be removed, with no qualms of conscience. If the woman is forced to have the baby *against her will*, by pro-life Christians and the patriarchal power structure, this and the groups that oppose her decision are evil. But in every case, *the will* is what bestows moral meaning. The left makes much of the will in its various "liberation" movements, but often so does the right, stressing the fulfillment of the individual's will in the distinctly libertarian understanding of freedom.

But as Christians have always known, the completely unfettered will is not free; rather, it becomes a slave to sin and to the *desires of the flesh* (John 8:36; Gal. 5:16–24). Desire is a function of what Shakespeare calls *appetite*. Traditionally and in all cultures, our appetites need to be controlled. But today's assumption is that we have a right to the satisfaction of our appetites. We see this most dramatically in the new sexual ethos. Young people have sexual desires, so they cannot be expected to wait until marriage to fulfill them. And if some people have sexual desires for someone of their own sex, there can be no moral objection. Having sexual desire for someone other than one's spouse is considered a valid reason for divorce and for abandoning one's children. Appetite supersedes all other considerations. Appetite also governs our economic lives, serving as the engine of consumerism, advertising, and our debt-based economy.

For Shakespeare, the coming together of power, will, and appetite forms a "universal wolf" that devours *everything*. As we have been seeing in contemporary thought and culture, this wolf is eating up universities, laws, technology, the family, the arts, the media, and churches. But, having done so, there comes a point, says Shakespeare, when the wolf starts eating up himself.

Modernism unleashed skepticism against all traditions and authorities, all in the name of reason; whereupon postmodernism unleashed that skepticism against reason itself. All that remains now is to be skeptical about skepticism. Universities have taken academic freedom so far that they now censor dissenting views, impose speech codes, and in other ways inhibit academic freedom. Humanism has advanced to the point of becoming antihuman. Progress has evolved to become neoprimitivism.

But when the universal wolf has finished devouring himself, his predation will be at an end. Life might start to flourish again. The course of post-Christian culture, when it ends in self-contradiction and catastrophe, may herald cultural rebirth. For example, the universal wolf of sexual permissiveness now has to face the #MeToo movement, in which women are rising up against their exploitation by the sexual revolution. Men and the society as a whole are realizing that the sexual appetite must be restricted and controlled after all. Whether this insight will lead to a renaissance of the family remains to be seen, but it demonstrates how the contemporary condition is making the Christian worldview and traditional values highly relevant again. Similarly, progressive education is failing so obviously and on such a vast scale that it has inspired a revival of classical education. Scholars from across the ideological spectrum, troubled by the nihilistic dead end that the universal wolf has brought them to, are trying to find ways to recover truth, community, morality, beauty, nature, and meaning.

To be sure, such efforts may, perhaps more likely, lead to new bad ideas and false worldviews rather than a return to biblical realism. But Christians should be undaunted at the post-Christian onslaughts, knowing that such onslaughts are ultimately doomed, in this world as well as the next.

In fact, some scholars and observers are seeing something genuinely different emerging after modernism and postmodernism and their offspring have devoured themselves. They are calling it "postsecular."

This Book

This book is divided into four parts, addressing four major facets of contemporary thought and culture: (1) how we relate to reality, including chapters on constructivism, science, and technology; (2) how we relate to our bodies, focusing mainly on issues of sex and having children; (3) how we relate to other people, including issues of culture and politics; (4) and how we relate to God, with discussions of the persistence of religion (or spirituality) even among those who claim not to be religious.

Each of these sections has an "arc," a consistent sequence of development. In each of these four sections, I describe the current picture and give its historical and cultural context. I also show the problems with the current state of affairs that even today's secularists are admitting. The last chapter in each section suggests how Christians can offer solutions to those problems.

The entire book also has an arc, a movement from the consequences of secularism to the prospects for a postsecular society.

PART 1

REALITY

1

Constructing Our Own Worlds

The Ptolomaic Counterrevolution

One of the greatest achievements of the last few centuries has been the rise of science. The systematic empirical study of the objective universe has opened up new vistas of knowledge, and applying this knowledge has given us technological marvels. The success of science has led many people to believe that religion is no longer necessary, either to explain existence or to solve our problems. Many people, so impressed are they with science, believe that the physical realm—what science can study empirically—is all that exists, a philosophy known as naturalism or materialism.

And yet a dominant worldview today rejects the very possibility of objective knowledge. There is no "nature," in the sense of an external physical order of which we are a part and to which we are subject. And the material realm is wholly subordinate to the mind, which shapes it at will.

Historically, from ancient times all the way through the age of science, human beings in the West have sought to understand reality by using their minds to discover the truth about things. Postmodernists and their successors, however, are *constructivists*. Truth is not something we discover, they say, but something we *construct*. Morality is not something built into human *nature*; rather, it is an individual or cultural *construction*. Knowledge comes not so much from a passively receptive intellect, but from the will; specifically, the will to power. And since different cultures and individuals can construct different truths, truth is relative.

It is difficult to imagine how science can continue to flourish in a climate of constructivism. Already, science is being "interrogated," as they say, for its patriarchal, imperialistic, and racist biases. While postmodernists and their successors continue to invoke science as a bastion against religion, they are mostly interested not so much in science but in technology. That is, what can be *constructed* from science.

Meanwhile, the public has drifted into what is essentially a gnostic worldview, in which the material universe is considered to be void of any significance. That the natural function of sexuality is to engender children must not be allowed to limit our sexual behavior. And if a man desires to be a woman, or vice versa, the body itself is subject to reconstruction.

With constructivism, human beings attempt to take on the role of creator. But when they do, they end up repudiating reality itself.

Reason, Empiricism, and the Self

So how did the Age of Reason dissolve into constructivism, relativism, and the conviction that we can never know any kind of absolute truth?

The classical thinkers of the ancient world, such as Aristotle and Plato, had already taken reason about as far as it could go. The scholastic theologians of the Middle Ages managed to Christianize that heritage, making reason foundational to Christian theology. Read Saint Thomas Aquinas, whose *Summa Theologica* balances reason and revelation in a web of logical *syllogisms* on everything from the existence of God to the nature of the soul. His logical proofs have been compared to the buttresses that support the soaring walls of a Gothic cathedral, buttresses that are also supported by flying buttresses of their own.

The role of human reason was so great in medieval theology that, according to the Reformers, it took the place of God's revealed Word in Scripture. Subjecting revelation to reason made human beings, not

God, the authority in Christianity, a human centeredness that the Reformers also saw in the institution of the papacy. The Reformers made the Bible the authority in Christianity, not the pope and not reason, but they did not reject reason altogether. They put reason in its place, as it were, that place being nature, as a function of God's orderly creation. Nature includes human nature. The human capacity for reason is a facet of God's image, so that reasoning is an important tool for problem solving, earthly government, and carrying out one's God-given vocations. So how could the Enlightenment of the late seventeenth and eighteenth centuries be more of an "Age of Reason" than that?

The medieval church insisted that they too believe in Scripture, faith, grace, and Christ, but the Reformation insisted on the "solas"— authority in the church is by Scripture *alone*, as opposed to the Roman formula of Scripture plus the church magisterium plus church tradition; we are saved by faith *alone*, not faith plus works; this is possible by God's grace *alone*, not grace plus our merits; our hope is in Christ *alone*, not the meditation of Christ plus the mediation of the saints plus the meditation of the church.

Similarly, the Enlightenment took a "solas" approach to reason. Disillusioned with the carnage of the seventeenth-century wars of religion, many thoughtful Europeans embraced "reason alone." Not by reason plus revelation, but what we could call *sola ratione*.

But this made the human mind, once again, the measure of all things and the authority over everything. Reason was once grounded in God and in nature; "logic" comes from the classical/Christian concept of *logos*, the cosmically ordering Word of God that underlies all creation and which became flesh in Jesus Christ (John 1:1–18). But then reason, while claiming the ability to determine objective truth, became grounded in human subjectivity. What the Enlightenment really promoted in its exaltation of reason and of "rational" values such as liberty, equality, and fraternity was a new humanism. *Sola humanitate.* This, in turn, led to the exaltation not so much of human beings in general but of the individual self. *Ego solus.*

Baylor theologian Ralph Wood traces this unmooring of reason from the objectivity of God and of nature, focusing on the pivotal role of the French philosopher René Descartes (1596–1650). Descartes sought absolute certainty, which rationalists insist upon to this very day ("prove to me *for certain* that God exists"; "I won't believe unless I can be absolutely *sure*"), even though achieving such certainty is impossible for our limited minds. So Descartes launched upon a mental experiment, systematically doubting *everything*, until he found something that could not be doubted. That bedrock truth, the only certainty, is that I exist: "I think, therefore, I am." I can doubt your existence, but not my own. Now upon this foundation, Descartes went on to prove the existence of other minds and of God himself. But his legacy is the radical skepticism that has come to characterize the post-Enlightenment world, in which every authority, institution, custom, truth claim, moral principle, and religious teaching is questioned and usually found wanting. (Notice today how logic, which is based on the notion of the objective *logos*, has been replaced by critical thinking, which in school curricula simply means learning to criticize.)

In making the thinking self the basis of certainty, Descartes separated reason from God and from nature. This sent the mind, the soul, and the body running in different directions. As Wood says:

> It is safe to say that, prior to Descartes, human reason seated itself either in the natural order or else in divine revelation. In the medieval tradition, reason brought these two thought-originating sources into harmony. Thus were mind, soul, and body regarded as having an inseparable relation: they were wondrously intertwined. So also, in this bi-millennial way of construing the world, was the created order seen as having multiple causes—first and final, no less than efficient and material causes. This meant that creation was not a thing that stood over against us, but as the realm in which we participate—living and moving and having our being there, as both ancient Stoics and St. Paul insisted. . . .
>
> After Descartes, by contrast, the sensible realm becomes a purposeless thing, a domain of physical causes awaiting our own mastery and manipulation. Nature no longer encompasses humanity as its crowning participant. The soul drops out altogether and is replaced by disembodied mind. Shorn of its spiritual qualities, the mind becomes a calculating faculty for bare, abstract thinking. To

yank the mind free from the body is also to untether it from history, tradition, and locality. After Descartes, the mind allegedly stands outside these given things so as to operate equally well at anytime and anywhere. Insofar as belief in God is kept at all, it is an entailment of the human. Atheism was sure to follow. Marx made truth itself a human production, whether social or economic. Nietzsche went further, insisted that nothing whatever can stand over against the human will to power, not even socially constructed truth.[1]

So, beginning with reason, the Enlightenment soon led to romanticism, with its exaltation of the self, and to constructivism, with its insistence that the mind creates what it perceives.

Though the Enlightenment is called the "Age of Reason," it was never about reason, as such. We already had reason. The main reason that the period of the late seventeenth and eighteenth century is hailed as the beginning of modernism is that it coincided with the rise of modern science. Deductive reason, with its abstractions and logical syllogisms, played an important role during this period, but it soon gave way to inductive reason, that is, to empiricism. Human beings not only knew reality by the intellect but *experienced* reality by means of the senses. Careful observation of nature led to one discovery after another. The observer, detached from nature, can now force nature to give up its secrets.

Kant's "Copernican Revolution"

There is a subjective element even in empirical observation. Our senses can deceive us. Direct perception falls short of capturing the full truth. Someone who says, "I only believe what I can see," must believe that objects get smaller when they are farther away. Or looking down a highway, the empiricist must conclude that the two sides of the road grow ever closer together until they meet on the horizon. This is what we perceive. But our *reason* tells us that despite what we see, the parallel sides

---

1. Ralph C. Wood, "Walker Percy's Funny and Frightening Prophecy," *American Conservative*, May 18, 2018, accessed June 10, 2019, http://www.theamericanconservative.com/articles/walker -percys-funny-and-frightening-prophecy/. Prof. Wood is discussing Percy's novel *Love in the Ruins* (1972), which explores the consequence of this "untethering" of mind, soul, and body and this alienation of human beings from God and from nature. In contrast to the way the Christian worldview reconciles them.

of the road will never intersect and that objects at a distance are the same size that they would be up close. Our intellect makes this analysis very rapidly so that we can go so far as to estimate how far away something is by how small it seems. Our senses take in data from the outside world, but then our minds shape it into a meaningful form.

This was the insight of the German philosopher Immanuel Kant (1724–1804). Hailed as the pinnacle of Enlightenment thought, Kant reconciled rationalism and empiricism. In doing so, Kant became the father of constructivism.

According to Kant, the human mind receives sense impressions from outside itself. It then actively organizes those impressions according to innate mental categories. These include *space*, so that we can orient ourselves with the perceptual illusion that objects seem smaller the greater their distance. Also *time* and *cause and effect*. Other fundamental concepts according to which the mind makes sense of reality include *quantity* (unity, plurality, totality); *quality* (reality, negation, limitation); *relation* (subsistence, causality, dependence, community); *modality* (possibility-impossibility, existence-nonexistence, necessity-contingency).[2]

Although we receive data from the outside world, Kant insisted that we can never know the "thing-in-itself." All we can know is *phenomena*; that is, the perceptions that the mind forms.

Kant was no relativist. He believed the objective universe exists, just that we cannot perceive it directly apart from the mental constructs that we impose upon it. He was a moralist, seeking to establish principles of morality in terms of innate mental categories rather than external laws or considerations. Kant the ethicist did much with "duty." He taught that we should always treat others as "ends" rather than "means." He formulated a version of the Golden Rule that he called the "categorical imperative": "Act only in accordance with that maxim through which you can at the same time will that it become a universal law."[3] In other words, judge your action by asking, "What if everyone did this?" (Killing is wrong because if everybody killed, there

2. Derk Pereboom, "Kant's Transcendental Arguments," *Stanford Encyclopedia of Philosophy* (Spring 2018), ed. Edward N. Zalta (Spring 2018), accessed June 10, 2019, https://plato.stanford.edu/archives/spr2018/entries/kant-transcendental/.

3. Quoted in Robert Johnson and Adam Cureton, "Kant's Moral Philosophy," *Stanford Encyclopedia of Philosophy*, accessed June 10, 2019, https://plato.stanford.edu/archives/spr2018/entries/kant-moral/>. See their entire discussion of Kant's ethics.

wouldn't be anyone left! We could apply this to abortion: if everyone committed abortion, the human race would die out. Conversely, you should be honest in your business dealings because you should want everyone's business dealings to be honest.) As for religion, Kant did not think we could know for certain that God exists or know him directly; then again, he did not think we could know *anything* outside ourselves certainly and directly. But since believing in God and practicing religion help to keep us moral, Kant thought it was rational to do so. (Notice, however, that Kant confuses religion with morality, with little to say about revelation, Christ, grace, salvation, prayer, or other tenets of a faith that comes from outside the self.) Kant was interested in finding "universals," not diverse "truths."

Nevertheless, Kant laid the groundwork for constructivism. He still looms large in contemporary philosophy. "Trying to summarize Kant's influence on philosophy is like trying to summarize Newton's influence on science," says Oregon State philosopher Jon Dorbolo in an online philosophy class. "The most accurate summation in either case may be: after Newton/Kant the entire approach to science/philosophy had changed. . . . Kant changed the entire world by providing a new way of thinking about how the human mind relates to the world."[4]

Kant is said to have brought about a "Copernican revolution." Just as Copernicus turned the model of the universe inside out by showing that the earth revolves around the sun, rather than vice versa, Kant changed the center of human thought. He wrote, going on to allude to Copernicus:

> Up to now it has been assumed that all our cognition must conform to the objects; but all attempts to find out something about them a priori through concepts that would extend our cognition have, on this presupposition, come to nothing. Hence let us once try whether we do not get farther with the problems of metaphysics by assuming that the objects must conform to our cognition.[5]

4. Jon Dorbolo, "Immanuel Kant," *InterQuest: Introducing Philosophy*, Oregon State University, accessed June 10, 2019, https://oregonstate.edu/instruct/phl201/modules/Philosophers/Kant/kant.html.

5. From Kant's Critique of *Pure Reason*, 10:130–31, quoted and discussed in Michael Rohlf, "Immanuel Kant," *Stanford Encyclopedia of Philosophy*, accessed June 10, 2019, https://plato.stanford.edu/archives/sum2018/entries/kant/.

No longer must our thinking conform to the objective world; the objective world must conform to our thinking. The center shifts away from objects to the mind that perceives them, away from external reality to the self.

But this is not a Copernican revolution! The error of the Ptolomaic model of the universe, in which the sun, planets, and stars revolve around the earth, is that it makes man the center of the universe. But man cannot be the center of the universe. Dante recognizes this when, after exploiting all of the symbolic possibilities of the geocentric universe, he turns the universe inside out after his character breaks through to heaven and sees the universe as it truly is. He looks back at where he has come from and sees that *God is the true center.*[6] Copernicus taught us that the universe is not as we perceive it to be—with the sun "coming up" every morning, traversing the sky, and "going down" in the evening—but that the reality is quite different. We human beings think that we are stable and that the universe revolves around us—indeed, this is how we experience our lives—but, in reality, *we* are the ones spinning, in constant motion, hurtling through space. But Kant has placed at the center of his cosmology the human mind. Once again, man is the center of the universe. We are back to Ptolomy's model. Kant has not given us a Copernican revolution. He has given us a Ptolomaic counterrevolution.

Constructing Our Own Realities

Kant's successors made their own contributions to Kant's revolution. The Romantic movement took the centrality of the self even further, emphasizing not just perception but the creative power of the mind to shape reality. Nietzsche stressed the creative power not just of the intellect but of the will. Specifically, the will to power.

This exaltation of the self, coupled with the continuing success of science (nevertheless), led to the attempt to study human beings scientifically. Thus arose the field of psychology. Also the social sciences, which began to discover the role of culture in determining how human beings act and think. What we consider to be reality began to be thought of as not just the construction of an individual's mind but

---

6. See Dante's *Paradiso*, Canto 28.

of the culture that formed that individual. Our beliefs, customs, and worldviews began to be seen as social constructions.

Indeed, the very concept of worldview, which has proven so helpful for Christian analysis, was first articulated by Kant. The term that he coined for the concept, *weltanschauung* (literally, worldview), was taken up by a host of psychologists and social scientists, as well as philosophers and theologians such as Abraham Kuyper.[7]

Social constructivism was weaponized by Karl Marx and his followers. Marx took Nietzsche's "will to power" and applied it to social institutions, particularly economic classes. He taught that cultural values and the institutions and artifacts that support them are the products of the dominant social class and are designed to facilitate their oppression of the other groups. Thus, for Marx and Marxists, art, literature, laws, political ideologies, morality, and religions are all "masks" of power, hiding the repressive agenda of the ruling class and making it palatable for those who are oppressed. For example, in the Middle Ages, the tales of knightly chivalry and heroism cause the peasants to admire their feudal masters. In our era dominated by the middle class, the political ideals of individualism, democracy, and liberty are "masks" to validate capitalism and to keep the wealthy bourgeoisie in power. For Marx, religion is the "opiate of the people," keeping the masses fixated on a future life and anesthetizing their suffering so that they will cooperate in their own exploitation.[8]

Today the post-Marxists adopt Marx's analysis but apply it not just to economic classes but to other dominant and oppressed groups. The rich still oppress the poor, as in classical Marxism, but other groups also "construct" reality to advance their will to power. Whites oppress blacks. Men oppress women. Heterosexuals oppress homosexuals. Humans oppress animals. And "intersectionality" unites the disparate victim groups, as they ally with each other to form a common front against the oppressors.

On university campuses today, much academic research is devoted to "deconstructing" these power relationships. Thus marriage, the

---

7. See David K. Naugle, *Worldview: History of a Concept* (Grand Rapids, MI: Eerdmans, 2002), 58. He cites Kant's first use of the term in his *Critique of Judgment* (1790).

8. See Derek Layder, *Understanding Social Theory* (London: Sage, 2006), 44–45.

nuclear family, sexual morality, and opposition to abortion are un-masked as being constructions of the patriarchy, means by which men control women. Activists, in turn, on and off campus, employ post-Marxist analysis and rhetoric in their own causes.

If you are among the oppressed, you can repudiate the social con-structions that bind you by purposefully transgressing the norms and by constructing your own alternatives. In the long run, though, the goal must be for *your* group to gain power. This might happen in an inevitable Marxist revolution, in which the workers will overthrow the middle-class property owners, or in the particular communities and social spaces that your group controls (campuses, political parties, pro-fessions, social media sites, etc.). Thus, the much-discussed political cor-rectness is, for the most part, a post-Marxist version of Marxist social control, as seen in the former Soviet Union, in which certain ideas and ways of expressing them were not permitted. In such contexts, appeals to freedom of speech or academic freedom do not carry much weight, since those are more "bourgeois" ideals that are masks for capitalism, patriarchy, heteronormativity, or other oppressive ideologies.

Editors of the *Oxford English Dictionary*, the custodians of En-glish language usage, declared that the 2016 Word of the Year was *post-truth*. We are said to be living in the post-truth era.[9] This has become a matter of alarm, as political parties from across the spec-trum turn out "fake news" to promote their agendas. But this should not be surprising. According to constructivists, journalists and other ostensibly objective writers choose particular bits of information from the avalanche of data available to them. They then construct an in-terpretive paradigm to connect those bits of data and to give them meaning. Guiding their selection of data and their interpretation is the writer's agenda, including the journalist's political beliefs, personal motivations, and "will to power." The pretense of objectivity is itself a construction, created by a particular rhetorical style. For the con-structivist, all news is "fake news."

One of the latest phrases in the academic field of education and in the teaching profession is *constructivist education*. Instead of learning

---

9. See, e.g., Ralph Keyes, *The Post-Truth Era* (New York: St. Martin's Press, 2004); and Lee McIntyre, *Post-Truth* (Cambridge, MA: MIT Press, 2018).

objective knowledge, children are taught to "construct" knowledge for themselves. They write their own reading textbooks by dictating stories, which the teacher writes down and which they then learn to read. They create their own math rules. More advanced students study different people's perspectives and then formulate their own. While much of the constructivist curricula is actually just "discovery learning," in which students discover information for themselves— an educational technique that is quite classical—that teacher training programs are latching onto the philosophy that children create their own truths and need to be taught how to do so is certainly telling.

Another popularized example of constructivism is the notion that moral principles are not objective standards that transcend the individual or the culture. Rather, morality is a contingent and relative human construction. This appears, as with other types of constructivism, in two forms: social constructivism and personal constructivism.

Many people today believe that morality is a social construction, simply a matter of culture. Since there are many different cultures, with no basis for saying that one is better than any other, morality is relative. Some Westerners excuse even the atrocities of Islamist terrorists by saying, "But that's their culture." That different cultures, in fact, show a high agreement on moral teachings is overlooked; and that traditional cultures tend to be quite conservative when it comes to morality, particularly sexual morality, is an embarrassment to progressive Westerners. So we are seeing now a different kind of cultural relativism, a temporal perspective emphasizing cultural change. Yes, sex outside of marriage used to be looked down upon, but the culture has changed. Our morality needs to change accordingly. Also we are seeing individual groupings—such as by generation, affiliation, or post-Marxist "identity"—exalted as "culture." Thus, we hear, "I can do that because that's my culture!"

The clearest example of constructivist ethics on a personal level can be seen in the abortion debate. Again, as was said in the introduction, abortion advocates do not say that they are pro-abortion but that they are pro-*choice*. The *content* of the decision does not determine its moral significance; only the authenticity of the decision as a free, noncoerced choice.

This mind-set is also evident in other issues. The killing of sick people, euthanasia, is justified if the person *chooses* to die. We may have sex with someone we are not married to as long as there is *consent*; that is, as long as there is a *choice*.

The exaltation of choice easily morphs into the libertine definition of *freedom*. Whereas the Bible defines freedom as liberation from the enslaving power of sin (John 8:34–36), and political freedom means that the state will not violate our God-given rights, libertines define freedom as the right to do whatever I want, whatever I *choose*. Thus, arguments for the legalization of prostitution, drugs, and the like tend to be framed in terms of "freedom of choice."

Constructivism at its most extreme can be seen in the transgender movement, which teaches that the self is so untethered to objective reality as to become disembodied. One's personal identity is distinct from one's body. A person might have been "born in the wrong body," a woman in the body of a man, or a man in the body of a woman. In those cases, the person is free, with the help of medical technology, to reconstruct his or her body accordingly. But even such reconstruction is not necessary, since the physical body has no bearing on sex or gender, only the individual's self-constructed identity.

We will discuss this phenomenon—another Kantian term—in a further chapter. We will also explore in greater depth other issues raised by constructivism: the tension between science and constructivism; the rise of technology and the loss of nature; identity politics; and the newly constructed religions that are emerging.

For now, notice what this particular post-Christian revolution means. Rejecting God, human beings are attempting to place themselves in his role as creator, lawgiver, and savior.

2

Knowing Nature

The Dominance of Science

In today's post-Christian world, human beings are cut off from nature. This is true even for those who assume that nature is all that exists. Those who believe that they understand nature and can make nature do their bidding and can even destroy nature nevertheless feel that they have no place in the universe. Being lost spiritually, of course, is the perennial problem of the human condition; but in our post-Christian times, people are also lost in the mundane, physical, natural world.

By "nature," I do not mean mountains, trees, and wildlife. When we hear the word *nature*, we immediately think of wilderness unspoiled by traces of humanity, which demonstrates my point. By "nature" I mean physical reality—that is to say, to use a theological term, *creation*.

We used to assume that we were part of nature, part of God's created order. We had been given dominion over it so that we could understand its operation up to a point and use its features to meet our needs. But we knew we were natural, created beings nonetheless. We were born into physical bodies with physical needs; we interacted with the world in order to survive; we engaged in sex and had children; we died; and our offspring started the natural cycle all over again.

Christians believe that God created and sustains this natural order. We fell from his created perfection, but he redeemed us and will raise us to life in a new creation that will last for eternity. There is a spiritual realm as well as a physical realm, a supernatural reality as well as a natural reality. Human beings inhabit both. So does God, who, to save us, became incarnate in Jesus Christ, who, after his resurrection and ascension, fills all things (Eph. 1:15–33).

But without God, nature and supernature, the physical and what remains of the spiritual, fly apart. Splitting the two realms has been disastrous. One way of doing so is to exalt the physical and to denigrate the spiritual. This was one strain of the Enlightenment, continuing to develop in nineteenth-century materialism and in the set of beliefs known as *modernism*. Another way of splitting the two realms is to exalt the spiritual (or the mental, or the interior) and to denigrate the physical. This was the way of the ancient Christian heresy of Gnosticism, which has continued to haunt the Christian tradition and which has taken a variety of secularist forms, including *postmodernism*. These two kinds of reductionism seem to be opposite, but, in effect, they are much the same. Without the Creator, we also lose the creation.

Lost in the Cosmos

In our last chapter, we saw how human reason, as part of the multifaceted soul, was reduced to a calculating machine. As Ralph Wood described the influence of Descartes, the mind becomes detached from the world, from the thinker's body and personhood, and from physical reality as a whole. The human mind is "a calculating faculty for bare, abstract thinking," Woods says. "To yank the mind free from the body is also to untether it from history, tradition, and locality. After Descartes, the mind allegedly stands outside these given things,"[1] contemplating them and understanding them, but from a distance.

The Enlightenment view of the human mind is thus not unlike its view of God. The religion based on reason alone—that is, deism— taught that God is detached from his creation, contemplating what

---

1. Ralph C. Wood, "Walker Percy's Funny and Frightening Prophecy," *American Conservative*, May 18, 2018, accessed June 10, 2019, http://www.theamericanconservative.com/articles/walker -percys-funny-and-frightening-prophecy/.

he has made without interfering in its self-contained operation. The human does much the same, though it interferes with nature when it can.

But what happens to the self—not just the mind but the individual person as a conscious, experiencing entity, situated in a particular place and time, with flesh and blood and an immortal soul? As science marched on, with the mind achieving an ever greater understanding and mastery of the world it contemplates, the self became a world of its own.

The physical world follows its own inexorable natural laws, which the new science was discovering, but it has no meaning, as such. The objective universe, such as it is, does not include meaning, morality, significance, or value. Such categories are subjective, having to do with the interior workings of the self. Nancy Pearcey has shown how the "fact/value distinction," a legacy of the Enlightenment and of the subsequent scientific materialism, divided the very concept of truth.[2] Strictly speaking, only "facts"—physical events and realities as determined by the scientific method—can be considered to be objectively true. "Values" exist only in the mind. Morality, religion, beauty, and other intangible values are on the order of subjective *feelings*.

Such a view reduces the natural and physical world to a dead mechanism whose orderliness is nothing more than a mindless repetition. If you want something more, you must go inside yourself. Nature is deterministic; freedom inheres in the self. Nature is void of meaning; the self can bestow meaning. Nature knows nothing of good and evil, beauty, joy, purpose, or spirituality. Those can be found only in terms of the self. In the nineteenth century, scientific materialists would denigrate such "values" in favor of hard and cold scientific fact, while some Romantics exalted the self to the point of scorning objectivity altogether.

With Kant, the objective world receded even further away. We cannot know the objective world in itself at all, just the phenomena as we perceive them. And yet the human mind, godlike but still detached from the world, imposes order on the chaos of sense perception.

---

2. See Nancy Pearcey, *Total Truth: Liberating Christianity from Its Cultural Captivity* (Wheaton, IL: Crossway, 2004).

Either way, whether you were a scientist or a Romantic, you were distanced from the natural, created order. Scientists tried to put themselves under their own microscopes, attempting to apply the scientific method to human society with the social sciences and to the self with the science of psychology. Romantics tried to heal their alienation by projecting themselves onto nature.

But this sense of not being at home in the universe persisted. And as science disclosed the utter vastness—yet emptiness—of the universe, the alienation intensified. The mathematician and pioneering scientist Blaise Pascal, a contemporary of Descartes who became a Christian apologist, anticipated these feelings and expressed them the best:

> When I consider the short duration of my life, swallowed up in an eternity before and after, the little space I fill engulfed in the infinite immensity of spaces whereof I know nothing, and which know nothing of me, I am terrified. . . . The eternal silence of these infinite spaces alarms me.[3]

Today, in our post-Christian times, the sense of being a lone consciousness, alienated not only from God but from reality itself, has only intensified. Walker Percy calls it being "lost in the cosmos." In his book with that title, he analyzes "the loneliness of self, stranded as it is as an unspeakable consciousness in a world from which it perceives itself as somehow estranged, stranded even within its own body, with which it sees no clear connection."[4] He concludes, "You live in a deranged age—more deranged than usual, because despite great scientific and technological advances, man has not the faintest idea of who he is or what he is doing."[5]

The Scientific Method

None of this being "lost in the cosmos" in any way diminishes the very real and praiseworthy accomplishments of modern science. The natural sciences have resisted constructivism and so have retained a grounding in objective, physical reality that keeps our culture from

---

3. Blaise Pascal, *Thoughts* [*Pensées*], trans. C. Kegan Paul (London: George Bell & Sons, 1905), 28.
4. Walker Percy, *Lost in the Cosmos: The Last Self-Help Book* (New York: Picador, 1983), 180.
5. Percy, *Lost in the Cosmos*, 76.

being sucked *entirely* into the black hole of subjectivity (to use a scientific metaphor). The triumphs of science give us abundant reason to question Kant's assertion, quoted in the previous chapter, that making our cognition conform to reality has "come to nothing."

And yet, though science has proceeded pretty much oblivious to Kant, it has had to take his insights into account. While the human mind, with its powers of perception and reason, can indeed understand the outside world, at least to a point, the human mind can also get in the way of understanding.

Thus, the *scientific method* operates so as to rigorously guard against both Kantian mental constructions and the limitations of empiricism. Here is the scientific method as described by University of Rochester physics professor Frank L. H. Wolfs, which he wrote up online for his physics students: "The scientific method is the process by which scientists, collectively and over time, endeavor to construct an accurate (that is, reliable, consistent and non-arbitrary) representation of the world." Notice that here too we see the language of constructivism: scientists "construct" a "representation" of the world. At the same time, Professor Wolfs describes the scientific method as an attempt to compensate for the active shaping of the human mind:

> Recognizing that personal and cultural beliefs influence both our perceptions and our interpretations of natural phenomena, we aim through the use of standard procedures and criteria to minimize those influences when developing a theory. . . . In summary, the scientific method attempts to minimize the influence of bias or prejudice in the experimenter when testing an hypothesis or a theory.[6]

Professor Wolfs then gives the four steps of the scientific method:

1. Observation and description of a phenomenon or a group of phenomena.
2. Formulation of an hypothesis to explain the phenomena. In physics, the hypothesis often takes the form of a causal mechanism or a mathematical relation.

---

6. Frank L. H. Wolfs, "Introduction to the Scientific Method," accessed June 10, 2019, http://teacher.pas.rochester.edu/phy_labs/AppendixE/AppendixE.html.

3. Use of the hypothesis to predict the existence of other phenomena, or to predict quantitatively the results of new observations.
4. Performance of experimental tests of the predictions by several independent experimenters and properly performed experiments.[7]

He goes on to explain that a hypothesis is the unproven explanation. If it is confirmed by experimental evidence, it can become a "model," which has at least some predictive validity. If the hypothesis and related hypotheses are confirmed by a large number of experiments, we have a "theory," or even a "law of nature."[8]

In addition, the hypothesis, model, theory, or law must be *falsifiable*.[9] It may not be possible to fully prove an idea to be true, but it must, in theory, be capable of being proven false. To use the example used by Karl Popper, who formulated the principle, Einstein's theory of relativity is scientific because if a particle were ever discovered that travels faster than the speed of light, the theory would collapse. Freud's theory of psychoanalysis, on the other hand, is unscientific because it purports to offer an explanation for every behavior, and there is no conceivable experiment that could prove it wrong. For Popper, psychoanalysis is therefore a pseudoscience. Popper admitted that there is a place for nonfalsifiable ideas. Metaphysical philosophy—including that of Descartes, Kant, modernists, and postmodernists—offers explanatory paradigms that account for all of existence, including any actual evidence that could be used against them. They may help our understanding, even though they are not falsifiable. That just means they are not scientific, that they do not accord with the scientific method.

Notice that Christianity *is* falsifiable. If when we die, there is *nothing*—no face-to-face encounter with God, no judgment, no everlasting life—then Christianity is not true and never has been. The Bible itself states how Christianity could be falsified:

---

7. Wolfs, "Scientific Method."
8. Wolfs, "Scientific Method."
9. Brendan Shea, "Karl Popper: Philosophy of Science," *Internet Encyclopedia of Philosophy: A Peer-Reviewed Academic Resource*, accessed June 10, 2019, http://www.iep.utm.edu/pop-sci/#H2.

If Christ has not been raised, then our preaching is in vain and your faith is in vain. . . . And if Christ has not been raised, your faith is futile and you are still in your sins. Then those also who have fallen asleep in Christ have perished. If in Christ we have hope in this life only, we are of all people most to be pitied. (1 Cor. 15:14, 17–19)

If Jesus was not raised from the dead, if somehow we could discover his bones, then Christianity would unravel. "But in fact Christ has been raised from the dead, the firstfruits of those who have fallen asleep" (1 Cor. 15:20). That Christianity is falsifiable does not mean that it is scientific, as such. But it does show that Christianity, like science, has to do with physical reality, with the realm of facts ("in *fact* Christ has been raised").

The experiments that are foundational to the scientific method must be empirical (drawing on data and evidence from the external world), and they should, as much as possible, be *controlled*. That is, they should test for a single variable. Typically, an experiment will consist of two parallel investigations. (Two seeds of exactly the same type are planted, and each is given the same measure of light and water.) One of which will have a single variation. (The only difference is that one of the plants is grown in acidic soil.) Then the two systems will be compared, whereupon any differences can be attributed to the variable. (If the plant that grows in acidic soil sprouts later and is smaller, we can draw a conclusion about the effects of acidic soil.) Such controls are not always possible. Experimentation on human beings is notoriously difficult, since people have too many features to fully control (age, sex, weight, metabolism, body type, allergies, personality, etc.).[10]

Experimental controls can take different forms, but the goal is to eliminate extraneous factors so that the scientist can zero in on specific effects. The variable can be *negative* (something left out) or *positive* (something added). Medical research makes use of *placebos* (pills or injections containing no actual medicine) as controls in testing new drugs. (If the group of patients that receives the drug being tested fares no better than the patients getting the placebo, the drug is proven to

---

10. Anne Marie Helmenstine, "What Is a Controlled Experiment?," ThoughtCo, accessed June 10, 2019, https://www.thoughtco.com/controlled-experiment-609091.

be ineffective.) Another type of control is the "blind experiment," in which the human subjects do not know to which experimental group they have been assigned. ("Am I getting the placebo or the real medicine?") Even more rigorous is the "double-blind experiment," in which *neither* the subjects *nor* the scientists know which group is getting what treatment. ("Am I administering a placebo or the real medicine?")[11] Notice how this is an attempt to prevent the observers from unintentionally shaping the results with their active intellects. It is a control against constructivism.

Another requirement of the scientific method is that an experiment must be replicable; that is, reproducible. If other scientists perform the same experiment, they must get the same results. If they do not, the original experiment lacks validity, and its findings become questionable. There must have been other factors at work that the original researcher did not account for. There must have been inadequate controls.[12]

Recently, the scientific community has been agonizing over what is being described as the "Replication Crisis."[13] It turns out that a surprisingly large percentage of published scientific research cannot be replicated.[14] The problem is especially acute in the social sciences, particularly psychology. One investigation found that only 39 percent of the psychological studies that were examined could be replicated.[15] That might be understandable, given that while chemicals can be expected to perform in a consistent way every time, human beings—in addition to having far more "variables," as noted above—also have agency, the ability to initiate their own actions according to their own choices. It should not be surprising that one group of human subjects would act in one way for one researcher, while another group of sub-

11. Martyn Shuttleworth, "Double Blind Experiment," *Explorable*, accessed June 10, 2019, https://explorable.com/double-blind-experiment.

12. Martyn Shuttleworth, "Reproducibility," *Explorable*, accessed June 10, 2019, https://explorable.com/reproducibility.

13. For a useful overview of the issue, along with links to the research that exposed the problem, see "Replication Crisis," Wikipedia, accessed June 10, 2019, https://en.wikipedia.org/wiki/Replication_crisis.

14. See John P. A. Ioannidis, "Why Most Published Research Findings Are False," PLoS [Public Library of Science] *Medicine* 2, no. 8 (2005): e124, accessed June 10, 2019, https://doi.org/10.1371/journal.pmed.0020124.

15. Monya Baker, "Over Half of Psychology Studies Fail Reproducibility Test," *Nature* 27 (August 2015), accessed June 10, 2019, https://www.nature.com/news/over-half-of-psychology-studies-fail-reproducibility-test-1.18248.

jects acts differently for another researcher. Nevertheless, if studies in psychology and sociology are not reproducible, then the social sciences are not exactly *sciences*, at least not in the way that chemistry and physics are. And yet there is also a replication crisis in the harder sciences, especially medical science.[16] Again, human subjects have so many *physical* variables that it is difficult to control for them. But the problem is even showing up in chemistry, biology, and physics.[17]

How to account for this? Investigations have turned up cases of overt dishonesty, including manufacturing data and purposefully distorting findings so that they accord with the hypothesis. But usually the mistakes are unintentional. Often the problem is just a flawed experimental design. Since much of the scientific research done today comes out of academia, the publish-or-perish pressure can lead scientists to publish their results before they are truly ready, encouraging shortcuts and sloppy research. A major problem seems to be math errors, particularly in statistical analysis. From the other side, journals exhibit a "publication bias," in which editors deciding which articles to select for publication favor positive, even dramatic findings, over more humdrum research. That would include replicating experiments that have already been done. Academic scientists hoping to make tenure have little incentive to redo other people's work.

This is to say, scientists are human too, and science as a whole is a human enterprise. Far from being the detached, disembodied application of reason to the physical world—as in the theoretical picture—the mind of the scientist is active, constructing, and it sometimes gets in the way. Though methodological rigor corrects for much of that effect, the scientist's biases, ambitions, mental states, personal problems, and worldview often come into play. This is not always a bad thing. Coming up with a hypothesis can be the product of the creative imagination, which, often, is confirmed empirically. The mind is connected to physical reality after all.

16. Ivan Couronne, "Beware Those Scientific Studies—Most Are Wrong, Researcher Warns," *Yahoo News*, July 5, 2018, accessed June 10, 2019, https://www.yahoo.com/news/beware-those -scientific-studies-most-wrong-researcher-warns-164336076.html.

17. Monya Baker, "1,500 Scientists Lift the Lid on Reproducibility," *Nature* 25 (May 2016), accessed June 10, 2019, https://www.nature.com/news/1-500-scientists-lift-the-lid-on-reproducibility -1.19970?WT.mc_id=SFB_NNEWS_1508_RHBox.

Nature, Red in Tooth and Claw

Science has explored the physical universe—its structures, its operations, its laws—in a way that discloses its wonders. (The application of
those discoveries—technology—is also wonderful, and this will be the
topic of the next chapter.) The eighteenth-century Enlightenment and
nineteenth-century materialism created the impression that science
would "disenchant" the universe, reducing its mysteries by explaining
them away, turning the physical creation into nothing more than an
eternally running machine. But such discoveries as DNA, electricity,
the structure of the atom, gravity waves, black holes, and quantum
physics (which we will discuss later) show that the creation is far more
complex and deeply ordered than anyone realized. And the more science learns about the universe, the more mysterious it becomes.

Yet in our post-Christian times, science is used to beat up on
Christianity, in many people's minds taking the place of religion.
People in the general public don't necessarily know much about
science, but that doesn't stop them from using it as an overarching, all-encompassing authority. For example, a doctor who per-
forms abortions explained to a British newspaper that he is actually
a Christian but justified his practice of killing children in the womb
by invoking science. "As a Christian doctor in the USA, you might
expect me to be anti-abortion," he told a British newspaper. "Yet
some church leaders insist on maintaining religious customs regarding human reproduction that were established prior to scientific
understandings about how that process occurs."[18] He never explains
what he has in mind, as if the ancients did not know where babies
come from and as if modern science has discovered a completely different explanation. Yet even if it had, scientific findings can never determine a moral judgment. That would violate Hume's Law, named
after the skeptical Enlightenment-era philosopher, who showed that
one cannot derive an "ought" from an "is."[19]

---

18. Willie Parker, "Voices," *Independent*, May 24, 2018, accessed June 10, 2019, https://
www.independent.co.uk/voices/catholics-choice-ireland-abortion-law-repeal-the-eighth-a836
6831.html.

19. Charles Pigden, "Hume on Is and Ought," *Philosophy Now* 83 (March/April 2011), accessed June 10, 2019, https://philosophynow.org/issues/83/Hume_on_Is_and_Ought.

But the abortion doctor's error is even greater. Modern science *has* improved our knowledge of reproduction. The more we know about it, the more reason there is to oppose abortion. In the Middle Ages, people assumed that the fetus did not become fully human until "quickening"; that is, when the mother could first feel her baby move. That was held to be the moment of "ensoulment," when the developing child is given a soul. Medieval Christians who believed this still opposed abortion, even though their science—while empirical (they were basing their beliefs on observation, on when the life is first perceived)—was faulty. And yet pro-abortion Christians are fond of invoking Saint Thomas Aquinas on ensoulment to justify their insistence that the child in the womb is not a human being.[20] But modern science has shot down the concepts of quickening (literally, becoming alive) and ensoulment. Instead, the field of embryology shows that a human being develops in a continuous process, beginning at conception and continuing after birth, through childhood, maturity, and old age, ending only at death. That quickening begins at conception, interestingly, is the view of the Bible, which depicts the incarnation as occurring at the angel's visitation to Mary, immediately after which the "fetus" John the Baptist leaped in the womb of Elizabeth, not because he just then became alive but because he recognized his just-conceived Lord *in utero* (Luke 1).[21] This passage must have puzzled medieval Christians, since it violated the science of their time, but they believed it anyway.

This abortion doctor invokes "Science" as a religious talisman. It banishes the old gods and the old moralities in favor of something new. He does not say anything that he has learned from science that bears on his conviction that abortion is good. Perhaps for him, though he claims to be a Christian, the word *science* is a shorthand term for the materialistic or naturalistic worldview, the notion that material objects and the natural realm are all that exist. To be sure, this is the only realm that science can study. To those who idolize science, the physical realm must comprise all there is. And yet they

20. See André Marie, "Ensoulment Theories and the Abortion Debate," Catholicism.org, September 22, 2007, accessed June 10, 2019, http://catholicism.org/ensoulment-theories-and-the-abortion-debate.html.

21. See John Piper, "The Baby in My Womb Leaped for Joy," *Desiring God*, January 25, 2009, accessed June 10, 2019, https://www.desiringgod.org/messages/the-baby-in-my-womb-leaped-for-joy.

can hardly deny nonphysical realities such as mathematics, natural laws, consciousness, and mental states. Modernists embraced science and materialism as an explanation for the external world, but they often turned to existentialism—the notion that they can create their own meaning in a meaningless world—for the internal world. Postmodernists went further, often questioning even scientific objectivity, which they saw as a construction of Western culture and the human mind.

Science, strictly speaking, cannot disprove or replace religion. It can only speak to physical reality, not other kinds of reality. There is nothing in the scientific method or in the exploration of the laws of nature that conflicts with Christianity. Quite the contrary. Most of the pioneers of modern science—the formulator of the scientific method Francis Bacon, the Lutheran astronomer Johannes Kepler, the groundbreaking chemist Robert Boyle, the father of the scientific revolution Isaac Newton, and many more—were devout Christians. For them, the order in the physical realm that science discloses is a function of God's creation, the details of what God has made.

But in the nineteenth century, science did strike a blow against Christianity and against religion in general, one that continues to reverberate today. Charles Darwin's theory of evolution has indeed undermined Christianity, as well as presented a worldview that has made even scientists more alienated from nature than ever.

During the Enlightenment, even non-Christians believed in the necessity of some kind of deity, if only to start the universe and to account for its laws. But in purporting to account for the origins of human life in purely naturalistic terms, Darwin seemed to have rendered God unnecessary. When Darwin's *Origin of Species* was published in 1859, it was seized upon by many in the educated public who were interested not so much in its technical scientific claims as in its potential for freeing them from the "shackles" of religion.[22] To this day, modernists and postmodernists and secularists in all of their variety invoke the theory of evolution as the definitive refutation of biblical faith.

---

22. See Tom Wolfe's account of Charles Darwin and the early days of his theory in *The Kingdom of Speech* (New York: Little, Brown, 2016).

That all life in all of its forms, including human beings, evolved over millennia through random natural selection has become a controlling paradigm not only for biology but also for geology, anthropology, cosmology, and science conceived of as a whole. In terms of the scientific method, evolution by natural selection is a theory in the sense of being an overarching hypothesis confirmed by extensive and wide-ranging experimentation. More than that, Darwin's theory has become what historian of science Thomas Kuhn calls a "paradigm," an explanatory structure that accounts for the observed data.

In his landmark work *The Structure of Scientific Revolutions*, Kuhn shows that the history of science consists of a series of "revolutions," in which old paradigms, after controversy and struggle, give way to new paradigms.[23] For example, the Ptolomaic theory of the universe, in which the sun, planets, and stars revolve around the stationary earth, fully accounted for the observational data over the course of many centuries. After all, we *experience* the earth as standing still, and we can·*empirically* see the sun and other celestial bodies traversing the sky. The Ptolomaic universe was mathematically predictable, making it possible to predict the seasons, the occurrence of eclipses, and navigational positions with great accuracy. Eventually, though, new data was discovered—for example, with the help of new technology such as the telescope—that could not easily fit into the Ptolomaic paradigm. The paradigm was revised accordingly. But eventually it could not bear the weight of all of the new findings. A completely new paradigm—the Copernican theory that the earth circles the sun—took its place. But first came a period of upheaval and dispute, as the stakeholders in the old paradigm tried to fight off the new evidence, sometimes by viciously attacking the scientists with the contrary data.[24]

If Darwin's theory of evolution by natural selection has become such a paradigm, that suggests that it too may someday be unable to account for all of the data and that it too will have to be replaced. The extreme vehemence with which the evolutionary paradigm is being

---

23. Thomas S. Kuhn, *The Structure of Scientific Revolutions* (Chicago: University of Chicago Press, 1962).

24. Similar paradigm shifts are evident in chemistry, studies of the structure of the atom, the shift from Newtonian physics to Einstein's theory of relativity, and in the new fields of quantum mechanics.

defended against a new cadre of critics—to the point that scientists skeptical of Darwinism are being fired from their positions—suggests a paradigm in jeopardy. The arguments of creationists and the sophisticated critiques based on intelligent design—such as the "irreducible complexity" of the simplest living organisms, whose DNA and ability to reproduce must exist prior to natural selection[25]—are angrily dismissed without a hearing. One soon realizes that for committed evolutionists, *no* evidence is accepted that could possibly undermine Darwinism. This suggests that for them, the paradigm is unfalsifiable, thus making Darwinism more of a philosophical commitment than a scientific theory, which must always be open to revision.

I remember in graduate school studying what had to be the greatest poem on Darwinian evolution, namely, "In Memoriam," by Alfred, Lord Tennyson. The poet is lamenting the death of a close friend. The comforts of Christianity, with its promise of everlasting life, are hard to hold onto in this new era of scientific materialism. The long, empty stretches of geologic time make a mockery of our brief lives. What we now know about the laws of nature make a mockery of Christian ethics. The one "who trusted God was love indeed / And love Creation's final law"[26] must face up to a different reality:

> Nature, red in tooth and claw
> With ravine, shriek'd against his creed.[27]

Nature used to be valued for its moral lessons, not only in the ancient world but in the Enlightenment with its trust in rational order and in early nineteenth-century Romanticism with its emphasis on natural harmony and vitality. But now nature at its essence is revealed to be bloody and violent, "red in tooth and claw." Natural selection has to do with "survival of the fittest," as mutations are passed on that offer an advantage in the ceaseless struggle for survival. Progress comes from the strong preying on the weak, with the "unfit" dying out. Evolution discredited not only the Christian doctrine of creation but also, as

---

25. See, e.g., Michael Behe, *Darwin's Black Box: The Biochemical Challenge to Evolution* (New York: Simon & Schuster, 1996).

26. Alfred, Lord Tennyson, "In Memoriam," stanza 56, lines 13–14, *Literature Network*, accessed June 10, 2019, http://www.online-literature.com/tennyson/718/.

27. Tennyson, "In Memoriam," lines 15–16.

Tennyson laments, the Christian teachings about love. Thus this new scientific paradigm took away the spiritual consolations, while also taking away the consolations one might find in the physical world.

In my study of the poem, I was impressed with how Tennyson was wrestling with Darwinism and exploring its implications in a profound way. And then I noticed that the poem was published in 1849, that is, a full ten years before Darwin published *The Origin of Species* in 1859. Not only that, Tennyson began "In Memoriam" as early as 1833!

Did the poet anticipate, by the sheer power of his imagination, the findings of the scientist? Not really. Darwin's theory of evolution was in the air long before Darwin. Geologists had already proposed an old earth. Philosophers had already developed the concept of gradual development. In his study of the Ptolomaic paradigm, C. S. Lewis, wearing his literary historian hat, makes this point:

> When I was a boy I believed that "Darwin discovered evolution" and that the far more general, radical, and even cosmic developmentalism which till lately dominated all popular thought was a superstructure raised on the biological theorem. This view has been sufficiently disproved.[28]

Lewis goes on to cite a number of writers who put forward the concept of evolution before Darwin, including Schelling in 1812, Robinet in 1786, and our friend Immanuel Kant (1724–1804). (I would add J. G. Hamann, whom we will discuss in chapter 3, who wrote in 1772, "The evolution of the human race from a swamp or slime continues to strike me like a beautifully-painted mask without a brain."[29]) Lewis concludes:

> The demand for a developing world—a demand obviously in harmony both with the revolutionary and the romantic temper—grows up first; when it is full grown the scientists go to work and discover the evidence on which our belief in that sort of universe would now be held to rest. There is no question here of the old Model's being shattered by the inrush of new phenomena.

---

28. C. S. Lewis, *The Discarded Image: An Introduction to Medieval and Renaissance Literature* (New York: Cambridge University Press, 1964), 220.

29. Quoted in John R. Betz, *After Enlightenment: The Post-Secular Vision of J. G. Hamann* (Oxford, UK: John Wiley & Sons, 2012), 160.

The truth would seem to be the reverse; that when changes in the human mind produce a sufficient disrelish of the old Model and a sufficient hankering for some new one, phenomena to support that new one will obediently turn up. I do not at all mean that these new phenomena are illusory. Nature has all sorts of phenomena in stock and can suit many different tastes.[30]

We can also find natural selection—the "survival of the fittest"— in the economic theory of Adam Smith, whose *Wealth of Nations* (1776) establishes the principles of free-market capitalism, whose "creative destruction" Darwin would have witnessed in the Industrial Revolution of his day. In many ways, Darwin's theory is nothing more than the "dog eat dog" competition of free market capitalism, with its inevitable progress, applied to biology.

We could say then that Darwin's theory of evolution is not just the result of disinterested observation of empirical phenomena. It is a cultural construction. Christians who find their faith in the Bible disturbed by the claims of Darwinism should consider whether this particular scientific paradigm will still be around in the next century or two, or if it is likely that some other paradigm—perhaps one equally caustic to Christianity—will arise to take its place. Such is the history of science, and it would be unusual for Darwinism to become the one exception to the provisional quality of all such paradigms.

By the way, Tennyson worked through his struggle with proto-Darwinism, his Christian faith intact. His conclusion makes the same point I have just tried to make:

Our little systems have their day;
They have their day and cease to be:
They are but broken lights of thee,
And thou, O Lord, art more than they.[31]

Quantum Physics and the Limits of Reason

There was a time when scientific discoveries reduced questions to "now we understand this," making the natural world seem somehow less won-

30. Lewis, *Discarded Image*, 221.
31. Tennyson, "In Memoriam," Prologue, lines 17–20.

derful than it was before. The early twentieth-century social scientist Max Weber wrote about the "disenchantment of the world" brought about by scientific progress.[32] The science of the nineteenth century, which includes Darwinism, transmuted everything to inert matter. In the public mind, the universe was nothing but an aggregation of atoms and electrons, which were pictured as tiny billiard balls orbited by marbles.

But the science of today is far more interesting. And instead of reducing the sense of mystery in creation, contemporary science is increasing our sense of mystery. The more we learn, the more the world seems enchanted after all. From the unimaginably huge scale of outer space—with its black holes, gravity waves, and dark matter—to the unimaginably tiny scale of subatomic particles and quantum mechanics, science is disclosing wonders that are awe-inspiring, mind-boggling, and hardly materialistic at all.

The key field here is quantum physics, in which scientific discovery takes us past the limits of human reason. Light, whose speed is the ultimate limit and the universal constant, bridges the near infinite gap between the subatomic realm and the galactic realm.

The utter mind-bending weirdness of quantum physics can be seen in an easily performed quantum experiment that I watched being conducted in a college science lab.[33] It is called the Double Slit Experiment.[34] Shine a beam of light through a slit onto a screen. The light that gets through will appear like a bar the size of the slit, consistent with the particles of light known as photons. Now shine the beam of light through two slits. This time the light acts like a wave, forming an interference pattern from each slit that shows up on the screen as alternating bright and black lines. *Light is both a particle and a wave.*

Now use a device that shoots one photon at a time at the two slits. Half the time the photon goes through one slit, and half the time it

32. Max Weber, *Science as Vocation*, translated from "Wissenschaft als Beruf" (Munich: Duncker & Humblodt, 1919), 20, accessed June 10, 2019, http://www.wisdom.weizmann.ac.il/~oded/X/WeberScienceVocation.pdf.

33. This experiment and the various effects it discloses are shown on a number of YouTube videos. See, e.g., Jim Al-Khalili, *Double Slit Experiment Explained*, accessed June 10, 2019, https://www.youtube.com/watch?v=A9tKncAdlHQ. For a lucid and informative animated treatment, see Dr. Quantum, *Double Slit Experiment*, accessed June 10, 2019, https://www.youtube.com/watch?v=DfPeprQ7oGc.

34. See Jay Bennett, "The Double-Slit Experiment That Blew Open Quantum Mechanics," *Popular Mechanics* 28 (July 2016), accessed June 10, 2019, https://www.popularmechanics.com/science/a22094/video-explainer-double-slit-experiment/.

goes through the other. These register on the screen on the other side as random dots. But keep sending them through, and eventually *the random dots accumulate until they form a pattern identical to the wave interference pattern!*

Now put a measuring device on the other side of the slits so that we can observe which of the two slits a particular photon goes through. This time the light is resolved into two simple bars on the screen. Unplug the observation device. The light forms the wave interference pattern. *How can the simple act of observation change and determine what is being observed? How do these particles "know" that someone is watching and change their behavior accordingly?*

Now rig up a device with a crystal at each slit that splits each photon in two, sending one to a detector and the other to the screen to form an interference pattern. Except that it doesn't. The unobserved photon is affected by its observed twin and refuses, as it were, to act like a wave. That is odd enough. But then comes the bombshell. I'd better let an expert say it (caps mine): "Even if the second photon is detected AFTER the first photon hits the screen, it still ruins the interference pattern. This means that observing a photon can change events that have *already happened.*"[35]

It turns out that the Double-Slit Experiment applies not only to light, the universal constant, but also to electrons and neutrons. And recently, the same effects were also found with complete, massive atoms.[36] *This means that the building blocks of all matter are both particles and waves, that their actions are affected by observation, that they can reverse causality in time.*

And all of these inconceivable facts derive from only one experiment. There are many more. For example, particles can become entangled with each other.[37] When photons are split into two, as we

35. Avery Thompson, "The Logic-Defying Double-Slit Experiment Is Even Weirder Than You Thought," *Popular Mechanics*, August 11, 2016, accessed May 22, 2019, https://www.popular mechanics.com/science/a22280/double-slit-experiment-even-weirder/; emphasis original. See also the video "How the Quantum Eraser Rewrites the Past" in the series Space Time from PBS Digital Studios, August 10, 2016, https://www.youtube.com/watch?v=8ORLN_KwAgs.

36. "Do atoms going through a double slit 'know' if they are being observed?," Quantum Mechanics Research Update, *Physics World*, May 26, 2015, accessed June 10, 2019, https://physics world.com/a/do-atoms-going-through-a-double-slit-know-if-they-are-being-observed/.

37. See Karl Tate, "How Quantum Entanglement Works," *Live Science*, April 8, 2013, accessed June 10, 2019, https://www.livescience.com/28550-how-quantum-entanglement-works -infographic.html. For the experimental evidence, see the video "Quantum Entanglement and the

described above, what happens to one happens to the other. Change the spin on one, and the other will start to spin in the opposite direction. *This happens no matter how far apart they are.* The effect has been experimentally detected at a distance of seven hundred miles. But, theoretically, the two entangled particles could be on the opposite sides of the universe from each other. *There is no contact between them.* Furthermore, *tampering with one particle affects the entangled particle on the other side of the universe instantly.* There is no time lag, no issue of speed, not even the speed of light. The effect is *instantaneous.* This is called "nonlocality," not being bound by place. Quantum physics also has shown that particles can be present in different positions at the same time. Scientists have also discovered that there is a "temporal nonlocality." Particles can be entangled over time. In fact, a recent experiment has shown that particles can be entangled that have never coexisted in the same moment.[38]

So what do all of these experimental findings do to the logical principle of noncontradiction? To causality? To time and space? What about the rest of Kant's categories that we mentioned in chapter 1, according to which the human mind organizes its sense perceptions and constructs its explanations? It would seem that quantum physics takes us beyond the capacity of the human mind to comprehend its own discoveries.

Theologians have always talked about the limits of human reason, and now we are bumping against them; that is to say, scientists, the very products of the Age of Reason, are bumping against those limits. And yet they are going forward.

Notice where this leaves us. Gone is the mechanical, clockwork model of the universe. Gone is simple materialism. The natural, at its deepest level, seems almost . . . supernatural.

I have heard that some Christians are appalled at the new physics, that its seeming lack of rationality shakes their faith. Surely, they think, the Creator would build the universe according to a more logical plan. But just as the infinite God—a union of three distinct

Great Bohr-Einstein Debate" in the series Space Time, PBS Digital Studios, September 21, 2016, https:// www.youtube.com/watch?v=tafGL02EUOA.

38. See Elise Krull, "If You Thought Quantum Mechanics Was Weird, Check Out Entangled Time," *Science Alert*, April 14, 2018, accessed June 10, 2019, https://www.sciencealert.com/if-you -thought-quantum-mechanics-was-weird-check-out-entangled-time.

persons, one of whom became incarnate within his creation—staggers the human intellect, there is no reason why his created order should not be similarly staggering.

It is said that the Big Bang began as a quantum event. Wouldn't that require an observer?[39] Might we think of God not just as a cosmic watchmaker but as the infinite creator who spoke reality into existence and as the observer who sustains all the quantum events that constitute the universe?

Conclusion: The Reality of Mathematics

Of course, quantum physics is not irrational at all, nor is the universe it discloses. How, one might wonder, can scientists penetrate such mysteries, if they go beyond their comprehension? They do so by means of a higher rationality that eludes our mundane, common-sense thinking. Namely, mathematics.

The discoveries of quantum physics are grounded in empirical observation and experimentation, but their foundation is mathematical equations, calculations, and proofs. Actually, the mathematics often comes first. What mathematics predicts is then confirmed in the laboratory. And this is the most remarkable phenomenon of them all.

Mathematics, which is the underlying basis for all of the sciences, is a mental construction. And yet it corresponds exactly to the external world. That mathematics "works" would suggest that there is a connection between mind and matter. Or that there is a Mind that has constituted the physical world, making it possible for lesser minds to apprehend it.

Mathematics bridges the subjective and the objective. Contrary to the modernist position that only matter is real, numbers—though accounting for material reality—are nonmaterial.

Contrary to the postmodernist position that because reality is a mental construction "there are no absolutes," numbers—mental construction or no—are absolute.

The mathematical order of the universe goes beyond this or that particular example of intelligent design. Mathematics shows that *everything* is designed. Even *randomness* can be accounted for mathematically.

---

39. See Stephen Hawking, *A Brief History of Time* (New York: Bantam, 1998), 138; and Bobbie L. Foote, *Beyond Science* (Colorado Springs, CO: Bobbie Leon Foote, 2012), 21–23.

The existentialists of the modernist era and the relativists of the postmodernist era were fond of saying that the universe, while mindlessly repeating its physical laws, has no order or significance as far as human beings are concerned. Rather, human beings must create their own order and significance. But the accord of mathematics to reality suggests that there is an objective order after all, and that its physical properties are far from mindless. That means that human beings do not have to be alienated from the physical world—from nature, from their bodies, from reality—but can embrace the creation and their own creatureliness through a relationship with their Creator.

3

Mastering Nature

The Achievements of Technology

Science, with its promise of explaining all things and exorcising religion, has been the preoccupation of modernists, past and present. Postmodernists in all their variations are preoccupied, on the other hand, with technology.

Science and technology are *not* the same, though they are related (just as modernism and postmodernism are related).

The word *science* means "knowledge," from the Latin word *scientia*. According to classical thought as it developed through the Middle Ages and the Renaissance, there are three categories of knowledge: natural science (knowledge of creation); moral science (knowledge of human beings); and theological science (knowledge of God).

Technology comes from the Greek word *techne* (τέχνη), meaning "art" or "craft." Technology is the capacity to make or to do things. Classical thought recognized three categories of art: liberal arts (mastery of language and mathematics to equip a free citizen for productive liberty); mechanical arts (involving the useful skills: agriculture, constructing buildings, waging war, hunting, trade, weaving, cooking, metalwork); and fine arts (making aesthetic works valuable in themselves: painting, sculpture, musical performance).

The post-Christian mind-set narrowed "science" so that the *only* recognized category of knowledge is natural science, going so far as to insist that knowledge of human beings and knowledge of God must also conform to its conventions, as in social science and critical scholarship of the Bible. A similar narrowing took place with the arts. Though the fine arts and the liberal arts continue to exist, often in a marginalized form, the only "technology" recognized today is the application of scientific findings in the mechanical arts.[1]

Scientists discover knowledge about the natural order, whereupon engineers, inventors, and designers turn that knowledge into technology. Technologists are, quite literally, the artists. They are the creators.

However great the accomplishments of science in our post-Christian world, the accomplishments of technology are even greater. Science understands nature, but technology *conquers* nature.

Today, in the euphoria of our technological triumphs—our information technology, our electronic media, biotechnology—we feel that we can make reality do our bidding. That we can make our own realities. No wonder we are constructivists. No wonder we deify ourselves.

Overcoming Our Limits

Technology has allowed us to overcome many of the limits imposed on us by nature. Technology has also extended our human powers.

Distance has been all but obliterated by automobiles, aircraft, and telecommunications. Scarcity—of food and other necessities, which has nearly always been part of the human condition—has been greatly mitigated by agricultural technology and the industrial revolution. And disease, the vulnerability of the human body, has been greatly mitigated by modern medicine, which has greatly extended our lifespans and enhanced the quality of our lives by minimizing sickness and suffering.

---

1. Universities continue to be organized around the "arts and sciences," but the "liberal arts" have become synonymous with the "humanities," into which are shoehorned the "fine arts" and what were once the "moral sciences" of history and government. Theological science, when it is present at all, is also crammed into the "liberal arts," which has lost most of its original subjects (the trivium of grammar, logic, and rhetoric; the quadrivium of arithmetic, geometry, music, and astronomy) and its purpose, the equipping of a free citizen. But all of this comes from the loss of classical education, which some Christians are recovering.

Yet for all our technology, we still exist in space and time. Many are still in want. And we still suffer physically. And technology has not cured us of death. But what formerly seemed natural—the vastness of the world, the constant effort to find enough to eat, getting sick, dying—now seems unnatural, as if there is something wrong when technology cannot let us transcend our physical limits.

Technology has also amplified our distinctly human powers. Our minds have a great capacity to reason and calculate, but these capabilities are multiplied by calculators, computers, and artificial intelligence. No longer are we limited to the use of our individual minds as, first, the technology of books allowed us to access the minds of others, including those long dead. And now the fruits of untold numbers of minds and an incalculable amount of information are all linked together, accessible to all, via the Internet.

Perhaps our greatest powers come from language, which allows us to communicate our very selves with others and binds us together into communities and societies. Writing is a technology, which made possible the preservation of oral language. Then the printing press made writing and reading available to everyone. Now the Internet ramps up the printing press exponentially so that virtually everyone can communicate whatever they wish and tap into global networks of relationships, doing so instantaneously. Our new information technology still depends on writing and reading—with its writing-based social media and hyperlinked information sources—but it also facilitates oral and visual communication, with cell phones, video, and streaming media.

Technology addresses not only what we need but what we want, improving not only our survival but our comfort; making us more productive not only in our work and our quest for knowledge but in our entertainment and pleasures. Air-conditioning has made habitable parts of the country with unbearable heat and humidity. Now Florida is one of the most populous states in the union. Some have blamed air-conditioning for the massive growth of the federal government, since now lawmakers and bureaucrats can stay in Washington, DC, all year round instead of leaving in the sweltering summers as they used to. One of my favorite new technologies, which I appreciate more than my computer, is my GPS navigation device. Despite lacking a sense of direction, I don't get lost anymore!

Technology, unlike some other human endeavors, is cumulative; that is to say, technology—unlike psychological theories, contemporary artistic movements, or liberal theologies—is not always starting over from ground zero. As they say, you do not have to reinvent the wheel. Once the wheel was invented, long ago, other inventors could add the refinement of an axle. Over the centuries, the wheel gave us the cart, and then the chariot and then the carriage. We replaced the horse with a steam engine and got the locomotive engine pulling railway cars. We devised an internal combustion engine, which can be much smaller, and we got the automobile. Year by year, refinements, features, and new technology were added. The next stage may be the self-driving car. (Notice how our language preserves the past while remaining capable of expressing whatever is new. "Car," meaning a vehicle with wheels, is the root word for cart, chariot, carriage, railway car, the Model-T car, the sportscar, the electric car, etc.)

The same conservative methodology—innovation by building on previous discoveries and putting them together in new combinations—applies to the way developments in symbolic logic, electronics, silicon chemistry, and mechanical calculators came together to form the computer. This, in turn, was integrated with separate developments in telecommunications, video technology, and satellite technology. All of which has come together into a critical mass, resulting in exponential advances year by year.

To be sure, there are technological revolutions—the Iron Age, the agricultural revolution, the printing press, the Industrial Revolution, modern medicine, the digital revolution—but these too were put into motion by building on previous discoveries. They were revolutionary because of the human and social impact of these technologies. Because technology, for all of its wonders, comes at a cost.

What Technology Does to Us

Socrates worried that the relatively new technology for the Greeks of writing—setting down oral speech with visual symbols—would mean the lessening of the power of memory. And, of course, he was correct.

Students who formerly memorized the complete works of Homer so that they could recite them began to just store the *Iliad* and the *Odyssey* on their shelves, to consult only when needed. Thus Socrates never wrote down his ideas, which emerged not while he was facing a blank piece of papyrus but when conversing with his friends and disciples. This allowed for a very high level of thought, but it would have been lost forever if it were not for his student Plato, who wrote down his dialogues and thus preserved them forever. (The same could be said of Jesus, who, in his earthly ministry, did not write but rather preached. He was the "living Word" [see below] whose life and teachings were put into writing by Matthew, Mark, Luke, and John and thus made accessible to us even today. Though since their words were divinely inspired, we could say that the Son, with the Father and the Holy Spirit, wrote down the Word of God into a book.)

But it is worth considering Socrates's critique of writing as an example of how even the most basic technology and the very best technology has its tradeoffs. In the dialogue *Phaedrus* (360 BC), Socrates recounts an Egyptian myth, in which the god Thamus questions the invention of his fellow deity Theuth, the inventor of the arts, including writing:

> **Socrates.** [Thamus says,] . . . This discovery of yours will create forgetfulness in the learners' souls, because they will not use their memories; they will trust to the external written characters and not remember of themselves. The specific which you have discovered is an aid not to memory, but to reminiscence, and you give your disciples not truth, but only the semblance of truth; they will be hearers of many things and will have learned nothing; they will appear to be omniscient and will generally know nothing; they will be tiresome company, having the show of wisdom without the reality. . . .

> **Socrates.** He would be a very simple person, and quite a stranger to the oracles of Thamus or Ammon, who should leave in writing or receive in writing any art under the idea that the written word would be intelligible or certain; or who deemed that writing was at all better than knowledge and recollection of the same matters?

Phaedrus. That is most true.

Socrates. I cannot help feeling, Phaedrus, that writing is unfortunately like painting; for the creations of the painter have the attitude of life, and yet if you ask them a question they preserve a solemn silence. And the same may be said of speeches. You would imagine that they had intelligence, but if you want to know anything and put a question to one of them, the speaker always gives one unvarying answer. And when they have been once written down they are tumbled about anywhere among those who may or may not understand them, and know not to whom they should reply, to whom not: and, if they are maltreated or abused, they have no parent to protect them; and they cannot protect or defend themselves.

Phaedrus. That again is most true.

Socrates. Is there not another kind of word or speech far better than this, and having far greater power—a son of the same family, but lawfully begotten?

Phaedrus. Whom do you mean, and what is his origin?

Socrates. I mean an intelligent word graven in the soul of the learner, which can defend itself, and knows when to speak and when to be silent.

Phaedrus. You mean the living word of knowledge which has a soul, and of which written word is properly no more than an image?[2]

Written words are lifeless. They cannot answer the questions of readers, defend themselves from objections, or explain what they mean to readers who cannot understand them. That is, they cannot participate in dialectic, in the give-and-take conversations that Socrates believes are essential for thinking and understanding, the living discussions that Plato captures and freezes by recording the "dialogues." This is in contrast to the "living word" and the living mind of an actual human being, whose thoughts are "graven in the soul."

---

2. Plato, *Phaedrus* (360 BC), trans. Benjamin Jowett, accessed June 10, 2019, http://classics.mit.edu/Plato/phaedrus.html.

Technology is an extension of this living mind, which creates ways to compensate for its limitations. Ironically, while technology overcomes those limits and multiplies human power, it underscores how limited we are, of ourselves. We are physically weak, an easy prey for animal or human predators—so we invented weapons. We are bound by time and space—so we invented ships and automobiles and airliners. Our lives are brief—so we invented medicine so that we can live longer. Our greatest thinkers die—so we devise ways of preserving and storing their words by means of writing. And though such technology mitigates our condition, we remain weak, bound, and dying. We remain that primal living soul. Though sometimes we like to forget about that fact.

There was a time when most people had never heard a great musician. Then recording technology was invented, so musical performances could be preserved, like writing, for anyone to hear whenever they wanted. As the technology kept improving—vinyl records, then cassette tapes, then CDs, then digital files; distributed by radio, then music stores, then computer downloads, then streaming services—music of every variety suited to every taste became accessible to everyone. This was a great advance for the arts and for the cause of aesthetic experience, which can enrich our lives with meaning and beauty. At the same time, though, the technology changed music.

I remember as a child—I am now very old—my parents inviting friends over for dinner. Afterward they would gather around the piano, and, as my mother played, they would sing. That is what people did before music was recorded. They sang and played musical instruments themselves. (We did have a small black-and-white TV, a radio, and a record player back in the 1950s, but our family had not yet been swept up in the media revolution.)

You can still find that "living music" tradition carried on in some parts of the country with, for example, blue-grass jam sessions (which recall the old family ensembles) and circle singing. In the old days, you might listen to a really good musician by going to a concert or dance hall or asking a talented friend or family member to perform for you. In those cases, the performer made music in front of the audience. In corporate music making, though, everyone gathered into a circle, so that you could hear each other. Think "Will the Circle Be Unbroken?" Some of that oral and aural tradition in music is preserved, like Plato writing down Socratic dialogues, in the recorded genre of folk music.

Today, people continue to love music. But we tend to receive it passively. We don't sing much anymore. As has been said, just about the only places where people sing today is at sporting events (the National Anthem; "Take Me Out to the Ballgame") and—significantly—church. And yet many churches have also been moving to a listening-to-a-performance approach to music.

There are certainly those today who learn to sing or play musical instruments, though not as many as there used to be. (Note the difficulty congregations now often face in finding a church organist, something that used to not be a problem. Today many traditional congregations are using .mp3 files to accompany their liturgy and hymns.) We still can learn to make music for our own satisfaction or for playing with friends. Much music education, though, is oriented to training professional performers. Even amateur musicians emulate the professionals, if only on the karaoke stage. Our default approach to music is not making music ourselves but listening to other people making music.

Technology has also changed music, as well as the other arts, by turning artistic expressions into mass-produced commodities to be bought and sold. The necessity to sell records (or CDs, or downloads) puts art at the mercy of market forces. Artists must create works that mass audiences will buy. Their art must be shaped not only by their creativity but by the desires of consumers.

Technology has turned live drama—the acting out of stories—into movies, television, and streaming videos. Interestingly, the entertainment media do not replace each other but rather multiply. (Contrary to the fears that movies would kill plays, and television would kill movies, we still have them all.) The simple act of imaginative play as practiced by children—pretending to be cops and robbers, gunfighters or swordfighters—has been taken up into gaming technology.

Entertainment technology has become so pervasive that we are constantly stimulated. And yet, ironically, this makes us susceptible to paralyzing boredom. At some point, we get so used to the stimulation that it fails to make an impression, and we need new and ever-increasing stimulations to keep us distracted. Otherwise, we sink into malaise.

Ken Myers has shown how the entertainment industry has created a pop culture that undermines actual culture, with its traditions and values. He also shows how pop culture creates a self-centered, please-me sensibility that has insinuated itself even into the church.[3]

But it isn't just us Christian critics who have been questioning our current technological utopia. In his book *Amusing Ourselves to Death*, media scholar Neil Postman shows how entertainment technology has carried over into education, politics, journalism, and—yes—religion.[4] Postman's book was published back in 1985 and considered mostly the effect of *television*. Now, television has itself transformed from a device that received only a handful of channels over the air into, first, a device that receives hundreds of channels via fiber-optic cables and satellite transmission. And now that device has become a video technology that is integrated with computers and cell phones, allowing viewers to binge-watch any program they want, on demand. What Postman saw happening in 1985 has accelerated exponentially, and all of his warnings have come true.

We have focused here on how music and the arts have been affected by a technology that reduces them to "entertainment" and then to an "industry" and a "culture." But that is only one example. All technology has these kinds of unintended consequences and ripple effects. As Robert R. Johnson has observed:

> Technology helps shape the discursive and material characteristics of cultures. As technologies emerge and are incorporated into a cultural context they alter not just the immediate activity for which they were designed but also have "ripple effects" that shape culture in defining ways.[5]

---

3. See Ken Myers, *All God's Children and Blue Suede Shoes: Christians and Popular Culture* (Wheaton, IL: Crossway, 1989). See also the 2012 edition with a new introduction, in which Myers updates and extends his observations.

4. Neil Postman, *Amusing Ourselves to Death: Public Discourse in the Age of Show Business* (New York: Penguin, 1985).

5. Robert R. Johnson, *User-Centered Technology: A Rhetorical Theory for Computers and Other Mundane Artifacts* (Albany, NY: SUNY Press, 1998), 89.

With the invention of gunpowder, a peasant with a musket could fire a shot that punctures a knight's armor and a cannon ball could knock down the walls of a castle, thus dooming the feudal system. The automobile and interstate highways led to commuting, the rise of suburbia, the decline of cities, and the loss of community.

As A. Trevor Sutton says, discussing Johnson's insight and applying it to social media:

> Far from an inert object waiting passively for an actor to arrive and decide how best to use it, technology is itself an actor networked with other human and non-human actors. Technology thus exerts societal influence, creates an "order," and even predetermines human behaviors. Technology is never neutral; it is always in the process of inclining users toward a certain action, value, or social arrangement.[6]

Though this has always been the case, today not only technology but a trust in technology drives everything else before it.

"Embedded in every tool is an ideological bias," says Postman, "a predisposition to construct the world as one thing rather than another, to value one thing over another, to amplify one sense or skill or attitude more loudly than another."[7] Today, he says, "technology imperiously commandeers our most important terminology. It redefines 'freedom,' 'truth,' 'intelligence,' 'fact,' 'wisdom,' 'memory,' 'history.'"[8] Postman, who died in 2003, says that our culture has surrendered to technology. We now live, he says, in a "technopoly."

Virtual Realities

It is plain to see why those whose culture has given way to a technopoly, whose sensibility is completely shaped by their technological consumption, would be constructivists. According to their experience, reality as they know it really *is* a human creation. They live in climate-controlled houses where they are immersed in their entertainment sys-

---

6. A. Trevor Sutton, "How Facebook Is Transforming Religion," *Sightings*, July 12, 2018, accessed June 10, 2019, https://divinity.uchicago.edu/sightings/how-facebook-transforming-religion.

7. Neil Postman, *Technopoly: The Surrender of Culture to Technology* (New York: Vintage, 1993), 13.

8. Postman, *Technopoly*, 8.

tems. They get in their automobiles, which have both climate-control and an entertainment system, and drive to work, where they use computers either to run their business or to be their business. At home, they interact with their friends, most of whom they have never met in person, on social media. They play video games on their computers or consoles in which they get to be the heroes in their own fantasy world. Even their sexual desires can be fulfilled by means of technology, rather than in a relationship with an actual human being, thanks to Internet pornography. And they may well invest in a virtual reality headset that immerses them in a three-dimensional, 360-degree, multisensory, simulated world. *Of course* those who are oriented to virtual-reality headsets will be constructivists. In their minds, all reality is virtual reality.

Throughout the course of modernism—the eighteenth-century Age of Reason, nineteenth-century materialism, and twentieth-century scientism—which exalted the objective knowledge disclosed by science, precursors of what would later be termed postmodernism—Kantians, Romantics, existentialists, and Nietzscheans—were insisting that the mind is not just a passive receiver of information about the outside world, but rather an active creator of that world. The postmodernists were triumphant in the late twentieth and twenty-first centuries—to the point of credibly maintaining that modernism was *finished*—but this did not mean they had to repudiate the findings of modern science. They thought of the findings of modern science as raw material for constructing reality.

Today's information technology has given us an online "world," as we say, that is the perfect embodiment (well, except the "body" part) of a mentally constructed alternative reality.

Online and video gaming immerses the player in different worlds. These are computer-animated projections of our fantasies, in which we can play the role of superheroes with magical powers. Often the game world is that of medieval-style fantasy literature, so that you play a knight on a quest, battling orcs and dragons, and inhabit three-dimensional realistic-seeming castles and supernatural landscapes. We might play that for awhile, then enter a different world, in which we can fantasize about being a soldier in World War II. Or a drug dealer. Or an assassin. Or a serial killer.

Our online worlds also have a social dimension. In the physical world, we are born into families and must live in communities, where we have friendships, interact with people we do not know, and are part of a culture. Today, many people's relationships are largely in online communities. On social media, they form networks of "friends," with whom they share their lives and their thoughts, even though they are not present with them, and even though they might not have ever met them. The online world also allows for affinity groups, where people can gather together—without, of course, actually gathering anywhere—to share their common interests, passions, and idiosyncrasies.

This is not a bad thing. In our current physical society, which has dysfunctions of its own, including a loss of community, individuals are often lonely, unable to find friends or people with common interests. The Internet allows them to do so. This can result in genuine connections and actual social bonds. For some people, online relationships are better than relationships in the real world, where people judge you on your appearance, where you must conform to social norms, watching what you say and putting on a polite façade. Online interactions, by contrast, are liberating. It is mind-to-mind communication, with no one knowing what you look like, what you do for a living, or what your racial, ethnic, or sexual identity might be (unless it is the bond of the web community you are taking part in at the moment).

Online, you are liberated from your history, your job, and your body, and you can even assume new identities, which is the whole point of many computer games. Of course, you are still stuck with your actual history, your job, your body, and your identity. We cannot completely inhabit the computer universe, at least not yet. But in the meantime, for many people, online is their haven, the place where they go to find meaning and connections in their lives.

One problem with the online society is that without the actual presence of other people, we lose our inhibitions. People post erotic pictures of themselves and circulate inflammatory Twitter comments and then are shocked when they get in trouble when the "real world" finds out about them.

Social conventions keep our outward behavior in line, at least to a certain extent, preventing our inner sinful nature from breaking out into vile and destructive behavior. But with the anonymity of online interactions, we do break out into vile and destructive behavior. Online communication, though sometimes praised as pure connection between two minds, is often, in practice, cruel, hateful, and tormenting. "Trolls" haunt blogs and discussion boards, intruding on affinity groups simply to mock, deride, and spread their poison.

But even the affinity groups, even the online communities of kindred spirits and Facebook "friends," can turn vicious. People may prefer online communities as a way to escape the social expectations and pressures of actual communities. But online groups tend to establish social expectations and pressures of their own, becoming as narrow-minded, conformist, and judgmental as the worst stereotype of the insular small town. But because online there are few moral inhibitions and little sense of the empathy we feel in the presence of another human being, the cliques and the shaming and the cutting words are intensified. The resulting sense of rejection is also intensified, leading some victims of online abuse to desolation or even suicide.

You may know someone like this: a friend who, in person, is the nicest guy you would ever meet. He is active in your church and always eager to help with whatever he can do. But online he is a monster. He is a troll, the kind of monster in the folktales who hides under bridges to prey on whoever passes by. Since he lives in multiple worlds, he has still more personalities: though a kind father and a loving husband, he becomes a rabid authoritarian when he gets on his political sites, a serial killer on his computer games, a pious Christian on his Bible study app, and a sexual predator on the porn sites. Though this individual is evidently sane, he has a form of multiple personality disorder. Which is his true self? Where is his "living soul"?

Such conflicting personalities and identities have become part of our post-Christian condition. The technology promotes the compartmentalization of our lives. We can inhabit so many worlds; it is as if we are each many different people. A man might play a game in which he is a superhero rescuing the defenseless. Then he switches to one in which he shoots defenseless women and runs over elderly pedestrians.

Then he takes part in his Bible study site. Then he makes constructive comments on a politically conservative blog. Then at night he hits the porn sites.

The virtual world we inhabit also distorts our notion of truth. The Kantians could talk about how the mind shapes what it considers to be true, and the postmodernists can complain that truth claims are little more than the cultural constructions of those who hold power. But the online world allows truth claims to be manufactured, promulgated, believed, and acted upon with little reference to the outside world at all.

Once again, the technology begins by offering something good. The Internet gives everyone a platform. No longer may a few gatekeepers—journalists, academics, and corporations that can afford a printing press—control what information and ideas are allowed to circulate through the culture. Our new information technology gives every individual access to a mass audience. New voices can be heard. Diverse opinions and beliefs can battle it out in the marketplace of ideas.

At the same time, though, the lack of gatekeepers means that truth is on an equal par with falsehood; and distinguishing between them is more difficult. Today's technology encourages the construction of plausibility paradigms and alternative perspectives of interpretation, to use the terms used by the postmodernists. Individuals can latch onto the "truths" (often put into quotation marks today) that they *want* to believe in or that accords with their *will to power* (the will taking the place of the intellect; power taking the place of reason). Different versions of "truth" can become the basis for the various contending online "communities." Such a climate becomes ripe for manipulation by political activists, ideological propagandists, and Russian trolls. As a result, *all sides* complain of "fake news." Verifying what is factual and what is fake is also fraught with difficulty, as fact-checking sites are themselves accused of operating from a political bias.

As a result, we don't know what to believe or whom to believe. At the same time, we will believe in anything. No wonder that in our post-Christian times we tend to assume that truth is relative and that we must live without it.

Conclusion

What are we to think of technology and our current online virtual technopoly as Christians? Are the Amish right in just repudiating modern technology altogether, from automobiles to the buttons on clothing? Of course, even the Amish do not reject all technology. They retain horse-drawn buggies and hand-operated farm implements. They keep the eighteenth- and nineteenth-century technology that they brought with them when they immigrated from the old country. But why draw the line at the nineteenth century? Already the printing press, which the Amish retain, was impacting society, making possible mass education, the individualism of private reading, and a new social mobility. Ironically, some Amish today are reportedly making exceptions in their antitechnology asceticism for computers and cell phones.

The Bible says little about technology, as such. Much of human civilization proceeded from Cain, the father of agriculture and the builder of cities, and from his immediate descendants: Jabal, "the father of those who dwell in tents and have livestock"; his brother Jubal, "the father of all those who play the lyre and pipe"; and their half-brother Tubal-cain, "the forger of all instruments of bronze and iron," who can thus be considered at least one of the fathers of technology (Gen. 4:17–22). Such a pedigree might suggest that civilization, including music and technology, is tainted by sin—which, of course, it is, from the fall not just of Cain but of Cain's father—but the Bible elsewhere has positive things to say about music, agriculture, and cities (including "the holy city, new Jerusalem, coming down out of heaven from God" [Rev. 21:2]). As for technology, in almost a paradigm of how it operates, young David multiplied his strength with the help of centrifugal force when he killed the giant Goliath with a sling (1 Sam. 17).

I feel ungrateful for criticizing the Internet and our new information technology since I myself use it so avidly. I am a blogger. I love having the world's information at my fingertips. I could never have written this book without access by means of a few clicks to information resources (Pew Research reports, online articles, Wikipedia factoids) and examples of what I am chronicling (surrogate mother advertisements, sperm donor sites, lists of newly discovered genders, and other telling illustrations of what I will be getting into in later chapters).

We have the Christian freedom to employ technology—look at what Christians have done with the printing press—and should thank God for blessing us through the vocations of inventors, engineers, and technicians. But Christians—indeed, all human beings—must also live in the real, physical, created world, not just be hunched over their computer screens.

4

Recovering Reality

The Story of Kant's Neighbor

So the human being stands outside of nature. The modernist imagines the human mind observing, understanding, and exploiting the natural order, thus mastering it. The postmodernist imagines the human mind creating reality, whether by constructing truth or by taking the raw materials of nature and technologically making new realities out of them, thus bending nature to the human will.

Christian critiques often accuse human beings of taking on the role of God. But notice what kind of god we try to make ourselves into. When we take the place of God, we do not emulate the Christian God who cares for his creation, is providentially involved in its every facet, and became incarnate for its redemption. Rather, we try to make ourselves into the god of deism, the impersonal, detached deity of the Enlightenment's "rational religion" that makes and observes. If we are gods, we are watchmaker gods.

The actual deists of the eighteenth century believed that their deity was, in some sense, righteous, overseeing a moral order. But in our role as gods, we are not righteous at all, demanding that reality serve and obey us but doing nothing that brings salvation. Our very attempts to exalt ourselves to the point of taking God's place disclose how sinful and small we are, as the god we turn ourselves into is pathetic, tyrannical, unloving, and unworthy of worship.

If the modern and postmodern condition is to stand at a distance from nature, what about the environmental movement? Surely environmentalism honors and cares for nature. Indeed, the great popularity of the environmental movement, which has become a de facto religion for many people today, demonstrates the human need to overcome their alienation from the natural order. But notice that by "nature," environmentalists tend to mean forests, mountains, and wildlife. Anything human is *not* "natural." To their mind, civilization, with its technologies and economics and communities, is the *enemy* of nature.

For today's environmentalists, human beings not only stand apart from nature, *they can destroy nature*. Nature is fragile. Nature is weak. It is at the mercy of "Man," whose plastic waste is wiping out wildlife, whose economic rapacity is ruining the landscape, and whose technologies are warming the earth to the point of an upcoming global apocalypse.

I am by no means minimizing environmental concerns, but my point here is that even those most committed to nature cannot help but think of human beings as being separate from the natural order. And, like the modernists and the postmodernists, as being godlike. A god can create the world; and a god can destroy the world.

We human beings need to recover our *creatureliness*. We must come to realize that for all of our scientific reasoning and our technological creations, we are creatures. We do not create the world, as the constructivists imagine. Nor do we create ourselves, as is the assumption of self-help videos and "you-can-be-whatever-you-choose" philosophies. Rather, we have been created by a creator other than ourselves, which makes us part of a created order. We are answerable to this created order and must live within its terms. This objective, physical creation is *not* meaningless, leaving human beings to make up their own subjective meanings, but is rather charged with meaning. But the Creator loves us. He is active in and through his creation, bestowing his gifts and carrying out his saving purposes.

Our civilizations, technologies, and communities are also part of this created order, no less than forests, mountains, and wildlife. As later chapters will show, our current problems with sexuality, our social dysfunctions, and our religious confusions also have to do with losing our sense of creatureliness. This entails going beyond nature to creation. And to embrace creation, we must know the Creator.

One way forward can be seen in a recently rediscovered eighteenth-century thinker who has become something of a sensation in philosophical and theological circles today: J. G. Hamann.

Kant's Neighbor

We began this section of the book by discussing the thought of Immanuel Kant, who was simultaneously the pinnacle of Enlightenment rationalism (thus one of the most important modernist thinkers) and the originator of constructivism (laying the groundwork for postmodernism).

Kant had a friend and neighbor in Königsberg, Prussia, a German city that, because of the fortunes of war, is now Kaliningrad, Russia. His name was Johann Georg Hamann (1730–1788). The two were part of a circle of bright young men who wholeheartedly and with great enthusiasm embraced the Enlightenment. Kant would summarize the spirit of the Enlightenment with the motto "Dare to Know!" and the group of friends eagerly cast down traditions and conventional ideas all in the name of Reason.

Hamann was brilliant and well educated, with a particular ability in languages, but he lacked the financial prospects and the sense of purpose of the other Enlightened young gentlemen. Hamann traveled back and forth between Germany and Latvia, trying various professions and trying to find himself. The father of one of the friends, who owned a trading company, took pity on Hamann and hired him to go to London to conduct some business. Hamann botched the assignment, which made him feel humiliated and depressed. He met a bon vivant and lived with him awhile, joining him in a life of debauchery. But then the two fell out, and Hamann moved to a rooming house—almost out of money, owing three hundred pounds, and now in failing health. Dejected, with nothing else to do, he bought a Bible.[1]

---

1. For the biographical details, see John R. Betz, *After Enlightenment: The Post-Secular Vision of J. G. Hamann* (Oxford, UK: John Wiley & Sons, 2012), 25–37. Betz's book includes summaries, partial translations, and discussions of all of his works and is probably the best introduction to Hamann and his significance.

Reading the Bible, for Hamann, was overwhelming. The insecure but prideful twenty-eight-year-old felt that God was addressing him personally in his Word. God's law was demolishing his every pretension, revealing his sins, and bringing him to repentance. And the gospel was revealing God's grace in Christ, which Hamann described as being even more shocking than the realization of his sin. Hamann described his experience of reading God's Word:

> The further I went, the newer it became for me, the more divine was my experience of its content and effect. I forgot all my books about it; I was even ashamed that I had ever compared them to the book of God, had ever set them side by side, and had ever preferred another book to it. I found the unity of the divine will in the redemption of Jesus Christ, so that all history, all miracles, all the commandments and works of God converge at this central point, in order to lead the human soul out of slavery, bondage, blindness, folly, and death from sin to the greatest happiness, the highest blessedness, and a reception of such good gifts, whose greatness, when they are revealed to us, must shock us more than our own unworthiness or the possibility of making ourselves worthy of them. I recognized my own offenses in the history of the Jewish people; I read the story of my own life.[2]

Thus, when he was reading about Cain killing Abel, whose blood cried out from the ground (Gen. 5), Hamann saw himself in Cain. And Abel's blood reminded him of Christ's blood. "I could no longer hide from God that I was the killer of my brother, the murderer of his only begotten Son."

> Despite my great weakness, despite the long resistance which I had, until now, put up against his witness and his tender touch, the Spirit of God kept on revealing to me the mystery of divine love and the benefit of faith in our gracious, only Savior, more and always more.

---

2. J. G. Hamann, "Thoughts on the Course of My Life," in *London Writings*, trans. John Kleinig (Evansville, IN: Ballast Press, forthcoming). Only excerpts from what we might call this personal testimony of his conversion, written soon after the fact, are currently available in English. The Australian theologian John Kleinig is working on a translation of the entire *London Writings*, and I am serving as editor. The quotations here are from an early draft of the translation.

Hamann was converted:

> "My son! Give me your heart!" [Prov 23:26]—Here it is, my God!
> You demanded it, as blind, hard, rocky, perverse, and stubborn as
> it was. Purify it, create it anew, and let it become the workshop of
> your good Spirit. It has deceived me so often, when it was in my
> own hands, that I no longer wish to acknowledge it as my own. It
> is a leviathan that you alone can tame—by your indwelling let it
> enjoy peace, comfort, and salvation.

He closes his testimony by confessing his faith. First, he rapturously
extols God's Word:

> I conclude, from the evidence of my own experience, with heart-
> felt and sincere thanksgiving for his saving Word which I have
> tested and found to be the only light by which we not only come
> to God, but also get to know ourselves. It is the most precious gift
> of God's grace that surpasses the whole natural world and all its
> treasures as much as our immortal spirit surpasses the clay of our
> flesh and blood. It is the most amazing and venerable revelation
> of the most profound, most sublime, most wonderful mysteries
> of the godhead, whether it be in heaven, on earth, or in hell, the
> mysteries of God's nature, attributes, and his great, bountiful
> will chiefly toward us poor people, full of the most significant
> disclosures throughout the course of all the ages until eternity.
> It is the only bread and manna for our souls, which a Christian
> can no more do without than the earthly man can do without his
> daily necessities and sustenance—yes, I confess that this Word of
> God accomplishes just as great miracles in the soul of a devout
> Christian, whether he be simple or learned, as those described in
> it. I confess that the understanding of this book and faith in its
> contents can therefore be gained by no other means than through
> the same Spirit, who inspired its authors, and that his unutterable
> sighs, which he creates in our hearts, are of the same nature as
> the inexpressible images, which are scattered throughout sacred
> scripture with a greater richness than all the seeds of the natural
> world and its realms.

Then Hamann confesses Jesus Christ:

Secondly, I confess with my heart and my best understanding that without faith in Jesus Christ it is impossible to know God and what a loving, unutterably good and generous being he is, whose wisdom, omnipotence and other attributes seem to be only, as it were, instruments of his love for humanity. I confess that this preference for men, the insects of creation, belongs to greatest depths of divine revelation. I confess that Jesus Christ was not only pleased to become a man, but also a poor and most wretched man. I confess that for us the Holy Spirit has published a book for his Word in which, like a fool or a madman, yes like an unholy and unclean spirit, he turned proud reason's children's stories, trivial, contemptible events, into the history of heaven and God (1 Cor. 1:25). I confess that this faith shows us that all our own deeds and the noblest fruits of human virtue are nothing but the sketches from the finest pen under a magnifying glass, or the most sensitive skin as seen under it. I confess that it is therefore impossible for us to love ourselves and our neighbor without faith in God which his Spirit produces and the merit of the only Mediator. In short, a person must be a true Christian to be a proper father, a proper child, a good citizen, a proper patriot, a good subject, yes a good employer and a good employee. I confess that every good deed, in the strictest sense of the word, is impossible without God, and that he indeed is its only author.

Notice that here too Hamann has discovered the doctrine of vocation.[3] But his own vocation emerged and was sharpened by the reaction of his friends.

Metacritic

Hamann's enlightened friends, including Immanuel Kant, were shocked by his conversion and appalled at the radical transformation they saw in his life. Your newfound piety, they said, is clearly excessive. Your religiosity is a return to outdated dogma and superstitions. You have abandoned the cause of Reason! They attempted to argue Hamann out of his new enthusiasm so that he would return to a state of rational enlightenment.

---

3. See my book *God at Work: Your Christian Vocation in All of Life* (Wheaton, IL: Crossway, 2002).

Fine, said Hamann. Reason did not bring me to Christ, he told them, so it is unlikely to take me away from him. And it did not.

But turn-about is fair play. Hamann then began challenging *his friend's* Enlightenment worldview. In conversations and letters, then in brief essays and reviews, and then in treatises on a wide variety of topics—aesthetics, language, philosophy, religion—Hamann launched what today has been called the most philosophically sophisticated critique of the Enlightenment.[4] This culminated when Kant published his *Critique of Pure Reason* in 1781, one of the monumental texts of Western philosophy; Hamann came back with his *Metacritique of the Purism of Reason*, a work which, in addition to coining the *meta*-prefix that would become popular among postmodernists, may be the definitive refutation of Kant.

Hamann's objection to the Enlightenment view of reason is, first of all, that it reduces reality—including tangible, physical things—to mental abstractions. Actual human beings become abstracted into a collective "humanity." What we experience with our senses in the fields, the mountains, and the arts cannot be understood, we are led to believe, unless we can turn them into abstractions. Even God becomes a philosophical concept rather than the highly specific, highly personal Holy One of Israel. The rationalists of the Enlightenment thus use reason, ironically, to distance themselves from existence.

Hamann also notes the rationalists' obsession with *certainty*. They are not content unless their knowledge is absolutely certain, beyond the shadow of a doubt, and they are convinced that reason can give them this assurance. We see this most explicitly with Descartes, who systematically doubted *everything* until he found the one thing upon which he could be absolutely certain, namely, his own existence. Note the irony: reason's quest for certainty tends to manifest itself in the opposite of certainty, namely, skepticism and doubt.

Descartes used reason to build upon the certainty that he thinks and that therefore he exists, arriving at what he considered to be other reliable truths. But then other Enlightenment thinkers—Leibnitz,

---

4. Ted Kinnaman, "Johann Georg Hamann (1730–1788)," *Internet Encyclopedia of Philosophy: A Peer-Reviewed Academic Resource*, accessed June 10, 2019, https://www.iep.utm.edu/hamann/.

Spinoza—challenged Descartes and countered with systems of their own, which also claimed to be built on reason and to offer certainty.

Kant took reason, including empirical reason, about as far as it could go, to the point of reasoning about reasoning and exploring how the mind makes sense of empirical sense impressions. But his project comes to the conclusion that all we can know is the "phenomena" as the mind perceives them and that we cannot know *anything* about the "thing in itself." Kant's achievement of rational certainty makes *everything* uncertain!

Hamann criticizes Kant for problematizing ordinary experience. We go through a day interacting with the world, including innumerable physical "things"—breaking an egg for breakfast, working with tools, talking with friends, walking through the garden, enjoying the sunset. Are you saying, Immanuel, that we are not *really* experiencing these things? Yes, when you reason about them so closely, simple perceptions become mind-bogglingly complex, but what good is a philosophy that makes ordinary life, in effect, disappear?

Notice how Hamann's "metacriticism" applies not just to modernistic rationalism but to postmodernist constructivism. In rejecting objectivity altogether, postmodernists will say that, yes, objective reality exists, but we can never know it, since our minds and culture get in the way. In addition to such overt Kantianism, others ascribe our experiences to power relationships or to political oppression or to human choices. But, again, all of this turns ordinary experiences and perceptions into philosophical or political *problems*, as complicated enigmas to be regarded with a "hermeneutics of suspicion." Hamann gives us a touchstone: what does this way of thinking do to ordinary life—walking the dog, going to the grocery store, spending time with your family?

The assumption that the only valid knowledge is what we can know with absolute certainty is commonplace today. It comes up all the time in conversations with agnostics: "If only I could be *sure* that God exists!" "I know there are reasons to believe in God, but there are also reasons not to. How can I know for *certain*?" Atheists, of course, *are* certain, basing their unbelief, they say, on reason: "Prove that God exists." "There is no evidence that God exists." "Belief in God is irrational."

Now, of course, there are rational proofs, grounded in reason alone, of God's existence. Not only Saint Thomas Aquinas but the rationalistic philosophers of the Enlightenment provided them: Descartes, Leibnitz, Spinoza, and even Kant. That atheists are seldom persuaded by them proves Hamann's point that reason is seldom as conclusive, even for rationalists, as they say it is.

But those who demand certainty today look not to philosophers but to science, and many people today believe that science provides that certainty. Scientific criteria—that is, empirical evidence analyzed by the experimental method—have become the *only* measures of rationalism broadly accepted today. This, of course, rules out, by definition, any consideration of "things that are unseen" (2 Cor. 4:18), which would include not only religious truths but other realities as well, such as mathematics, with its invisible laws that science relies on.

Hamann showed that, in fact, *reason cannot give certainty*. Even reason at its best. "The system of today, which provides the proof of your presuppositions," he observed, "will be the fairytale of tomorrow."[5] One philosopher, ideology, and school of thought succeeds another. Even scientific empiricism, which Hamann would appreciate for its attention to the physical realm, cannot provide total certainty once the data is processed through an intellectual hypothesis and then a more abstract theory. One scientific theory gives way to another, as more and more data are discovered.

But this lack of absolute certainty does not mean that science, the various schools of thought, and reason itself cannot give us reliable knowledge and even truth. All knowledge, according to Hamann, including the knowledge disclosed by reason, *depends on faith*.

Faith has to do with trust, acceptance, and reliance. Faith gives a different kind of knowledge than the discursive process of reasoning. It is more like perception. Hamann describes faith as being similar to tasting and seeing.[6]

Reason itself rests on assumptions that elude rational proof but that are taken on faith. Reasoning requires accepting the validity of logic, the correspondence of thought to the world, the consistent order

---

5. Quoted in Betz, *After Enlightenment*, 96, from "The Magi of the East."
6. See Betz, *After Enlightenment*, 83.

of the universe, the laws of mathematics, and trusting the contributions of others.

Hamann makes use of the radical skeptic David Hume, of all people, to make his case. Hume showed that there is no *logical* connection between cause and effect. The conviction that A causes B is a "belief." The same holds true for inductive reasoning itself, since we can never know *for certain* that one empirical observation will hold true for other cases at a future time. These, along with other foundational assumptions—such as the uniformity of nature, the existence of other people, the existence of the self—are all "beliefs," though ones that we can generally rely upon.

But what Hume intended for skepticism, Hamann utilized for the defense of faith. Whereas his Enlightened friends exalted reason and derided faith, Hamann showed that reason needs "belief," that is, faith. And whereas his Enlightened friends, along with Hume, had the agenda of undermining Christianity, Hamann, in making the case for faith in general, was also making the case for faith in Christ.

When Hume said that believing in miracles takes a miracle, he meant to disparage Christianity. Hume wrote:

> So that, upon the whole, we may conclude not only that the Christian religion was at first attended with miracles—but even to this day cannot be believed by any reasonable person without one. Mere reason is not sufficient to convince us of its veracity, and whoever is moved by faith to assent to it is conscious of a continual miracle in his own person, which subverts all the principles of his understanding and gives him a determination to believe what is most contrary to custom and experience.[7]

But Hamann agreed! "Hume may have said this with a scornful and critical air," he commented, "yet all the same, this is orthodoxy and a witness to the truth from the mouth of an enemy and persecutor."[8] Faith in Christ is a gift of God. That Christians have faith in Christ is God's continual miracle.

---

7. Quoted in Walter Leibrecht, *God and Man in the Thought of Hamann* (Philadelphia: Fortress Press, 1966), 14–15. The quotation is from Hume's *Enquiries Concerning Human Understanding*.
8. Quoted in Leibrecht, *God and Man in the Thought of Hamann*, 15, from a letter to Kant.

Similarly, that we can know anything—the faith that makes reason possible—is also God's gift. Reason is not autonomous because we are not autonomous. For Hamann, reason is impossible without God, as is knowledge, faith, and the human mind.

Hamann's most devastating criticism of Kant and the argument that would have the greatest influence in the field of philosophy is that Kant ignored *language*. Kant's attempt at "pure" reason failed to take language into account. The fact is, Hamann pointed out, we cannot think without language. There can be no reason apart from language. "Reason is language."[9]

Furthermore, the language that shapes our thoughts and our reasonings brings with it culture and tradition. The figure of the disinterested rationalistic observer, working with no preconceptions or biases and without any personal investment, applying reason and reason alone—the human being as deistic god—is a myth. Any philosophy or account of human nature must take language into account.[10] Hamann's emphasis on the role of language, as we shall see, would become a major theme of both modern and postmodern philosophy.

Hamann did not stop with a "metacritique" of the Enlightenment. He went on to offer a different basis for language and for nature—also aesthetics, reason, ethics, society, and humanity—namely, the Word of God, the creation, and Jesus Christ.

The Self-Giving of the Father, the Son, and the Holy Spirit

Hamann's insight that language underlies all thought is now recognized as beginning the "linguistic turn" in modern philosophy, which culminated with Ludwig Wittgenstein.[11] But in the hands of later philosophers, this attention to language would take different forms.

A movement of twentieth-century analytic philosophers practiced "linguistic analysis." These thinkers were logical positivists, believing that only the material world as accessed by the scientific method holds any claim to truth. They believed that thoughts about nonmaterial

---

9. Quoted in Oswald Bayer, *A Contemporary in Dissent: Johann Georg Hamann as Radical Enlightener*, trans. Roy A. Harrisville and Mark C. Mattes (Grand Rapids, MI: Eerdmans, 2012), who devotes a chapter to these issues, 156–70.

10. See Betz, *After Enlightenment*, 248–57.

11. See Lauri Snellman, "Hamann's Influence on Wittgenstein," *Nordic Wittgenstein Review* 7.1 (2018): 59–82; DOI 10.15845/nwr.v7i1.3467.

reality, including not only religion but most abstract ideas, were made possible only because of language. So they took on the project of examining the classic issues of philosophy—free will versus determinism, the nature of the soul, the existence of God—and arguing that they are nothing but words. The language makes it sound as if conversations about such concepts mean something, but they are only "language games" and so are technically meaningless. After World War II, this kind of logical positivism was mostly abandoned—after all, its central claims about materialism, science, and language are themselves abstract ideas rather than material facts—though attention to language, as well as logic, remains a hallmark of the "analytical philosophy" that dominates the discipline of philosophy in England and the United States.

The postmodernists took the "linguistic turn" in another direction. A number of the formative postmodernist thinkers were literary critics who stressed the instability of language. They emphasized the arbitrary relationship between the "sign" (e.g., the word) and the "signified" (what the word refers to in the world) so as to cast doubt on the ability of language to convey any kind of objectively reliable meaning. Not just literature but laws, constitutions, philosophies, religions, and all cultural expressions and institutions can be thought of as texts, that is, linguistic constructions. Language creates an illusion of objective meaning. Since there is no "transcendental signified," meaning is a subjective construction. And yet because language is cultural, it is the mechanism for cultural control and cultural oppression from those in power. We inhabit the "prison house of language."[12] We can escape this prison only by taking advantage of the gap between the sign and the signified, which allows for slippage, ambiguity, and linguistic change and by exposing the linguistic contradictions and power relationships, thereby "deconstructing" the text.

Notice that neither the modernists nor the postmodernists had a *positive* basis for language. It either gives us the illusion of meaning,

---

12. The phrase was coined by Nietzsche in *The Will to Power*. For its appropriation by postmodernists, see Michael Mahon, *Foucault's Nietzschean Geneology: Truth, Power, and the Subject* (Albany, NY: SUNY Press, 1992); and Frederic Jameson, *The Prison-House of Language: A Critical Account of Structuralism and Russian Formalism* (Princeton, NJ: Princeton University Press, 1972).

or it constitutes a prison house. Either way, language is something we have to escape. For Hamann, though, human language, despite its limitations, is related to the language of God, that is, to God's Word.

If language is a property of thought, it is also a property of God's thought. This is the teaching of John 1:

> In the beginning was the Word *[Logos]*, and the Word *[Logos]* was with God, and the Word *[Logos]* was God. He was in the beginning with God. All things were made through him, and without him was not any thing made that was made. In him was life, and the life was the light of men. The light shines in the darkness, and the darkness has not overcome it. . . . And the Word *[Logos]* became flesh and dwelt among us, and we have seen his glory, glory as of the only Son from the Father, full of grace and truth. (John 1:1–5, 14)

For the Greeks, the *logos* refers to the underlying order and design of the universe. For the apostle John, the *Logos* is the mind of God, and thus, God himself, who became incarnate in Jesus Christ.

The *Logos,* that is to say, God's Word, is the means by which God created the universe. "And *God said,* 'Let there be light,' and there was light" (Gen. 1:3). God's Word is thus foundational to all creation. The objective universe is *not* meaningless, as both the modernists and the postmodernists say, because meaning, a function of language, is not merely a human construct; rather, meaning inheres in all things because of the creative *Logos.* And because human beings, created in God's image, also, like God, are persons who have language, they can hear and respond to God's Word. This includes the capacity, however limited, of understanding God's creation. Because of the *logos*, there can be its derivative *logic.*

Furthermore, since we too are creatures, we can relate to God's creation in ways other than simply trying to understand it and using it for our purposes. We certainly do not stand outside the creation, and we approach the creation—ourselves included—as God's self-expression. This enables us to *love* the creation and to respond to its *beauty.* One of Hamann's major preoccupations was aesthetics. Whereas the Enlightenment rationalists were trying to understand beauty by reason, including figuring out rules that a beautiful object had to follow, Hamann saw beauty as the "perception" of the *Logos* in creation, a glimpse of God's glory hidden in the lowliest details of what he has made.[13]

Physical reality in all of its fullness is not just as an impersonal nature—much less a clockwork machine or inert matter—but *God's creation*; indeed, as a manifestation of God's Word, it calls to us. "Creation," said Hamann, is "address to the creature through the creature."[14] We human beings are fallen sinners, alienated from God, from which derives our alienation from other people, from ourselves, and from creation. But God employs his creation to reach us and to restore us. God became incarnate—"the Word became flesh"—in Jesus Christ, who shared our human life and who died on the cross for our salvation. This salvation is, in turn, communicated to us by physical means: the water of baptism, the bread and wine of the Lord's Supper, the pages of the Bible, the pastor in a pulpit. Hamann might add, the London bookstall where he felt moved to buy a Bible and the wretched rooming house where he started to read it.

Hamann was a Lutheran. The German theologian Oswald Bayer, who played a major role in the recent rediscovery of Hamann, suggests that many of Hamann's ideas were simply sophisticated applications of Luther's theology: the limitations of reason, the exaltation and efficacy of the Word of God, the depths of human sin, justification by faith, the sacraments as physical means of grace, and a continual Christological perspective.[15]

One of Hamann's theological accomplishments, much needed today as well, was to present God not as a far-off, distant figure far beyond the universe, as the deists and even some Christians thought of him, but as a close, personal, all-encompassing reality in whom "we live and move and have our being" (Acts 17:27). This God, for all of his infinite and incomprehensible glory, is full of grace. He loves us, sinners though we be, and deigns to descend to our level in order to save us.

Hamann does a great deal with *kenosis*, that Christ, in the words of the epistle to the Philippians, "emptied" himself:

---

13. Betz, *After Enlightenment*, 20, 100, discussing Hamann's *Aesthetica in Nuce* [*Aesthetics in a Nutshell*].

14. Quoted in Oswald Bayer, *Martin Luther's Theology: A Contemporary Interpretation* (Grand Rapids, MI: Eerdmans, 2008), 108. The quotation is from Hamann's *Aesthetica in Nuce*.

15. See Bayer's book on Hamann, *A Contemporary in Dissent*, and his "contemporary interpretation" of Luther, *Martin Luther's Theology*, in which he appropriates Hamann.

> Have this mind among yourselves, which is yours in Christ Jesus,
> who, though he was in the form of God, did not count equality
> with God a thing to be grasped, but emptied himself, by taking the
> form of a servant, being born in the likeness of men. And being
> found in human form, he humbled himself by becoming obedient
> to the point of death, even death on a cross. (Phil. 2:5–8)

Hamann marvels that God the Son, the second person of the Trinity,
would so empty himself, becoming, as we quoted from his London
testimony, "not only a man, but also a poor and most wretched man."
The *Logos*, by whom all things were created, embraced a shameful,
humiliating death on a cross.

God the Father, according to Hamann, also empties himself and
humbles himself in his creation. For all of his glory, God has created
and attends to the lowest insects and vermin, what human beings
recoil from, as if their sins were not far more repulsive. God providentially governs and cares for everything that he has made. He attends
to every sparrow that falls and has numbered every hair on our heads
(Matt. 10:29–30). He works through ordinary human beings, even the
lowliest, to give daily bread to feed the human race, including those
who rebel against him; he creates new life by means of fathers and
mothers; and he generously gives his other earthly gifts by means of
human vocations. Though he is the most exalted king, God deigns to
serve his creatures.

Similarly, God the Holy Spirit empties himself and humbles himself in the Holy Scriptures. The Holy Spirit renders God's Word—the
Logos, the template for all of creation who became flesh in Jesus
Christ—in ordinary human language. "For us the Holy Spirit has published a book for his Word," says Hamann in his London testimony,
which includes what "proud reason" considers "children's stories,
trivial, contemptible events."[16]

> The whole Bible seems to have been written for just this purpose,
> to teach us the kingdom of God by way of trivial details. He is a
> God who hears the thoughts and words of a midwife when we
> enter the world and writes them down (Gen 38:27–30), and the

---

16. Hamann, "Thoughts on the Course of My Life."

rather insignificant exchange of words between Leah and Rachel about the mandrakes that Reuben had found (Gen 30:14–15). Our religion is arranged so completely for our needs, weaknesses, and deficiencies that these are all transformed into blessings and things of beauty.[17]

Hamann dealt with some of the early practitioners of the higher critical method, which subjects the Bible to a rationalistic critique. They stand apart from Scripture, judging it, just as the Enlightened rationalists stand apart from the creation. But the Bible is not just a text to interpret; rather, it is a text that interprets us. Nor is it just a collection of historical and doctrinal facts—a set of signifiers distinct from what they signify—though the Bible does refer to real events. Above all, though, the Holy Spirit *uses* the words of Holy Scripture to impact the lives of its readers and hearers, convicting them of sin and converting them to the gospel of Christ. Parallel to the Son of God's incarnation of the Word of God in human flesh, the Holy Spirit makes the Word of God incarnate (so to speak) in human language.

Thus, the triune God, in every person of the Trinity, gives himself to us. As Oswald Bayer puts it, summarizing Luther by way of Hamann:

> The *Father* gives himself to us absolutely in the creation; the *Son* gives himself to us in the redemption and opens for us thereby once again the access to the Father; finally, the *Spirit* gives himself to us in the *promissio* [the promise of God's Word], which constitutes faith, and at the same time gives us the Son and the Father.[18]

This self-giving of the Father, Son, and Holy Spirit has implications for all of human life and for restoring what has been lost due to the ravages of sin and unbelief. Here is how John Betz summarizes Hamann's thought, what he describes as his "most fundamental point":

> The *transcendent* God is kenotically hidden *within* language—just as he is kenotically hidden within creation, just as he is kenotically hidden within human history, just as he is kenotically hidden within the humanity of Christ, and just as the Holy Spirit is kenoti-

---

17. Hamann, "Thoughts on the Course of My Life."
18. Bayer, *Martin Luther's Theology*, 341.

cally hidden within the "rags" of Scripture. In sum, on the basis of this vision of the kenosis of transcendence, which is able to find the *transcendent* God *in* this world under the various guises of his love, Hamann points the way to a theological recovery of nature, history, language, and art.[19]

Hamann's Legacy

Hamann is not an author one can just pick up casually and read. One good legacy of the Enlightenment, in my opinion, is its clear and lucid writing style; but Hamann maintains that truth is not necessarily as clear and lucid as the rationalists wanted to make it seem. Hamann's style is gnomic and playful, full of jokes and ironies, as well as complex webs of allusions—to the Bible, classical literature, and contemporary events. I have been told that you cannot really understand Hamann unless you read him in German, and translation of his writing into English is extremely challenging. Not all of his works are even available in English, though some are, if only in excerpts.[20] Perhaps his most accessible work—as well as his most direct treatment of theology, in which many of his other ideas are anticipated—is his *London Writings*. As noted earlier, the Australian theologian John Kleinig is currently translating that book into English in its entirety (I am the editor), so you might watch for that. In the meantime, I recommend approaching Hamann through one of the books about him.[21] You need a Virgil to lead you through Hamann's *Divine Comedy*.

In his time, Hamann was well-known and influential. The poet Goethe called him "the brightest mind of his day." Hegel hailed his "penetrating genius." Kierkegaard ranked him with Socrates, calling him one of the "most brilliant minds of all time" and the "greatest humorist in Christendom." J. G. Herder and F. H. Jacobi, who would become influential in German thought in their own right, considered themselves his disciples.[22] Literary scholars say that Hamann helped

19. Betz, *After Enlightenment*, 340.

20. See Johann Georg Hamann, *Writings on Philosophy and Language*, trans. Kenneth Haynes (New York: Cambridge University Press, 2007).

21. I recommend John Betz's *After Enlightenment*. Also Bayer's *A Contemporary in Dissent*; Walter Leibrecht's *God and Man in the Thought of Hamann*; and James C. O'Flaherty, *Johann Georg Hamann* (Boston: Twayne, 1979).

22. Betz, *After Enlightenment*, 2–3, 14.

inspire the *Sturm und Drang* ("storm and stress") movement in German literature, which was a precursor to the romantic movement. But then, partly due to his eccentric writing style, Hamann faded from the cultural memory. In the twentieth century, scholars such as Isaiah Berlin classified him as an "irrationalist," a member of the "Counter-Enlightenment," whose rejection of reason would lead to the Third Reich.[23] Never mind that Hamann gave reason another foundation, that he defended the Jews as the people of the Bible, and that he opposed political tyranny (such as that of the Prussian King Frederick the Great, a major patron of the Enlightenment, whose rationalism, according to Hamann, led to his authoritarianism).

With postmodernism, though, Hamann suddenly made sense. He was recognized as anticipating the postmodernists' critique of modernism while avoiding their relativism and radical skepticism. John Betz says that in his "metacritique" of Enlightenment rationalism Hamann belongs with the reigning "postmodern triumvirate" of Nietzsche, Heidegger, and Derrida. But those three, according to Betz, lead to the dead end of nihilism. Hamann, though, offers a way forward. The *only* choice we have, according to Betz, is between Hamann (with his Christian faith) and nihilism:

> Anticipating the collapse of secular reason, Hamann thus brings us to a decidedly postmodern crossroads, at which point one can take the road of faith, which, as an inspired tradition attests, leads to ever greater enlightenment; or one can take the road of postmodern unbelief, which leads to nihilism. Simply put, the alternative is one between Hamann and postmodernity.[24]

The Hamann alternative Betz describes as "post-secular."[25]

Another reason Hamann has come back into prominence is his appropriation by the theological movement known as radical orthodoxy. Started by the Anglicans John Milbank, Catherine Pickstock, and Graham Ward,[26] and adopted by some Catholic and Orthodox theolo-

23. Isaiah Berlin, *The Magus of the North: J. G. Hamann and the Origins of Modern Irrationalism* (New York: Farrar, Strauss & Giroux, 1993).
24. Betz, *After Enlightenment*, 319.
25. Betz, *After Enlightenment*, 312, 337–40.
26. John Milbank, Catherine Pickstock, and Graham Ward, eds., *Radical Orthodoxy: A New Theology* (London: Routledge, 1999).

gians, radical orthodoxy uses postmodernism to attack liberal theology, with its modernistic assumptions. For this critical purpose, they make good use of Hamann.[27] But in my opinion, the radical orthodox stop short of fully applying Hamann's insights. With their interest in restoring something like patristic and medieval Christendom, they blame Luther and the Reformation for modernity! They are also interested in a neoplatonic spirituality rather than recovering, as both Luther and Hamann did, the physical creation. Thus, the radical orthodox do little with Hamann's Lutheranism and his evangelicalism. More promising, in my opinion, is the Protestant appropriation of Hamann from the Lutheran theologian Oswald Bayer. And one of my favorite comments about Hamann comes from the Reformed theologian Peter Leithart: "It takes a prophet to contribute to debates two hundred years before they start."[28] Leithart goes on to cite

> Hamann's importance to today's debates about language and meaning, religion and science, God and time, reason and faith, postmodernity, liberal political order, and theological interpretation of Scripture. No century has needed Hamann's profoundly Christocentric dissent more than ours.[29]

But much more needs to be done.

If, as Bayer says, Hamann's insights derive mainly from Luther, that would make Hamann not so much a particular genius as an ordinary Christian applying his faith to the issues of his day. Some Christians today might balk at some of what Hamann says, but he serves as an inspiring role model and offers some stimulating ideas for contending with and evangelizing our current post-Christian mentality.

---

27. The opening chapter in the manifesto of the movement is John Milbank's "Knowledge: The Theological Critique of Philosophy in Hamann and Jacobi," in *Radical Orthodoxy*, 21–37.

28. An editorial review of Bayer's *A Contemporary in Dissent* at Amazon.com, accessed June 10, 2019, https://www.amazon.com/Contemporary-Dissent-Johann-Radical-Enlightener-ebook/dp/B007FP06UW/ref=sr_1_1?ie=UTF8&qid=1534982620&sr=8-1&keywords=oswald+bayer+dissent.

29. Review of Bayer's *A Contemporary in Dissent*, Amazon. See also Peter J. Leithart, "Hamann's Century," *First Things*, September 23, 2011, accessed June 10, 2019, https://www.firstthings.com/web-exclusives/2011/09/hamanns-century.

PART 2

THE BODY

5

The End of Sex

The Exaltation of Barrenness

"Sexual love," observed Wendell Berry, "is the force that in our bodily life connects us most intimately to the Creation."[1] Indeed, sex has to do with the body. Also with our drives and instincts that we share with our fellow creatures in the animal world. Also with our physical senses and pleasures. Sex reminds us that we are not disembodied spirits but creatures of flesh and blood. But, more deeply, sex also connects us to the very process of creation, as God uses the passions and physiology of sex to create new life. Biologically, the purpose of sex is reproduction, and just as the life of animals centers on their fertility and the care of their young, sex for human beings gives us culture: marriage, parenthood, the family; and thus communities, economics, and governments. Hence, sex ties culture to creation.

If the characteristic infirmity of our time is a repudiation of the creation and our creatureliness, as we have been arguing, it is no wonder that sex has been thrown into such disorder. We have been attempting to pursue sex apart from what it means. Having untethered sex from the family, we have taken something that is life giving

---

1. Wendell Berry, *Sex, Economy, Freedom, and Community* (New York: Pantheon, 1994), 133. Quoted in Rod Dreher, *The Benedict Option* (New York: Sentinel, 2017), 197.

and made it barren. Having untethered sex even from the body, we are, with the help of technology, coming close to eliminating sex altogether.

In this hypersexualized age, how can I say that sex is being eliminated? Consider what sex is from a biblical perspective. Jesus himself, summing up a continual theme throughout Scripture, explains what sexuality in the created order entails:

> Have you not read that he who created them from the beginning made them male and female, and said, "Therefore a man shall leave his father and his mother and hold fast to his wife, and the two shall become one flesh"? So they are no longer two but one flesh. What therefore God has joined together, let not man separate. (Matt. 19:4–6)

Sex creates a "one flesh" union between a man and a woman that is intended to be permanent. Thus, sex, according to the Bible, is inextricably connected with marriage, though, as the apostle Paul points out, it is also possible to become "one flesh" with someone you are not married to, which is the problem with sexual immorality (1 Cor. 6:12–20). Notice that the purpose of sex is not *only* procreation—the Bible actually says little about that—though this is certainly the physical, biological purpose of sex, for which every organ of the reproductive system is designed. To say that two become "one flesh" speaks of *relationship*. Another word for the union of distinct persons is *love*, mirroring the union of the persons in the Trinity, so that we can say that "God is love" (1 John 4:8). The Bible further teaches that marriage—indeed, the sexual dimension of marriage, the becoming "one flesh"—is an embodiment of the relationship between and the union of Christ and the church (Eph. 5:31–32). All of this is grounded in creation and in God's design ("He who created them from the beginning . . .").

So, to summarize the biblical teaching, we can say that sex creates a one-flesh union between a man and a woman, intended for the permanent relationship of marriage, a vocation that by the design of sex can lead also to the vocation of parenthood. The nature and purposes of sex are built into creation, and they also speak to us of redemption.

Now notice the course of the "sexual revolution" in our post-Christian times. First, God, with his commands and his creative and redemptive purposes, is removed from consideration. Next, sex is detached from its physical function of conceiving children. Next, sex is detached from the sexual distinctions of male and female. Next, sex is detached from relationship altogether—from the impersonal pursuit of "sex objects" to sex with oneself, in the solitary eroticism of pornography. Thus, sex as a created reality is repudiated at every level. Instead, we are left with an attenuated alternative that reduces sex to little more than a spasm of pleasure and relief.

And yet as we shall see, human beings cannot escape their creation, and the richer dimensions of sexuality—love, parenthood, morality—keep asserting themselves, whether the secularists want them to or not.

Sex and Contemporary Thought

That sex has become disconnected from creation and from its purposes by no means implies that sex is fading from people's consciousness—far from it! When you minimize the objective, physical, created order, the self—along with all of its passions, drives, and pleasure seeking—remains. Sex untethered from the family expands *everywhere*, and because the desire for sex is so powerful, it takes over *everything*. Today, preoccupation with sex characterizes our politics, our technology, and our worldviews. In fact, I would argue that a major *cause* of contemporary secularism—the individual or collective impulse to throw out religion—is the fear that religion threatens sexual freedom, that is, sex that is "freed" from permanent relationships, the family, and the body.

Through most of American history, our political issues have had to do with economic policies, international relations, legal priorities, and factional interests. Rival political ideologies offered alternative solutions to the nation's problems, which made for political conflict, exacerbated by the competing interests of different regions, social classes, and economic sectors. Only recently has sex become a *political* issue. National elections and local elections have turned on candidates' attitudes toward sex and what they think the government should do about it: acceptance of homosexuality by establishing same-sex marriage, the right of a woman to abort a child that she did not want to conceive, whether the federal government should force employers to provide their employees free contraceptives.

These "gay rights" and "women's health" issues became the defining causes of liberal political activists, often—since these were mainly middle-class concerns—at the expense of their former commitment to the interests of racial minorities and blue-collar workers. At first, conservatives opposed these "culture war" measures. But many conservatives, in large part, eventually came around, supporting same-sex marriage and sometimes even abortion, all in the name of their "freedom" agenda. Christian activists, however, dissented. And although they remain politically influential, their rejection of homosexuality and abortion has made Christian political conservatives increasingly vilified and culturally marginalized. Then again, many Christian conservatives have put aside their concerns for sexual morality in order to pursue their other agendas.

Not only our politics but our technology has become sexualized. Our computer and Internet technology is a wonder of the human race, one of humanity's most remarkable and impressive achievements. And one of this technology's most common applications is *pornography*. The statistics are a matter of dispute, but between 10 percent and 30 percent of Internet use is for porn.[2] Three of the top ten most-visited websites in the United States in 2018 were porn sites.[3] And the major application for virtual reality technology is shaping up to be pornography.[4]

Our current obsession with sexual pleasure as the *summum bonum*, the highest good, is shaping the very way we think, our ideologies and philosophies. Quite a few young people reject the religion of their childhood when they go off to college not so much because of the

---

2. Michael Castleman, "Dueling Statistics: How Much of the Internet Is Porn?" *Psychology Today*, November 3, 2016, accessed June 10, 2019, https://www.psychologytoday.com/us/blog/all-about-sex/201611/dueling-statistics-how-much-the-internet-is-porn.

3. "Top Website Rankings," *Similar Web*, July 1, 2018, accessed June 10, 2019, https://www.similarweb.com/top-websites/united-states.

4. David M. Ewalt, "The First Real Boom in Virtual Reality? It's Pornography," *Wall Street Journal*, July 11, 2018, accessed June 10, 2019, https://www.wsj.com/articles/the-first-real-boom-in-virtual-reality-its-pornography-1531320180.

arguments of an atheist professor but because they want to plunge into the sexual debauchery of the campus culture. Their religion holds them back, and their sexual desires make the atheist professor's arguments more plausible than they otherwise would be. In fact, the atheist professor may well have first rejected God so that he could indulge his sexual appetite without guilt. This would be a variation of what I call the "Saint Augustine syndrome," after the great theologian of the early church who had become convinced that Christianity is true but nevertheless refused to become a Christian because he knew that if he did, he would have to give up his illicit sexual relationship. Eventually, Augustine—who prayed, "Lord, make me chaste, but not yet!"[5]—was broken and changed by God's Word, but the syndrome, I believe, is a common one. As is, conversely, choosing *not* to believe in order to pursue one's sexual desires.

While the decline in religious belief was a factor in the outbreak of the sexual revolution, one can also make the case that the sexual revolution led to the decline in religious belief. In our hypersexualized culture today, it should not be surprising that *religion* has become taboo. Sex, of course, used to be taboo, something not to be discussed in polite company, but now religion is. As with Flannery O'Connor's character, "Christ in the conversation embarrassed her the way sex had her mother."[6] In fact, the secularism that defines our post-Christian times, the conviction that our advanced Western culture can do without religion altogether, may well be caused, at least in part, by the desire to cast off everything that might inhibit our sexual freedom.

And yet such an unmooring of sexual desire changes the very nature of that desire. It makes sexual love all but impossible. And, ironically, it leads to the repudiation of actual sex.

Preventing Birth

What is unique about sex in our times is *not* simply sexual immorality. It is a shift in the *meaning* of sex, a change that has reverberated throughout the culture.

---

5. Augustine, *The Confessions* (New York: Penguin, 1961), book 8, section 7, 169–70.

6. Flannery O'Connor, "The Displaced Person," in *Collected Works* (New York: Literary Classics of the United States, 1988), 317.

Sexual sins of every kind have been a perennial problem through-out human history. Every age has its extramarital affairs, mistresses, and babies born out of wedlock. Prostitution was *rampant* in the ancient world, in the Middle Ages, and all the way through the Victorian era. Ironically, the word *Victorian* has become a byword for sexual propriety, and yet the streets of nineteenth-century London and the boomtowns of America's Wild West were notorious for their brothels and sexual exploitation. Prostitution was not made illegal in the United States until the early twentieth century, due largely to the activism of the Woman's Christian Temperance Union.[7] The so-called sexual revolution that began in the 1960s and that has been running its course ever since had to do largely with preventing birth, that is, disassociating sex from having children.

Even the non-Christians of the Enlightenment and nineteenth-century materialism tended to support the principles (if not the personal applications) of Christian sexual morality, not because of the moral absolutes of God's commandments but on the basis of utilitarian ethics. Sex outside of marriage is wrong, they reasoned, because that can result in children born out of wedlock, which can be catastrophic for the mother and a burden to society. But once that concern was addressed, via technology, those utilitarian reasons for limiting sex to marriage evaporated.

The Roman Catholic Church, which officially teaches that *all* sex without the intention to procreate, even within marriage, is sinful, condemned the new birth-control technology and forbade its use. Most Protestants do not go that far, but the Catholic warnings that the technology separating sex from propagation would have far-reaching moral and cultural consequences have surely come true.[8]

The birth control pill was approved by the Food and Drug Administration on June 23, 1960. We can think of this date as the beginning of the sexual revolution, just as the fall of the Bastille marks the beginning of the French Revolution, though both had long

---

7. See "Prostitution," Wikipedia, accessed June 10, 2019, https://en.wikipedia.org/wiki/Prostitution#20th_century.

8. For the moral and theological issues surrounding the birth control controversy, see my book with Mary Moerbe, *Family Vocation: God's Calling in Marriage, Parenting, and Childhood* (Wheaton, IL: Crossway, 2012), 109–12.

antecedents. Margaret Sanger, who was born in 1879, had crusaded for "birth control," a term that she coined, mainly for eugenic reasons. Sanger promoted the technologies available to her—the "barrier methods" and sterilization—even though for most of her career contraception devices and even distributing information about them were illegal. But in the 1950s the organization she founded, Planned Parenthood, invested in the research that led to the development of the birth control pill, an invention that Sanger, who died in 1966, lived to see.

Of course, 1960, when the pill became available, was also the beginning of the sixties. That decade was a time of reaction against a whole array of traditional cultural values in favor of a counterculture in which sexual freedom became a dominant theme. Hippies practiced "free love." The youth movement was energized by "sex, drugs, and rock 'n' roll." The various liberation movements often preached rebellion against the traditional family structure.

The pill seemed to be a safe, simple, easy-to-use way to prevent pregnancy. (The health side effects would not be known until later.) Women, in particular, felt empowered. The condoms that Margaret Sanger was selling gave *men* the ability to prevent pregnancy, but the pill gave *women* the power to choose whether or not to have a baby. Now women could fill jobs normally associated with men, since they no longer had to worry about having to stay at home to raise children, unless they wanted to. The pill bolstered the cause of feminism, of "women's liberation," liberating women from the restrictions of marriage, child bearing, and child raising. Now women could claim complete equality with men.

Of course, in reality, the pill "liberated" men. Now they could have sex with women without having to deal with the consequences. No longer did men need to worry about getting a girl pregnant and feeling the obligation to marry her. Now men could talk women into having sex with them by banishing her fears of pregnancy and dismissing her instincts of resistance as outmoded psychological hangups. Now men could use women sexually with no inhibitions. In the 1960s, as women went to consciousness-raising groups, men were enjoying *Playboy* magazine.

The sexual revolution, with its technological prevention of birth, was a cultural revolution, one that proved devastating to the basic unit of any culture: the family. Though marriage was no longer necessary to have sex, couples still got married. But they began to see marriage sheerly in terms of romantic attraction. And when that romantic attraction faded, or was shifted to someone else, the marriage was considered no longer valid. Self-fulfillment replaced love and service to one's spouse and children as the purpose of family life. Couples still had children, but since children had become optional in marriage, rather than a primary purpose, they were not enough to hold a marriage together. Consequently, the divorce rate soared:

> From 1960 to 1980, the divorce rate more than doubled—from 9.2 divorces per 1,000 married women to 22.6 divorces per 1,000 married women. This meant that while less than 20% of couples who married in 1950 ended up divorced, about 50% of couples who married in 1970 did. And approximately half of the children born to married parents in the 1970s saw their parents part, compared to only about 11% of those born in the 1950s.[9]

Among the legacies of the sexual revolution are single-parent families, fatherless children, heartache, loneliness, poverty, and a host of other personal and cultural dysfunctions.

The mind-set that we should prevent birth in the name of our self-fulfillment has given us something even more horrible and more corrupting: abortion. It turned out that using the birth control pill and other contraceptive devices do not always prevent conception. So with the Supreme Court's *Roe v. Wade* decision in 1973 legalizing abortion nationwide, women who found themselves pregnant had a "plan B."[10] If they could not prevent birth before they conceived a child, they could always prevent birth afterward by aborting the child.

---

9. W. Bradford Wilcox, "The Evolution of Divorce," *National Affairs* (Spring 2019), accessed June 10, 2019, https://www.nationalaffairs.com/publications/detail/the-evolution-of-divorce.

10. "Plan B" is now the brand name of a morning-after pill designed to kill the fertilized egg immediately after conception. Plan B is sold over the counter, without as much as a doctor's prescription. The acceptance of abortion has led to other types of abortifacients now sold as birth control devices. They are not contraceptives, since they do not prevent conception but destroy the life after it is already conceived.

Preventing birth by killing the baby before he or she is born—somehow, this became culturally acceptable. Progressives made abortion their defining issue. Feminists turned having an abortion into a virtue. Modernists rejected reason and science in maintaining that an unborn child is not human. Postmodernists threw out their concerns about power and oppression in insisting on the right of a woman to exert her power to destroy her baby.

And, of course, though abortion was championed in the rhetoric of "women's health" and "women's choice," the procedure was mostly to the advantage of predatory men. One study found that almost three-quarters of women who had abortions (73.8 percent) felt pressured to do so. A majority (58.3 percent) said that they had their abortion to make someone else happy. Nearly a third (30 percent) said that they feared losing their partner if they did not abort their child.[11] So much for abortion proponents being pro-choice.

Abortion is not only heinous in itself; it is deeply corrupting. What happens to the institution of the family when mothers and fathers are willing to kill their own children? Politically, it is hard to take progressive politicians seriously when they purport to champion the poor and the marginalized while, at the same time, they defend the killing of the poorest and most marginalized of them all, the infants in the womb. It is hard to respect a legal system that allows for executing innocent children without a trial. Mainline Protestants have embraced abortion, with some feminist theologians going so far as to call it a "sacrament,"[12] rendering any of their claims to moral or spiritual authority absurd. The medical profession is corrupted when those with the calling to heal their patients are engaged in killing their patients. Such noble concepts as freedom, choice, and rights are corrupted when they are used as pretexts for abortion.

"Daughters of Jerusalem," said Jesus on the way to his crucifixion, "do not weep for me, but weep for yourselves and for your children.

---

11. Jonathan Abbamonte, "Many American Women Have Felt Pressured into Abortion, Study Finds," Population Research Institute, January 24, 2018, accessed June 10, 2019, https://www.pop.org/many-american-women-felt-pressured-abortions-study-finds/. The published study is by Priscilla K. Coleman et al., "Women Who Suffered Emotionally from Abortion: A Qualitative Synthesis of Their Experiences," *Journal of American Physicians and Surgeons* 22 (Winter 2017): 113–18.

12. See, e.g., Ginette Paris, *The Sacrament of Abortion* (Washington, DC: Spring, 1998).

For behold, the days are coming when they will say, 'Blessed are the barren and the wombs that never bore and the breasts that never nursed!'" (Luke 23:28–29). Rejecting child bearing and caring for children will be a herald of God's judgment (v. 30). It will be a sign of the end.

Sex without Sexual Difference

The word *sex* literally refers to the two categories of human beings and most other kinds of life: the male sex and the female sex. These two sexes have different reproductive systems and play different parts in the all-important task of creating new life. But this is not all: the two sexes are different in every cell of their bodies. (Females have two X chromosomes and males have an X and a Y chromosome. This is true of humans, other mammals, and other living creatures, including many plants. Some birds, reptiles, insects, and other kinds of organisms have similar genetic distinctions between the sexes. Though some creatures can reproduce asexually, most require a male and a female.) The distinction between the sexes, which the Bible indicates also has a spiritual dimension, is built into creation. "Male and female he created them" (Gen. 1:27).

So sex, as in "sexual intercourse," means, technically, the physical union of the two sexes. Sometimes, though, sexual desire can be directed elsewhere. Some people are attracted to members of their own sex. Again, this is nothing new. In the ancient world, homosexual unions were commonplace, not just as a particular orientation but as a practice that many otherwise heterosexuals would enter into. The Theban army used same-sex ties to build unit cohesion, and pederasty was socially acceptable when older men would mentor adolescent youth. This was never to the exclusion of marrying and having children. This, along with other evidence, suggests that there is a cultural component to homosexuality, in addition to the psychological, genetic, or volitional explanations being advanced today. For whatever reason same-sex attraction exists, Jews and Christians have always rejected homosexual unions as violations of the created order.

But once sex began to be detached from procreation in people's minds, thanks to birth control and the sexual revolution, it became harder and harder to see anything wrong or even abnormal with homosexuality. If sex does not have to be about conceiving children, why should it be restricted to members of the opposite gender? If we want to have sex while preventing birth, what better way to do so than for men to have sex with men and women to have sex with women?

Even non-Christians through much of the twentieth century tended to disapprove of homosexuality, which was still on the books as being illegal. Homosexuals were looked down upon by much of the public, who found their sexual practices repellent, and, sadly, were often mistreated.

But in one of the most remarkable cultural turnarounds of all time, public opinion shifted almost overnight. Homosexuals gave themselves a name with a more positive connotation: "gay." They wrapped themselves in the mantle of civil rights and organized into the lesbian, gay, bisexual, transgender (LGBT) movement. They came out of the closet; instead of living their sexual lives in shameful secrecy, they became open about their orientation and claimed it as their identity. This meant that more members of the general public were personally acquainted with someone gay, which increased acceptance of the practice. When AIDS struck, the sexually transmitted plague that killed hundreds of thousands of homosexuals—and millions worldwide[13]— one might have thought that it would put homosexuality in a negative light. But instead, the horror of AIDS made people feel sympathy and compassion for its victims. The turnaround has been complete: in 1973, 70 percent of Americans believed that same-sex relations are always wrong.[14] In 2017, 70 percent of Americans believed that same-sex relations are morally acceptable.[15]

The LGBT movement crusaded for the ultimate marker of social acceptability: same-sex marriage. After years of conflicting state laws and legal rulings, the United States Supreme Court legalized same-sex

13. "HIV by the Numbers: Facts, Statistics, and You," *Healthline*, May 9, 2018, accessed June 10, 2019, https://www.healthline.com/health/hiv-aids/facts-statistics-infographic#location.

14. "Americans Move Dramatically Toward Acceptance of Homosexuality Finds GSS Report," National Opinion Research Center (NORC), University of Chicago, accessed June 10, 2019, http://www.norc.org/NewsEventsPublications/PressReleases/Pages/american-acceptance-of-homosexuality-gss-report.aspx.

15. "Homosexuality, Gender, and Religion," Pew Research Center, October 5, 2017, accessed June 10, 2019, http://www.people-press.org/2017/10/05/5-homosexuality-gender-and-religion/.

marriage nationwide in 2015. Opponents had difficulty marshaling arguments for why individuals of the same sex should not be allowed to marry each other. As late as 2001, 57 percent of Americans opposed gay marriage;[16] in 2018, 67 percent supported it.[17]

By this time, heterosexual marriage had changed, in people's minds, so that it had become the kind of institution that homosexuals too could enter into. The traditional view of marriage legitimizes sex between a man and a woman, both to create a "one-flesh" relationship and to conceive children, making for a family whose members share the "flesh" of biological relationship. But if the basis of marriage instead is romantic attachment, why shouldn't same-sex couples who feel romantically attached to each other get married? Furthermore, feminism had the effect of leveling the different roles of husband and wife. If the husband and wife are completely equal and have the same roles—both working, both taking care of the house, both taking care of the children, if there are any—why should the distinctions of sex matter at all in marriage?

Gay marriage has become almost the template of the post-sexual-revolution marriage. When the issue was being debated, gays threw in the face of their opponents the failures of heterosexual marriage. The divorce rate is so high, they would say, it looks like heterosexuals want to get out of marriage! We want to get into marriage! We will save the institution of marriage! One way they would do so is to loosen up the sexual exclusivity of traditional marriage, the notion that one should have sex only with one's spouse. Many gays who marry have open marriages, which allow for occasional extramarital flings, while still preserving the permanence of the marriage. This could be a model, some are saying, for reforming "straight marriage."[18]

The influence of homosexuals goes far beyond their numbers. A sympathetic study found that 4 to 5 percent of Americans identify as

---

16. "Changing Attitudes on Gay Marriage," Pew Research Center, June 26, 2017, accessed June 10, 2019, http://www.pewforum.org/fact-sheet/changing-attitudes-on-gay-marriage/.

17. Aamer Madhani, "Approval of Same-Sex Marriage in U.S. Reaches New High," *USA Today*, May 23, 2018, accessed June 10, 2019, https://www.usatoday.com/story/news/nation/2018/05/23/same-sex-marriage-poll-americans/638587002/.

18. See Emily Esfahani Smith, "Are Gay Marriages Healthier than Straight Marriages?" *Politico Magazine*, June 26, 2015, accessed June 10, 2019, https://www.politico.com/magazine/story/2015/06/gay-marriages-better-than-straight-marriages-119465_Page2.html.

LGBT. But of that number, nearly half, 46 percent, consider themselves bisexual. If that many feel sexually attracted to both sexes, they could presumably be encouraged—or converted—so that they could enter into a traditional marriage. Once the other categories in the study are factored in, such as the various kinds of transgender identities, it would appear that only 2 to 2.5 percent of Americans are exclusively homosexual.[19] But they have won over the culture.

Not only has the LGBT movement vanquished Christians in the culture wars; they want revenge on those who have mistreated them in the past and on those who refuse to accept them today. Homosexuality used to be classified as a mental illness; today, homophobia—the fear or, in practice, the rejection of homosexuality—is the mental illness. Opposing homosexuality is considered a form of bigotry, like racism. Businesses that have contributed money to organizations that oppose the LGBT agenda and entire states that are accused of being insufficiently gay-friendly are subject to boycott. Nondiscrimination statutes and hate-crime laws are being brought to bear against Christians who refuse to take part in same-sex weddings, Christian adoption agencies that will not place children with same-sex couples, and, in some countries, pastors who preach about the sinfulness of homosexual relations. The LGBT agenda is pitted against religious liberty, and often religious liberty is the loser.

Meanwhile, the influence and prestige of gay sex has become so pervasive that the ways homosexuals have sex with each other—the various practices long defined as "sodomy"—are now commonplace among heterosexuals.

Sex without Another Person

Homosexuality is not the definitive distortion of sex in our time. One distortion is separating sex from conceiving children. Another is pursuing sex without sexual difference. But the farthest departure from God's design is pursuing sex apart from any relationship whatsoever,

---

19. See Dominic Holden, "Who Are LGBTQ Americans? Here's a Major Poll on Life, Sex, and Politics," *BuzzFeed News*, June 13, 2018, accessed June 10, 2019, https://www.buzzfeednews.com /article/dominicholden/lgbtq-in-the-us-poll#.cxLA003Mpp. The data from the study, sponsored by *BuzzFeed*, can be accessed at https://assets.documentcloud.org/documents/4564749/WINS-amp -Buzfeed-LGBTQ-in-America-Poll-Topline.pdf.

sex without so much as another person, just a solitary individual masturbating to a computer screen.

Sex, in its essence, has to do with a relationship between a man and a woman, a desire for each other and a consummation that makes them "one flesh." Thus, sex and marriage, according to the Bible, are about love. "Husbands, love your wives," says the apostle Paul, "as Christ loved the church and gave himself up for her" (Eph. 5:25). Concludes Solomon, "Enjoy life with the wife whom you love, all the days of your vain life that he has given you under the sun" (Eccles. 9:9).

Even those who rejected Christianity with its sexual morality tended to hold on to the love part. Romantic love became an ideal, a dream that men and women yearned to find. But then romantic love was thought to justify all things, including adultery and premarital sex. "But how can it be wrong? We love each other!"

But in our times, we are pursuing sex without love. A major theme of popular music has always been romantic love, and, while this can still be found, much of today's music is about just sex. On many college campuses, dating has become passé, being replaced with hooking up; that is, going to events or parties with lots of peers, then pairing off with someone for sex, with no strings attached, no romantic feelings, once and done. Sometimes the two having sex do not even know each other's names.

Having sex with no love, commitment, or ongoing relationship is, of course, nothing new. There are no relationships in one-night stands, prostitution, seductions, the anonymous sex of the gay subculture. But now, with the aid of today's technology, we have taken impersonal sex to an even lower level.

I am referring to Internet pornography, which has made the dominant sexual experience of our time the utterly solitary act of masturbation. Sex by yourself. Sex with yourself. When pornography is your sexual outlet, you do not have to worry about attracting anyone or being rejected, getting emotionally involved or getting hurt. You can pursue your fantasies at their most perverse without having to persuade anyone to take part in them with you.

Besides violating *every* aspect of God's design for sexuality—creation, conception, relationship—pornography actually *disables* those who indulge in it from experiencing actual sex. Pornographic stimulation desensitizes people sexually so that they must go to greater and greater extremes to get aroused. A real, flesh-and-blood woman (or man, since women too are now using pornography) is not enough. And because porn conditions its users to make sex *impersonal*—the stimulating figures in the videos being merely objects, things—users will find it all the harder to form romantic relationships and to experience sexual love with an actual person.[20]

Internet pornography corrupts marriage as married men engage in mental adultery with the aid of their computers.[21] And that pornography has become the major source of sex education is disastrous for young people.

We see what this can lead to in Japan, in which hundreds of thousands of teenagers and young adults (though some are in their thirties and forties by now), isolate themselves entirely from any social interaction, still live at home, and spend the entire day playing video games and watching pornography. These so-called *hikikomori* young people (meaning "pulling inward") show no interest at all in romantic relationships or even actual sex. Their sexual desires are fulfilled by pornography, and their need for love is satisfied by playing a video game in which they romance an anime character. The *hikikomori* are a factor in the precipitous drop in Japan's marriage and birth rates, which are bringing that country to a demographic crisis.[22]

Pornography technology keeps advancing. Even virtual reality is no longer the cutting edge. We now have sex robots, animatronic

20. See Freda Bush, "The Problems of Pornography: Sexual Dysfunction and Beyond," *Focus on the Family*, accessed June 10, 2019, https://www.focusonthefamily.com/marriage/facing-crisis/problems-of-pornography-sexual-dysfunction-and-beyond.

21. See Juli Slattery, "The Impact of Pornography on Marital Sex," *Focus on the Family*, accessed June 10, 2019, https://www.focusonthefamily.com/marriage/sex-and-intimacy/when-your-husband-isnt-interested-in-sex/the-impact-of-pornography-on-marital-sex.

22. See Greg Wilford, "Young Japanese Adults Are Not Having Sex," *Independent*, July 8, 2017, accessed June 10, 2019, https://www.independent.co.uk/news/world/asia/japan-sex-problem-demographic-time-bomb-birth-rates-sex-robots-fertility-crisis-virgins-romance-porn-a7831041.html. Also Emiko Jozuka, "Why Won't 541,000 Young Japanese Leave the House," CNN, September 12, 2016, accessed June 10, 2019, https://www.cnn.com/2016/09/11/asia/japanese-millennials-hikikomori-social-recluse/index.html. For scholarly treatments, see Carmen Conde, "The Social Isolation of the Hikikomori: Voluntarily Imprisoned and Glued to the Screens," *Family and Media*, May 3, 2017, accessed June 10, 2019, http://www.familyandmedia.eu/en/internet-and-social-network/the-social-isolation-of-the-hikikomori-voluntarily-imprisoned-and-glued-to-the-screens/; and Emmanuel Stip et al., "Internet Addiction, Hikikomori Syndrome, and the Prodromal Phase of Psychosis," *Frontiers in Psychiatry*, March 3, 2016, accessed June 10, 2019, https://doi.org/10.3389/fpsyt.2016.00006.

mannikins with "artificial intelligence" features that can carry on a conversation, flatter the user, and moan with pleasure. Sex robot "brothels" are opening worldwide, though they are not really brothels, since they don't use real women and so don't violate any laws. These are proving very popular. There are reports of wives who drop off their husbands to have "sex" with the mannikins, waiting in the car until they finish. The wives don't consider this adultery, since no women are involved. Men can fulfill their darkest fantasies, dressing the dolls like children or beating them or raping them. After all, no one is hurt. What could possibly be wrong with this?

Thus we have reached a new phase in treating women as sex objects. Having sex with objects.

What has been lost is not just the Christian dimension of sex but the human dimension. Repudiating the end of sex—that is, its purpose—we have reached the end of sex, in which it has nothing to do with love or procreation or a personal relationship or bodies. It is just a spasm.

Conclusion

When I published *Postmodern Times* back in 1994, the main sexual issue we discussed was premarital sex. It was astonishing to me that 67 percent of Americans at that time believed that it was morally acceptable to have sex before marriage. As late as 1969, well into the sexual revolution, 68 percent believed premarital sex was *not* morally acceptable, a complete turnaround similar to what we documented here about the acceptance of homosexuality.[23] Today, 62 percent of Americans are fine with sex before marriage, which is actually a slight drop from the 1990s.[24] But in the meantime, the other sexual issues that we have discussed in this chapter have risen to the fore.

I have described them as a progressive repudiation of sex in all of its physical and relational aspects. And yet the creation cannot long be put aside. In our post-Christian times, men and women continue

---

23. See my book *Postmodern Times: A Christian Guide to Contemporary Thought and Culture* (Wheaton, IL: Crossway, 1994), 17.

24. See Kathy Frankovic, "Moral Judgments Often Break on Party Lines," *YouGov*, March 19, 2018, accessed June 10, 2019, https://today.yougov.com/topics/philosophy/articles-reports/2018/03/19/moral-judgments-often-split-along-party-lines.

to marry, love each other, and have children. Even the attempts to overthrow God's design for sexuality are haunted by his created order. Gays want to be married. Impersonal hookups and masturbating to pornography are not, in the long run, satisfying. Popular among the *hikikomori* in their parents' basement is a computer game called Love Plus, which allows them to have an *imaginary* relationship, but it testifies to a desire for the reality. Women are realizing the extent to which they have been victimized by the sexual revolution. Both men and women, after years of doing everything they could to prevent birth, are reaching the age when they yearn to have children, though it now may be too late. The desires may be disordered, but there is often a desire behind the desire, one that can only be fulfilled in God's design.

6

Repudiating the Body

Engineering Children and Oneself

Christians have often been accused of denying the body, but even the most neo-Platonic, hyperspiritual mystics hold our physical bodies in higher esteem than the post-Christians.

In our last chapter, we saw how sexuality—which one would think is all about our physical flesh—is being divorced from the actual body: from the reproductive organs; from sexual distinctions; from physical relationship with other flesh-and-blood human beings to stimulation by images on a computer screen or inanimate plastic objects. This is repudiation of the body.

We saw how science and technology posit a human mind over against and apart from the creation, contemplating the natural order in order to understand it, and then manipulating it for human use. Thus, science has learned an enormous amount about the universe, and technology has created marvelous inventions that enhance our lives. But these come at the cost of detaching ourselves from the creation, leading to a sense of alienation from existence and to the assumption that objective reality is void of meaning and that the only mind in the universe is ours.

This can perhaps be seen more clearly when we realize that this is the approach we tend to have to our own bodies. We look at our bodies as if we are separate from them. We want to alter our bodies so that they conform to our desires.

Just as science and technology have accomplished much in their approach to nature, medical science and medical technology have immeasurably improved our lives by curing our diseases and extending our lifespan. But combined with the spirit of constructivism that characterizes our age, medical science is attempting to remake the human organism with a synthesis of biology and technology known as "genetic engineering."

The mind-set that we are distinct from our bodies, which we can remake accordingly, is also manifested in the utterly unscientific and antimedical notion of transgenderism. This rests on the belief that a person can be "born into the wrong body," so that a female can mistakenly be born with the body of a male, and vice versa. Such a Platonic view of the self cannot be justified scientifically, and yet scientists seem to accept this culturally popular concept uncritically. And, astonishingly, medical doctors are willing to perform "sex reassignment surgeries" involving removal of the reproductive organs, even though they must know that such radical, mutilative surgery has no medical basis.

Meanwhile, we are seeing the rise of "transhumanism," an ideology that seeks the union of human beings and machines. We would first be made into cyborgs, a combination of both organic and mechanical components. But eventually, the "meat computers" of our physical bodies could be dispensed with altogether, so the dream goes, once our consciousness can be downloaded into cyberspace.

Engineering the Body

The God of Christians is one who heals diseases (Ps. 103:3), and the incarnate Son of God went about "healing every disease and every affliction" (Matt. 4:23). Disease may be part of the fallen human condition, but Christians have always given it battle. The apostles followed their Lord in performing miracles of healing. The Council of Nicaea not only formulated the Nicene Creed, affirming Christ as both true God and true man; it also ordered that hospitals be built in every cathedral town, thus creating the first health-care system throughout the

Roman Empire and establishing the foundational institution of Western medicine.[1] Missionaries have always brought medical care, along with the gospel, to the peoples they were ministering to. According to the doctrine of vocation, God continues to bring healing by working through the men and women whom he has called to the medical professions. So Christians should be thankful for the great progress that has been made in curing illness and alleviating the physical afflictions that have always plagued the human race, honoring doctors, nurses, and other health-care professionals for carrying out genuine works of mercy.

But in our time, the medical profession has also been asked to cure conditions that are not diseases. Having a baby is not a disease, and yet, as we discussed in the last chapter, medical technology has gone to great lengths to prevent birth, both in finding ways to prevent conception and in aborting the child who has been conceived. Not being beautiful is not a disease, and yet we now have cosmetic surgery. Medical techniques that at first were used to repair bodies disfigured in accidents or by disease—and thus were great blessings—are now used to make smaller noses, tighter skin, and bigger breasts. In order to remove wrinkles, doctors inject into their patients, at their request, one of nature's most potent poisons, the botulism toxin.

Notice the Platonism implicit in cosmetic surgery: it begins with an ideal of beauty, to which the patient aspires to conform. Then, like a classical sculptor, the doctor carves the patient's body to approximate that ideal. The ideal in the patient's mind—shaped by the culture, a construct of the entertainment industry—is what has value, with the body being merely raw matter in need of form.

Engineering Birth

Medical science has been enlisted in another more important cause: reproductive technology. We have made it possible to have sex without procreation. Now we have made it possible to have procreation without sex.

---

1. Cassandra Price, "Hospitals: A Historical Perspective," *Clearly Caring* 25 (September/October 2007), accessed November 7, 2019, Christian Life Resources, https://christianlife resources.com/2018/05/04/hospitals-a-historical-perspective/.

Again, this began with the laudable effort to help infertile couples bear children, a worthy goal, especially in a culture oriented to preventing birth. Fertility drugs and various kinds of surgery can help a couple to conceive a child. Then a method was devised in which the woman's egg is fertilized with her husband's sperm outside the womb, where the embryo is then implanted. Such in vitro fertilization constitutes procreation without sex. The Catholic Church opposes this procedure, but other Christians see no problem with it, since the baby is still conceived by a husband and a wife, so that the child is genetically related to both the father and the mother.

But then fertility treatments were devised that violate the one-flesh union of marriage and the sanctity of embryonic life. In vitro fertilization can now be carried out using an anonymous sperm donor or an egg donor or both. Thus the child is not genetically related to one or both of the parents. Conversely, the man who donates his sperm by masturbating into a collecting vial becomes a *father* without ever knowing or taking responsibility for his child.

Another method is hiring a surrogate mother to bear the child. Either the baby is conceived in vitro from the egg and sperm of the married couple, then implanted into the surrogate's womb, or she is impregnated by the injection of the husband's sperm (an adulterous approximation of Abraham's fiasco with Hagar [Gen. 16]). In this approach, the mother must give away the child she has given birth to.

The demand for surrogate mothers has soared now that same-sex marriage is legal. Typically, two men married to each other will have their sperm mixed together, then injected into a surrogate mother— either a friend or family member or, in states where it is legal, someone hired for the job.

Other fertility treatments involve the conception of lots of embryos, to save time. Sometimes multiple embryos are implanted, since in these procedures they do not always successfully attach to the womb. If only one attaches, the others are allowed to die. If more than one attaches, if the mother is up for twins or triplets or quadruplets, fine, but otherwise the others are aborted. Often, though, multiple embryos are conceived, but implanted one at a time. The others are frozen, in case they need to be used for a future pregnancy. If not, eventually they can be discarded.

Such treatments are no longer just therapies to help infertile couples have children. Same-sex marriages, whether between two men or two women, must have recourse to them in order to have children. Some celebrities and other wealthy couples have paid surrogates to have their babies just to avoid the discomforts of pregnancy and childbirth. Single women who want to have a baby without the burden of a husband can buy sperm from a donor.

Engendering children without sex has moved beyond the bounds of medical health care to become a commercial industry. A clinic in California, where commercial surrogacy is legal, charges from $90,000 to $130,000 for a baby, with the surrogate mother getting $50,000.[2] That seems like small compensation for nine months of pregnancy, enduring labor and childbirth, and then handing over the baby. The woman is treated like nothing more than a baby factory.

Another option is for a woman to donate her eggs, via a surgical procedure. For-profit clinics pay $9,000 for an egg,[3] then turn around and sell it for $26,700.[4] Men also are dehumanized. Sperm donors get paid up to $1,500 per month for donating three times per week. That comes to about $125 per masturbation. The vial of semen, in turn, is sold for $995 per vial. Motherhood and fatherhood are reduced to nothing more than a financial transaction.

Those in the market for sperm or eggs can go to the clinic's website where they can find photographs of donors and information about them so that they can choose the perfect genetic partner with whom they can conceive their perfect baby. You can do a search for a donor by any combination of eye color, hair color, ethnic origin, or other physical traits. You can also search for education level and religion, as if those traits were also hereditary. At the clinic I checked out, you can also search for look-alikes, with a drop-down menu of movie stars, singers, athletes, and other celebrities. Thus, if a woman has a crush

---

2. See West Coast Surrogacy, accessed June 10, 2019, https://www.westcoastsurrogacy.com/surrogate-program-for-intended-parents/surrogate-mother-cost.
3. See Circle Surrogacy and Egg Donation, accessed June 10, 2019, https://www.circlesurrogacy.com/donors/process.
4. See Circle Surrogacy and Egg Donation, accessed June 10, 2019, https://www.circlesurrogacy.com/costs/egg-donation.

on Leonardo DiCaprio, she can find a donor who looks like him, who may give her a baby that looks like Leonardo DiCaprio![5]

The sperm or egg shopper can see photos of the prospective "parent," along with physical details (height, weight, etc.) and paragraphs about the donor that read like personal ads on dating sites. For example, here is the description for a donor listed as "Altruistic Engineer (6'3–Brown Eyes–Brown Hair)":

> Ambitious, confident, and charismatic, donor 15468 is a natural problem-solver that enjoys helping others. He volunteered for Habitat for Humanity, mentored children, and made community service a priority when he was elected president of his fraternity. Intellectually curious, this mechanical engineer is an avid reader and enjoys exploring nature. He has an easy-going personality and our staff enjoys his sense of style and humor. You can catch a glimpse of both in his Adult photos.[6]

I can imagine a single woman who yearns for a baby poring over this site, looking for the ideal man to be the father of her child. Attractiveness, job prospects, likeable personality, and common interests are all factors she is looking for and responding to. It's much like dating and looking for a mate, only there is no actual relationship that can spoil it. Just her consumer choice.

She is also indulging in eugenics, in selective breeding. Her choice of a donor is based, above all, on the traits she hopes her baby will inherit. Cynics and Darwinists say that women always do this, if only unconsciously, when they decide on someone to marry. Some of the qualities women are supposedly looking for have to do with whether the man would be a good protector and provider for her and her children, but such concerns don't matter when the father is merely a sperm donor.

Engineering Genetics

Such informal eugenics pales in comparison to the current efforts to engineer the genetic code itself. It is no longer necessary to improve

---

5. See California Cryobank, accessed June 10, 2019, https://cryobank.com/search/.
6. California Cryobank, accessed June 10, 2019, https://cryobank.com/donor/15468/.

a living organism or a human being by selective breeding. We are developing the capacity to manufacture living organisms or human beings to order by means of manipulating and altering their DNA. It is not even any longer necessary to join a sperm to an egg in order to generate a new life. We can completely dispense with any remnants of what used to be sex!

Every cell in the body contains the genetic information necessary to generate every other cell and the entire body. This is an astonishing fact, a miracle built into creation, evidence that we are "fearfully and wonderfully made" (Ps. 139:14). This means, though, that all we need to conceive a new life is a single cell from anywhere in the body— a hair, a drop of blood, a flake of skin. The cell's DNA can then be caused to replicate, just as the fertilized egg does in sexual reproduction. The resulting offspring would be a "clone" of the cell donor, an exact replica, with the same genes and the same appearance.

As of this writing, cloning still makes some use of the natural reproductive system. The way cloning is generally carried out today is to replace the DNA in an egg cell with that taken from the donor cell. Since it has a full genetic complement, the egg will often start multiplying and forming differentiated cells. The resulting embryo is then implanted into the womb of a surrogate mother, leading eventually to the birth of the clone. Biotechnologists cannot "create life" and they remain dependent on the created order, whether they want to be or not, though they are drastically distorting that order.

Human cloning is currently illegal, though biotechnologists are reportedly experimenting with the concept in nations that lack the legal restrictions. But animals are being cloned. The commercial cloning of livestock is already available, so that prize-winning cattle—the ones that produce the most beef or the most milk—can be duplicated to create entire herds of identical champions.[7] Pets too can be cloned. A beloved dog or cat that dies can be replaced by a genetically identical copy. A cloning service charges $25,000 for a cat and $50,000 for a dog.[8]

---

7. See the ViaGen website, accessed June 10, 2019, http://www.viagen.com/.
8. See ViaGen Pets, accessed June 10, 2019, https://viagenpets.com/faq/. But see Jacob Brogan, "The Real Reasons Why You Shouldn't Clone Your Dog," *Smithsonian.com*, March 22, 2018, accessed June 10, 2019, https://www.smithsonianmag.com/science-nature/why-cloning-your-dog-so-wrong-180968550/.

A human clone, the generation of which I suspect is only a matter of time, would not be a monster. Nor is cloning a way to cheat death, as if a person could save a cell, get cloned after dying, and come back to life. A clone is simply an identical twin. When a developing embryo splits, the two children that are born have identical genes. But they are not identical people. They each have a different consciousness, and, while they will look the same and have many similarities as determined by genetics, they often have quite different personalities. The same would hold true for a clone. Pet owners who clone a gentle-spirited dog that died may get for their $50,000 a snarling biter that only looks like their late pet. Contrary to what many people believe today, genetics cannot account for everything.

More problematic than cloning, in my opinion, though much more acceptable to the general public, is genetic alteration. Biotechnologists actually make changes in the DNA of the developing organism, taking away genes or adding others.

As is so often the case, the technology can be used for altruistic ends. Eliminating a genetic disease by clipping the problematic gene from a strand of DNA is surely a legitimate extension of medical surgery. Biological engineering is also being applied to agriculture, adding genes to seeds that will produce insect- and disease-resistant crops. Tomatoes are being genetically modified to increase their shelf life, and potatoes are being genetically modified to be more nutritious.

Some consumers fear genetically modified food, thinking it could be dangerous, though studies have shown that it is as safe as unmodified food and, for insect-resisting modifications, probably safer than food grown with pesticides. Consumers in the United States and countries that receive American food exports have pushed through laws requiring "GMO" (genetically modified organisms) to be labeled as such, so that they can be avoided. Though GMO foods arguably can increase production and reduce world hunger, I suspect the real reason some people recoil from these products is the perception that they are "unnatural," a sentiment that however ill-informed it might be points to our instinctual ties to creation.

And, indeed, as so often happens, with technology, innovations developed for laudable purposes, such as medicine and food production, then get taken to extremes. A company began to sell GloFish, aquarium fish with a genetic modification that causes them to glow with a red, orange, or green neon light. Such a violation of nature, without so much as a genuine benefit to anyone, is surely perverse. The GloFish, like innumerable genetically modified animals, are *patented*. Is it perverse for a corporation to patent a living organism, something that is not a human invention or a manufactured product but a creation of God? What about this blend of medicine and livestock technology? Researchers are developing the capability of genetically modifying pigs so that they will grow *human* organs to be used for transplants. Is that a legitimate life-saving technology, or is it an un-natural abomination? Would you accept an organ transplant from a pig, or would you rather die? What if a loved one needed the organ?

Such blurring of species, organism and machine, and the natural and the unnatural, also blurs moral boundaries. The moral issues can be confusing even for Christians who, unlike the secularists, have a basis for knowing moral truth. Is such genetic engineering a supreme example of the dominion that God gave to human beings "over every living thing that moves on the earth" (Gen. 1:26–28)? Or is it a violation of that dominion, a kind of tyranny that abuses nature, no more a legitimate ex-ercise of a lawful domination than an evil king who abuses his subjects?

Genetic engineering has not yet reached its full potential, though it is developing rapidly. Another application, currently on the hori-zon rather than a reality, is the ability to fulfill the dream of eugeni-cists: to custom design human beings. Would-be parents could order "designer babies," choosing the color of hair and eyes, selecting for size, strength, intelligence, and—perhaps above all—attractiveness. Embryos that fall short of the parental standards could be identified, destroyed, and replaced. Or perhaps operated upon, adding and sub-tracting genes until the genetic makeup will be just right to produce what the parents consider to be the perfect child.

Or people could be bred to meet specific social needs. This could mean selecting for highly specialized traits. The government could use genetic modification to generate super-soldiers, with extraordinary strength and courage. Others could be engineered for high intelligence and mathematical ability, thus assuring the supply of scientists. We could engineer high-performing blue-collar workers, athletes, musicians, and artists. This might produce a genetic caste system, but we could breed skillful and beneficent leaders to rule us.

All that is needed now to completely liberate human reproduction from sex, marriage, relationships, and undirected random genetic pairings is the perfection of the artificial womb. Already an artificial womb designed for sheep has brought a lamb to term, though the technical challenge of designing one that would work for humans is daunting and said to be a long way off.[9] But think of the possibilities! An artificial womb would represent the ultimate liberation of women, freeing them from the constraints and pains of pregnancy and childbirth. It would undo the curse of Eve! No longer would we need marriage or parents. The family would be technologically obsolete. The government could take over the necessary but freedom-inhibiting function of reproduction, opening hatcheries that could produce children genetically customized according to social needs. From the hatchery, the children could be raised in nurseries that would transition into schools, where they could be culturally conditioned to fulfill their roles as determined by the state.[10]

Begotten, Not Made

What could possibly be wrong with this? Well, to start with, genetic engineering when applied to human beings is profoundly dehumanizing. In God's design, children are conceived in the context of the most intimate personal relationship of husband and wife, and they are brought up in the highly personal relationship of motherhood and fatherhood. Children are not commodities to be bought and sold, or products to be manufactured, or objects to be designed for someone else's use.

The Nicene Creed makes a biblical distinction that can clarify what is wrong with the genetic engineering mind-set.[11] The second article of that Trinitarian confession says:

9. See Sabrina Stierwalt, "Could Artificial Wombs Be a Reality?" *Scientific American*, January 24, 2018, accessed June 10, 2019, https://www.scientificamerican.com/article/could-artificial-wombs-be-a-reality/.

10. This is the starting point of Aldous Huxley's dystopian novel *Brave New World* (1932; repr., New York: Alfred A. Knopf, 2013).

11. Thanks to my friend Rev. Richard Eyer for the application of "begotten, not made." See his article "An Approach to Bioethics," LCMS, accessed June 11, 2019, www.lcms.org/Document.fdoc?src=lcm&id=506.

> I believe . . . in one Lord Jesus Christ, *the only begotten Son of God, begotten of His Father before all worlds,* God of God, Light of Light, very God of very God, *begotten, not made,* being of one substance with the Father, by whom all things were made.[12]

Jesus Christ, the Son of God, is "begotten, not made." The creed quotes John 3:16: "For God so loved the world, that he gave his only begotten Son" (KJV). Most modern translations of the Bible leave out "begotten," though this is a critical concept for orthodox Christology.[13] To "beget" means to generate from one's own substance. The Lord Jesus Christ is "begotten," which means that he is "of one substance with the Father." This is distinguished from another way of coming into being, namely, being "made"; that is, created. Christ was not created; he is not one of God's creatures. He was "begotten," so that he is the same kind of being that God the Father is. Thus, the Son of God is "very God of [with the meaning "from"] very God." Far from being "made," according to the creed, as the divine *Logos,* he is the one "by whom all things were made."

Furthermore, Jesus Christ is the *"only*-begotten Son of God." There is no other like him. We, on the other hand, are "made." We are God's *creatures.* This means that we are *not* deities of any sort. Though we were created in God's image, we do not share his substance, unlike Jesus.

But isn't God our Father too? Yes! We are God's children *by adoption.* So says the apostle Paul:

> But when the fullness of time had come, God sent forth his Son, born of woman, born under the law, to redeem those who were under the law, *so that we might receive adoption as sons.* And because you are sons, God has sent the Spirit of his Son into our hearts, crying, "Abba! Father!" So you are no longer a slave, but a son, and if a son, then an heir through God. (Gal. 4:4–7)

---

12. Quoted from the Nicene Creed, the Three Ecumenical Creeds, at The Lutheran Confessions, accessed June 11, 2019, https://www.lcms.org/about/beliefs/lutheran-confessions; emphasis added.

13. For the scholarly dispute about whether the Greek monogene (μονογενη) means "only begotten" or "only one of a kind," as well as a defense of the translations that retain the creedal language, see Charles Lee Irons, "Let's Go Back to 'Only Begotten,'" The Gospel Coalition, November 23, 2016, accessed June 11, 2019, https://www.thegospelcoalition.org/article/lets-go-back-to-only-begotten/.

> For all who are led by the Spirit of God are sons of God. For you did not receive the spirit of slavery to fall back into fear, *but you have received the Spirit of adoption as sons,* by whom we cry, "Abba! Father!" The Spirit himself bears witness with our spirit that we are children of God, and if children, then heirs—heirs of God and fellow heirs with Christ, provided we suffer with him in order that we may also be glorified with him. (Rom. 8:14–17)

Through the Son and through the Holy Spirit, we "receive" adoption. So although we are made, not begotten, we too become sons of God, entitled to call him not only "Father!" but the most intimate, loving word for Father, "Abba!" Not only that, we become his "heirs." As "fellow heirs with Christ," we adopted children will receive the same inheritance the begotten child will receive—eternal glory.

Adoption is the very description of our salvation. And here we see the biblical solution to many of the problems that reproductive technology attempts to address. There are medical treatments that can help infertile couples who yearn to have a baby, but rather than go to the extreme measures involving sperm or egg donors, surrogate mothers, or conceiving disposable embryos, *adopt a child.* Yes, this is becoming more and more difficult, largely due to the practice of abortion, which ends the life of children who otherwise would have been put up for adoption. But it is still the optimum, God-pleasing, life-affirming solution.

Adoption is also the solution for problems that lead women to commit abortion. Are you pregnant with an unwanted child, one that you cannot or are not ready to support? Put the baby up for adoption! There are too few babies available for couples who do want a child, and you could both save your baby's life and be an immeasurable blessing for a childless couple.

In an innovative pro-life initiative, women who want to give birth are adopting frozen fertilized embryos from fertility clinics, which are implanted and brought to term as "snowflake babies." In this kind of surrogacy, mothers are saving the life of someone else's discarded embryo. Instead of giving away the baby, they keep the child they have given birth to.[14]

---

14. See "Snowflakes Embryo Adoption Program," Nightlight Christian Adoptions, accessed June 11, 2019, https://www.nightlight.org/snowflakes-embryo-adoption-donation/embryo-adoption/.

Adopted children—who have the same love, rights, and privileges as naturally born children, as the Romans and Galatians passages we just quoted make clear—are still "begotten," as are artificially conceived children, even if one or both of their parents was a sperm or egg donor who promptly forgot about them. That they are begotten means that they are human beings. Machines, on the other hand, are made. Human beings, sharing God's image if not his substance, can also be creative, so we can also "create" or make things. We cannot create from nothing, as God does, but remain dependent on his creation, which we make use of in our own technologies. We can even make things in our own image, sort of—androids, artificial intelligence programs, and robots, including sex robots—though these fall far short of personhood.

Reproductive technology and genetic engineering can create the impression that human beings too are "made," and that we are making them. Thinking about babies in this way, in line with the consumer culture that we inhabit, is to make children disposable, valuing them as material possessions or fashion accessories, but denying their dignity and innate worth. Clients ordering a baby and the technicians manufacturing one to their specifications are, literally, playing God in presuming to design a human being according to their will. But, again, they are pathetic, superficial gods, unlike the radically personal God revealed in Scripture, who creates persons and places them in families (Ps. 68:6).

When we treat people as objects, we use them as we do other objects for our own benefit. That is, indeed, how many parents treat their children. But they are begotten, not made. They are a part of us, and yet independent of us.

The "begats" in the Bible, the genealogies that are the bane of Bible reading projects (e.g., Gen. 5; Num. 26; Matt. 1), remind us of a truth that we probably understand better, with our scientific knowledge of genetics, than the ancients did, that our DNA gives us not just our individual genetic blueprint. We carry in our every cell the genes of our parents—even if they were merely gamete donors—and of all of our ancestors, going all the way back to Adam and Eve. We contain within ourselves everyone who preceded us. So we are not just autonomous individuals, but members of a family and part of human history.

Yes, we are genetically inclined to sin. But in the further words of the Nicene Creed:

> The only-begotten Son of God . . . for our salvation came down from heaven and was incarnate by the Holy Spirit of the virgin Mary and was made man; and was crucified also for us under Pontius Pilate. He suffered and was buried. And the third day He rose again according to the Scriptures and ascended into heaven and sits at the right hand of the Father. And He will come again with glory to judge both the living and the dead, whose kingdom will have no end.

Because of the work of God's Son, we too, by faith, are children of God.

Transgender

Genetic engineering is not the most extreme example of today's repudiation of the body. That would be transgenderism—not just the small number of individuals who attempt to change their sex, either by surgery or by simple affirmation, but the ideology that accompanies it, which has become widely accepted by the general public.

There have always been a tiny number of men and women who would like to be of the opposite sex.[15] Cross-dressers—men who dress up like women—have been staples of pagan religions, the Renaissance stage, and modern music halls. Sometimes this is just acting or a heterosexual fetish, but often it has to do with homosexuality, with men wanting to be the object of desire of other men. Such "gender dysphoria" can also be found among women who cultivate masculine traits and pose as men.

But then came the technology of plastic surgery. Physicians became willing to mutilate these poor, confused people for no medical

---

15. A study calculates that one out of every 250 people identifies with the other gender, a percentage of four tenths of one percent (.4 percent). The number, however, is growing, according to the study, especially among young people, suggesting a cultural and not just a physiological or psychological component to the phenomenon. See Esther L. Meerwiik and Jae M. Sevelius, "Transgender Population Size in the United States: A Meta-Regression of Population-Based Probability Samples," *American Journal of Public Health* 107 (2017): e1–e8; doi: 10.2105/AJPH.2016.303578.

reason. "Sex reassignment surgery" could remove a man's sexual organs, shape something similar to those of women, and make artificial breasts, with massive injections of female hormones to give the man other female traits. For a woman who wants to be a man, sex reassignment surgery involves the complete removal of her reproductive system, removal of her breasts, the construction of a prosthetic male sexual organ, and hormones to make her grow facial hair. Men could actually become women, and women could become men. Or so it was thought. Never mind that every cell in their bodies continues to have either XX chromosomes (defining a female) or XY chromosomes (defining a male).

But then being "transgendered" became an ideology. Feminists had already separated sex from gender, defining the former as one's biological makeup and the latter as social roles. Feminists taught that one's sex is irrelevant to gender roles, so that women could do anything that a man can do. But transgenderism brought gender and sex back together. Changing one's gender had come to entail physically changing one's sex. This was a blow to feminist ideology, though most feminists out of solidarity with the LGBT movement went along with it.

But then the idea grew that one's sex is sheerly a matter of how a person chooses to self-identify. The surgery was not even necessary! If a man self-identifies as a woman, then "she" must be accepted as a woman. And if a woman self-identifies as a man, then "he" must be accepted as a man. *One's actual body makes no difference whatsoever.*

The transgendered and their allies speak of being born in the wrong body—of being a woman but being born into the body of a man, or being a man born into the body of a woman. They have, as they say, a "gender assigned at birth," but that is not their true gender. In that light, the medical profession has given a new name to sex reassignment surgery. It is now called "gender confirmation surgery." The procedure simply confirms—by radical mutilation of the body—what the person's gender actually is.

Again the self is standing over and against the physical world. A disembodied self is standing over and against his or her own body. The assumption seems to be that there is a soul of some sort, which is the essence of a person, which exists prior to the assumption of a physical body. That soul is either male or female, but sometimes the physical shell that it is made to inhabit gets it wrong. The shell can be repaired so that it confirms the correct gender. But that is not necessary, since the body, being a mere physical shell for the soul, really doesn't matter.

One might think that such a view would be hard to accept given the naturalistic, scientific worldview that is thought to dominate our secular culture. Are the transgender apologists really maintaining the existence of a soul? If so, this is not the Christian view of the soul, which comes into existence at conception. (Abortion-favoring, reproductive-engineering secularists certainly do not want that!) Rather, it is the gnostic view of the soul, the creation-denying, body-repudiating heresy that teaches the "transmigration of souls," which is similar to the Hindu belief in reincarnation and the Mormon belief in the preexistence of the soul. Still, such a view would seem to be even more problematic for a secular materialist than the Christian understanding. Perhaps such materialism is fading away in the general contempt for creation that we have been writing about, giving way to a more broadly based gnostic worldview.

At any rate, the transgender worldview has become almost unquestionable among our cultural elite, particularly in academic and left-wing circles (as well as the scientifically trained physicians who perform the lucrative "gender confirmation" surgeries). The general public is skeptical by a small and probably shrinking margin. A 2017 Pew Research study asked respondents if they believed that "whether a person is a man or a woman" is "determined by sex at birth" or "can be different from sex at birth." On the whole, 54 percent of Americans believe that sex is determined at birth, with 44 percent accepting the premise of transgenderism. But there is a political dimension to the belief. Among Democrats, 64 percent believe that one's sex can be different from the sex at birth. Among Republicans, only 19 percent accept that.[16] There is also a religious dimension. Among Christians, 63 percent say that sex is determined at birth. In another of our exactly opposite statistics, among the religiously unaffiliated,

---

16. Anna Brown, "Republicans, Democrats Have Starkly Different Views on Transgender Issues," Pew Research Center, November 8, 2017, accessed June 11, 2019, http://www.pewresearch.org/fact-tank/2017/11/08/transgender-issues-divide-republicans-and-democrats/.

62 percent believe that one's sex can be different from that of the body one was born with. Interestingly, among atheists, whom one would think would be most resistant to neo-Platonic mysticism, a whopping 71 percent accept that view![17]

The ideology of transgenderism demonstrates both the detached distance from creation that is a characteristic of modernism and the constructivism that is characteristic of postmodernism. If my body is not the gender I want it to be, I can, with the help of technology, change it according to my will. Such constructivism raises the question, if the "gender assigned at birth" is incorrect, who or what made that assignment? One might think, God. Others might think, nature. There was a time when God and nature were acknowledged to have an authority over us. If God wanted me to be a man, then I am a man, and any of my personal desires to the contrary must be either overcome or lived with. Or, if we leave religion out of it, if nature made me a woman, then I am a woman. If I demand rights equal to those that men have, I might be a feminist woman. If I have sexual desires for other women, I might be a lesbian woman. But I am still a woman, no matter what.

But transgenderism says that whatever gender you have been "assigned" by God or nature *makes no difference*. Your gender is however *you identify*. Identification used to be thought of as an empirical exercise: observe something and then identify what it is. But now identification is a construction, an imposition of the will. What you desire to be is what you are. Your gender is however you self-identify. If you identify as a man, you are a man. If you identify as a woman, you are a woman. Your reproductive system, your genetic code, your body are all irrelevant.

This principle, which is being written into laws and regulations, is being manifested in strange permutations. Now a (self-identified) man (without the surgery) can be pregnant and have a baby. There are cases when both of a child's parents are transgendered so that the child's mother is a man and the father is a woman. There are men who, declining the surgery, identify as women. They further identify

---

17. Gregory A. Smith, "Views of Transgender Issues Divide Along Religious Lines," Pew Research Center, November 27, 2017, accessed June 11, 2019, http://www.pewresearch.org/fact-tank/2017/11/27/views-of-transgender-issues-divide-along-religious-lines/.

as lesbian. So, in engaging in sex with other women, their gay sex is actually heterosexual sex. Transgendered women—that is, men who self-identify as women—are starting to dominate women's sports. In women's mixed martial arts, a transgendered "woman" takes advantage of her/his male strength to beat biological women to a bloody pulp. And there is nothing anyone can do about it.[18]

And though self-identification defines being male or female, some individuals refuse to identify with either of these two genders. Theorists are now criticizing the "binary" gender distinction of male and female. A person can have multiple genders. Now that gays have won their argument that sexual orientation is innate, permanent, and immutable—a notion that influenced the legal arguments for same-sex marriage, as well as popular acceptance of homosexuality—LGBT scholars are changing their story, saying that gender and sexual preference can be "fluid." Some say that the LGBT acronym should be made more inclusive—a prime and overarching value today—so as to include other possibilities. One proposal is LGBTQQICAPF2K+. Here is what the new proposed acronym stands for:

L—lesbian
G—gay
B—bisexual
T—transgender
Q—queer
Q—questioning
I—intersex
C—curious
A—asexual
A—agender
A—ally
P—pansexual
P—polysexual
F—friends and family

---

18. See "Fallon Fox," Wikipedia, accessed August 15, 2019, https://en.wikipedia.org/wiki/Fallon_Fox. Sports organizations, such as the one governing mixed martial arts, can require transgendered athletes to have the sex reassignment surgery before accepting them as female competitors. Some contend that the surgery and hormone treatments make males weaker, on a par with females. But studies show that this effect is minor, and the surgery does not affect size and musculature.

2—two-spirit

K—kink

+—the possibility of more, to be added later.[19]

By including "allies" and "friends and family," LGBTQQICAPF2K+ is so inclusive that it includes heterosexuals!

Meanwhile the number of genders keeps multiplying. A website devoted to keeping track of the number of genders currently lists fifty-six, with the provision for continually adding more. These include:

Adamasgender: a gender which refuses to be categorized

Aerogender: a gender that is influenced by your surroundings

Affectugender: a gender that is affected by mood swings

Agender: the feeling of no gender/absence of gender or neutral gender

Amaregender: a gender that changes depending on who you're in love with

Cisgender: the feeling of being the gender you were assigned at birth, all the time (assigned (fe)male/feeling (fe)male)

Demi-smoke: A transcendental, spiritual gender roughly drifting to other genders that are unable to be foreseen and understood, shrouded in darkness within your inner visual. Elevating through mystery. Caused by a lack of inner interpretation and dark emotional states

Egogender: a gender that is so personal to your experience that it can only be described as "you"

Espigender: a gender that is related to being a spirit or exists on a higher or extradimensional plane

Genderpunk: a gender identity that actively resists gender norms

Hydrogender: a gender which shares qualities with water

Mirrorgender: a gender that changes to fit the people around you

Multigender: the feeling of having more than one simultaneous or fluctuating gender

Vapogender: a gender that sort of feels like smoke; can be seen on a shallow level but once you go deeper, it disappears and

---

19. Katherine Timpf, "Some Activists Want to Turn 'LGBT' into 'LGBTQQICAPF2K+' for Inclusion," *National Review*, February 6, 2018, accessed June 11, 2019, https://www.national review.com/2018/02/lgbt-new-acronym-meaningless/.

you are left with no gender and only tiny wisps of what you thought it was.[20]

Scientists? Would any of you like to comment on these genders and the evidence for them?

Advocates are insisting that the language be changed to reflect this new gender ideology. Gender is embedded in most languages, though not all. In German, every noun has a gender. English lacks grammatical gender but retains gender distinctions in pronouns. Instead of saying "he" or "she," those who are "gender fluid" or otherwise object to such binary gender might prefer "they," since plural pronouns do not have different forms for gender. But using a plural form for a singular is confusing and ungrammatical. The neutral "it" also lacks gender distinction, so some prefer that, though others object that "it" is impersonal. So some gender activists are making up *new* pronouns: ne/nem/nir/nirs/nemself; ve/ver/vis/vis/verself; ey/em/eir/eirs/eirself; ze/zir/zir/zirs/zirself; xe/xem/xyr/xyrs/xemself.[21]

But language doesn't work that way, as if it can be changed by fiat. Language is organic, communal, and historic. New words are constantly being introduced—languages have provisions for how this happens—but new grammatical elements, which is what pronouns are, might take centuries to change and never by individual initiatives. Language, unlike the new approach to gender, is not self-generated.

Nevertheless, since language shapes thought, jurisdictions are passing laws and regulations to require language that accommodates the transgendered. Canada and California have passed laws that, at least in some cases, penalize failing to refer to transgendered individuals by their preferred pronouns. That seems to refer to the binary genders, calling a transgendered woman (formerly a man) as "he," or a woman now self-identifying as a man "she." No one could possibly enforce the bewildering array of self-invented pronouns for the nonbinary genders or the gender fluid, since hardly anyone knows what ne, ve, ey, ze, or xe mean, much less how to conjugate them. Nevertheless, the

---

20. "Gender Master List," Genderfluid Support, accessed June 11, 2019, http://genderfluid support.tumblr.com/gender.

21. "The Need for a Gender-Neutral Pronoun," *Gender Neutral Pronoun* Blog, January 24, 2010, accessed June 11, 2019, https://genderneutralpronoun.wordpress.com/.

new etiquette advice when meeting someone new is to first ask, "What pronouns do you use?"[22] Meanwhile, the British Medical Association has instructed its members to stop saying "expectant mothers," replacing it with "pregnant people," since self-identified men can also be pregnant. Medical professionals should also avoid saying "male" or "female"; instead, when referring to the patient's biological makeup, they should say "assigned male" or "assigned female."

Much of this sounds merely comical, but an area where the transgender ideology can have serious consequences is in child raising. If the "gender assigned at birth" is not the real, self-determined gender but a potential problem that can thwart the child's true nature, something must be done. Most states now allow for birth certificates to be changed retroactively when someone gets a sex change operation, with some states allowing them to be changed according to the individual's self-identity and to use "non-binary" options.[23] Some parents don't want a gender put down for their baby at all, since they want the baby to make that decision for zirself.[24] Other parents are going so far as to raise their children without any gender designations whatsoever, keeping the child's biological sex a secret from family, friends, and even the child. These so-called they-bies, babies who are referred to with the neutral but plural pronoun *they*, are sheltered from any gender influence in their dress, toys, or treatment. Once they are older, they can decide which gender they want to be, if any.[25]

But the most horrible consequence happens if they do decide. Gender dysphoria does happen in young children, with boys acting like girls, and vice versa. But, according to pediatricians, this clears up in between 80 percent to 95 percent of the cases.[26] Nevertheless, some

22. Emily Zak, "Proper Etiquette When You're Unsure of Someone's Gender Identity," Care2, January 22, 2017, accessed June 11, 2019, https://www.care2.com/causes/proper-etiquette-when -youre-unsure-of-someones-gender-identity.html.

23. "State-by-State Overview: Rules for Changing Gender Markers on Birth Certificates," Transgender Law Center, April 2017, accessed June 11, 2019, https://transgenderlawcenter.org /resources/id/state-by-state-overview-changing-gender-markers-on-birth-certificates.

24. Maryse Zeidler, "Parent Fights to Omit Gender on B.C. Child's Birth Certificate: Judicial Review Is Part of a Broader Effort Not to Include Gender on any Government Documents," CBC News, June 30, 2017, accessed June 11, 2019, https://www.cbc.ca/news/canada/british-columbia /parent-fights-to-omit-gender-on-b-c-child-s-birth-certificate-1.4186221.

25. Julie Compton, "'Boy or Girl?' Parents Raising 'Theybies' Let Kids Decide," NBC News, July 19, 2018, accessed June 11, 2019, https://www.nbcnews.com/news/amp/ncna891836?_ _twitter_impression=true.

26. See Michelle Cretella, "Gender Dysphoria in Children," American College of Pediatricians, June 2017, accessed June 11, 2019, https://www.acpeds.org/the-college-speaks/position-statements

parents, when they see signs of cross-gender identification, subject their young children to massive drug treatments to prevent puberty, despite their severe side effects, including infertility, heart disease, and interference with brain development. The antipuberty drugs also become self-fulfilling prophecies, since by suppressing the child's natural sexual development, they tend to cause the child to emulate the opposite sex.[27] And then when the child reaches adolescence and "self-identifies" as the other gender, these parents often find a surgeon who will perform the mutilative surgery. This is child abuse and malpractice.

Conclusion: Transhumanism

The secularist ethical ideology that prevailed through most of the modern era was humanism, the quasi-religious exaltation of humanity. You don't hear much about humanism any more. Human beings, after all, are destroying nature, cause wars, and are radically limited. They have bodies and will eventually die.

Humanism today has been replaced in cutting-edge circles by *transhumanism*. The goal is to go beyond being merely human. This will be accomplished when human beings are merged with machines. The goal is to become a posthuman. As a transhumanist website explains it:

> Posthumans could be completely synthetic artificial intelligences, or they could be enhanced uploads, or they could be the result of making many smaller but cumulatively profound augmentations to a biological human. The latter alternative would probably require either the redesign of the human organism using advanced nanotechnology or its radical enhancement using some combination of technologies such as genetic engineering, psycho-pharmacology, anti-aging therapies, neural interfaces, advanced information management tools, memory enhancing drugs, wearable computers, and cognitive techniques. . . . Radical technological modifications to our brains and bodies are needed.[28]

/gender-dysphoria-in-children. This is a thorough, balanced, objective medical discussion of the issue, which gives important evidence to undercut the transgenderist ideology and practices, especially as they apply to children and adolescents.

27. Cretella, "Gender Dysphoria in Children."

28. "What Is a Posthuman?" Transhumanism FAQ, accessed June 11, 2019, https://whatis transhumanism.org/.

Again, the body is expendable, something to overcome with technology. Some hi-tech fans deride the human brain as a "meat computer." The assumption is that computers made of plastic and silicon are much better. Never mind that the meat computer invented and made the artificial computers. And that, in fact, as we will discuss, the mind is *nothing like* a computer. Transhumanism can stand as a final example of how our post-Christian culture recoils from organisms, creation, life, and anything not under our control.

7

Sexual Counterrevolution

Toward a Theology of the Body

Whatever mental ideology we hold and however we try to adjust our psychology, we can only defy our bodies and our physical makeup for so long. Creation has a way of reasserting, whether we want it to or not. And so it will prove for sex, parenting, and our embodied existence.

Luther, in arguing against a very different denial of the body from what we see today—namely, enforced celibacy for the religious orders—said:

> Just as God does not command anyone to be a man or a woman but creates them the way they have to be, so he does not command them to multiply but creates them so that they have to multiply. And wherever men try to resist this, it remains irresistible nonetheless and goes its way through fornication, adultery, and secret sins, for this is a matter of nature and not of choice.[1]

We are so made, what with our sexual desires and also our yearning for a family, that we *have* to multiply. Even Darwinists know that

---

1. Martin Luther, *The Estate of Marriage* (1522), trans. Walther I. Brandt, *Luther's Works* (Philadelphia: Fortress Press, 1962), 45:11. Also at https://www.1215.org/lawnotes/misc/marriage/martin-luther-estate-of-marriage.pdf.

procreation is one of our strongest instincts, and yet, in another of those internal contradictions that characterize contemporary thought, they tend to buy into today's antibirth mentality. When this "matter of nature" is thwarted, says Luther, not allowed to find expression in the God-created institutions of marriage and parenthood, our sexual desires become disordered and immoral.

This is a matter not just of "nature," as the Darwinist would have it, but of God's creation. Advocates of the sexual revolution said that free sex is natural, pointing to the promiscuity of certain animals and claiming that marriage and morality are cultural and therefore unnatural. Again we see the falsehoods that nature is just about wildlife and that human beings with their cultures are not part of the natural order. Human nature, though, calls for marriage, families, and cultures. Roman Catholics have formulated an ethic, derived ultimately from Aristotle, based on "natural law," though the concept is confusing and controversial for people today. Just as "creation" may be a better category than "nature," while including it, perhaps we could think of "the laws of creation." They differ from "the laws of nature" mainly because it is by the revelation of God's Word that we know what they are, though they are embedded in everything that exists.

Environmentalists too love nature, as should Christians. An appreciation of creation, though, must extend not just to the wilderness but to families, communities, cities, even technology as an application of creation's laws. We human beings may not feel as if we are part of nature, but we are definitely part of creation. I do think the environmental movement, along with the desire for natural food and organic products, is a reaction against the scientism of modernity and the technology worship of postmodernity. Concern for the environment, however misguided it can be, is nevertheless a manifestation of the human need to be part of the created order once again. Just as environmentalism has taught us about ecology, the way every facet of the ecosystem contributes to all of the rest, we can see that the creation has its moral ecology, its cultural ecology, and its spiritual ecology. In our times, all of these have suffered from pollution and man-made degradation, and, like nature, are in need of conservation, restoration, and sustainability.

The sexual revolution is not sustainable. The antibirth mind-set is not sustainable. The distortion and neglect of our bodies is not sustainable. There are already signs that the culture is starting to realize this. Christians have an opportunity to restore marriage, parenthood, and the family. But first the church must be cleansed of its own complicity in sexual sin, whereupon it can live out a biblical theology of the body that may be increasingly attractive to the casualties of the sexual revolution.

Signs of a Counterrevolution

In the aftermath of the sexual revolution, it was often said that sex is no big deal. And the variation: "It's only sex!" Men would try to talk women into having sex with them by using that kind of rhetoric. Natural and moral inhibitions against recreational sex were portrayed as psychological hang-ups, a mental problem that the seducer would be glad to help the object of his attention to overcome. Whereas people used to feel ashamed for their sexual transgressions, the sexual revolution made people feel ashamed for their sexual morality.

Men tried to make women feel that there is something wrong with them if they refuse to have sex. If the man talked a woman into having sex, she may well have felt guilty about it. The man, thinking sex is no big deal, may have actually forced himself on the woman, without her consent and against her will. Women who were groped—which is sexual assault—or harassed or abused or raped were devastated at their violation. But they were expected to be quiet about it. Any negative feelings were "their problem." After all, "sex is no big deal."

But how could sex not be a big deal? Sex is all about the generation of new life. And women, who have the superpower of birthing children, have always and in all cultures been protective of their sexuality. They have known that they dare not risk having sex except with a man who is committed to her—committed enough to help her raise any children they might have—and in a relationship of mutual love. That man should be worthy of her. He should not exploit her, or harm her, or just use her. Rather, he should respect her, want the best for her, and protect her.

Women know this deep down, in their very bodies. And contraceptives and a sexually permissive culture do not change this reality. To be sure, this knowledge can be broken down. A woman has her own sexual desires, and she can seize on falsehoods ("sex is no big deal"; "it's only sex"), though more often her sexuality is distorted because of the way she has been manipulated, abused, or otherwise mistreated by a man.

Men too know that sex is a big deal, that to beget children they must find the right woman and be committed to her. A man, properly, is in awe of a woman. Feelings of romance, impulses to chivalry, and the yearning for acceptance by a woman are all manifestations of this primal masculine need. And yet all of these realities embedded in a man's createdness can be overcome, with effort. There is seemingly less at stake for men—they are not the ones who get pregnant—so they are tempted toward promiscuity, getting sexual pleasure apart from romance, commitment, or any regard whatsoever for the object of their desire.

The sexual revolution took place by overthrowing inhibitions and casting off every moral, cultural, and personal restraint on sexual desire. And women were its main casualties.

Recently, though, women have risen up. They are rejecting being reduced to the status of mere objects that exist—like the sex robots—for the sexual gratification of men, particularly for men who have power over them. Women are fomenting a sexual counterrevolution.

The catalyst was revelations about the sexual predations of Hollywood mogul Harvey Weinstein. Dozens of women came forward, recounting how over the course of three decades, Weinstein had sexually assaulted, sexually abused, or raped them. He also demanded that actresses have sex with him if they wanted to be cast in his movies, threatening the careers of those who refused him. Investigative journalist Ronan Farrow, the son of Mia Farrow and Woody Allen (a family with its own sexual controversies), wrote an article for the *New Yorker* detailing the allegations of thirteen women who had been misused by Weinstein. After the article appeared in October 2017, more women came forward with their stories, both about Weinstein (the number of his accusers is now ninety) and other powerful men.[2]

---

2. See "Harvey Weinstein Sexual Abuse Allegations," Wikipedia, accessed June 11, 2019, https://en.wikipedia.org/wiki/Harvey_Weinstein_sexual_abuse_allegations.

A social media initiative called #MeToo asked women in the general public if they had ever been subjected to such treatment. In one day, some 200,000 women tweeted #MeToo. By the end of the week, the number grew to half a million.[3] Outrage that had been building for decades was released in a torrent. Women reopened painful memories to blast the men who had mistreated them and made it clear that they would no longer tolerate being exploited sexually.

The #MeToo movement swept away hundreds of successful, prominent, powerful men who had treated women as their sexual perks. Weinstein was fired from his own company and put on trial for rape. Meanwhile, more accusations were bringing down other producers, directors, actors, comedians, journalists, executives, politicians, CEOs, musicians, artists, television personalities, restauranteurs, athletes, coaches, talk show hosts, academics—even church figures (more on those cases later). Charges of sexual misconduct took down the heads of Fox News, CBS, NPR News, the Paris Review, and the New Republic.[4] In the eighteen months after the story about Weinstein was published, 417 "high-profile" men were accused. Of those, 193 lost their jobs and another 122 have been suspended pending further investigations.[5]

Even before the Weinstein story broke, the public was unsettled by revelations that the once-beloved comedian Bill Cosby had been sexually abusing women throughout his career, including by slipping them drugs that made them unconscious so that he could rape them. Also from college campuses came reports from female students that they had been subjected to nonconsensual sex.

Some saw a mob mentality in the #MeToo movement, with many accusations being unfounded and at least some of the men being treated unfairly. Some of the incidents go back as early as the 1970s. One defender of Weinstein excused him by saying that he came of age

---

3. See "MeToo," Wikipedia, accessed June 11, 2019, https://en.wikipedia.org/wiki/Me_Too _movement.

4. See "Post-Weinstein, These Are the Powerful Men Facing Sexual Harrassment Allegations," *Glamour*, June 15, 2018, accessed June 11, 2019, https://www.glamour.com/gallery/post-weinstein -these-are-the-powerful-men-facing-sexual-harassment-allegations.

5. Jeff Green, "#MeToo Snares More Than 400 High-Profile People," *Bloomberg*, June 25, 2018, accessed June 11, 2019, https://www.bloomberg.com/news/articles/2018-06-25/-metoo -snares-more-than-400-high-profile-people-as-firings-rise.

in a time when such behavior was more acceptable than it is today.[6] That is hardly an excuse—why would sexual assault be acceptable in the 1970s?—but it does locate the origin of the problem in the sexual revolution. Much of the discourse of the #MeToo movement is in the language of feminism—female empowerment; women standing up against male oppression—but what other language do they have to condemn such sexual misconduct, given the eclipse of moral absolutes? But the realization that there is such a thing as sexual misconduct is a sign that moral absolutes still hold true.

This is evident too in the difficulty of the current moral frames of reference to fully deal with the problem. As we have discussed with the abortion debate, for contemporary secularists, what determines the morality of an action is the will; that is, whether or not there was a choice. If a woman chooses to have an abortion, then that is right for her; but if she is forced to have a child against her will, this is evil, as are the pro-lifers who would deny her that choice. Similarly, the current discussions about sex center upon consent. Sexual actions that are quite acceptable if they are done by consenting adults are heinous and repellant if they are not consensual for one of the partners.

It is indeed true that consent is an important factor in traditional sexual morality. Even in the Middle Ages in the cases of arranged marriages, according to canon law, there can be no marriage unless both the groom and, importantly, the bride give their "consent."[7] This is why wedding services require both parties to say, "I do." (Many arranged marriages, including those with dynastic importance, were thwarted when a young princess—perhaps exercising the greatest power that she was allowed to have at the time—refused the prince whom her family had arranged for her.) Similarly, lack of consent defines rape and is a factor in other crimes and transgressions.

The problem today is that if consent is the *only* criterion, the morality of an action becomes uncertain. It depends on an interior in-

---

6. As reported by Cal Thomas, "Why Criticize Harvey Weinstein? Restraint Is Passé and Uncool, Right? So Anything Goes," *Fox News*, October 10, 2017, accessed June 11, 2019, http://www.foxnews.com/opinion/2017/10/10/cal-thomas-why-criticize-harvey-weinstein-restraint-is-passe-and-uncool-right-so-anything-goes.html.
7. See James David O'Neill, "Consent (in Canon Law)," *Catholic Encyclopedia*, vol. 4 (New York: Robert Appleton, 1908), accessed September 11, 2018, http://www.newadvent.org/cathen/04283a.htm.

clination of the will that cannot easily be discerned objectively. One principle put forward in the campus sexual assaults is that someone under the influence of alcohol cannot consent. There is validity to this point, but it would turn virtually every sexual encounter on campus, given the booze-soaked fraternity and party culture, into rape. When Harvey Weinstein demanded that an actress have sex with him or she would lose the part in his movie, if she decided to do so to save her career, was this consent? Yes, but also no. Consent can be coerced. What about the man who persuades a woman to have sex with him, using the bogus "It's only sex" and "Get over your hang-ups" argument? She may consent, even though she didn't want to. In other cases, consent is given, then withdrawn. Or the man might have *thought* the woman consented, even though she did not, but failed to say anything to the contrary. The point is, while consent is an important factor, when it is the only factor, these cases become very difficult to adjudicate.

Far better and easier to enforce are objective criteria, as many organizations are realizing: "There is to be *no* sexual talk, sexual contact, or sexual relations with an employee." "Professors must have *no* sexual involvement with students." Even better, though, is traditional sexual morality as defined in the Bible: "No sex outside of marriage."

The #MeToo movement, with the harsh retribution that it wreaks, has created a different sexual climate. Executives and office holders with female employees and subordinates are starting to realize that sexual misbehavior risks throwing away their careers. Organizations are implementing strict policies against sexual harassment, including inappropriate language and off-color joking. On university campuses, the hookup culture is being questioned, with some male students wondering if having sex after an alcohol-soaked party might put him on a sex offender registry for the rest of his life.

None of This Is Working

Indeed, some men are concluding that relationships with women, sexual or otherwise, are simply not worth it. Romantic entanglements are too dangerous, what with consent claims and the future prospect of alimony payments. At their best, relationships are too fraught with emotion, with the potential for rejection and heartbreak. These men are trying to repress any instincts they might have for marriage and fatherhood, living as untethered individuals and channeling their sexual impulses into pornography.

This manifestation of the *hikikomori* syndrome, in which men (and some women) withdraw completely from their sexual and social roles, is actually no solution at all. We see that in the "incel" phenomenon, the online "community" of involuntary celibates. Pornography, far from satisfying sexual desire, only makes it worse. The user, sexually frustrated already if he has to resort to porn, becomes even more sexually frustrated. It is not enough to watch other people having sex. He wants to be the one in the video! To make it worse, these frustrations find expression in extreme resentment toward women for not having sex with him. The incels become hostile to women, bitter over their (false) perception that everyone else is having sex but not them, hurt and then furious because in their limited experience women have rejected them. Incels, withdrawing into an online existence, often become trolls, the bane of the Internet, posting on comment threads and discussion boards obscene, hateful rants against women. There have been cases when incels ventured into the real world to commit mass shootings! As of this date, twenty-five people have been killed in three cases of incel terrorism. The incels not only hate women; they hate themselves—specifically, their own bodies—dwelling on how unattractive they are, calling themselves "subhuman." The irony is that the members of the incel community have made themselves so vile in their personalities that of course no woman would want to have anything to do with them.[8]

The successful, high-status alpha males being brought down by the #MeToo movement and the misfit, socially inept incel males might seem to be opposites, but they have much in common. They both demand sex, while being oblivious to women. And they have both lost their masculinity, which is about far more than just sex.

Not just men but many women too are drawing away from marriage. The reason they often give is that the men they meet are not marriage material. The men are passive. They are emotionally needy. They

---

8. See Jia Tolentino, "The Rage of the Incels," *New Yorker*, May 15, 2018, accessed June 11, 2019, https://www.newyorker.com/culture/cultural-comment/the-rage-of-the-incels.

don't want to protect a woman. They want to be protected. Instead of being capable of providing for a wife and a family, many of the men they know want a woman to provide—emotionally, materially—for *them*. I have heard women complain that the men they know really want a mother, not a wife.

But if men have given up their traditional masculine roles, women have also given up their traditional feminine roles. Feminism has obliterated the gender roles for both sexes. Women can hold any job that a man can. Men can stay home to take care of the children. Women can kill an enemy in combat. Men can be soft-hearted and cry. If there is to be *no difference* between men and women, as feminism dictates, no wonder men can marry men and women can marry women. Homosexuality itself has to do with the interchangeability of women and men.

Ironically, transgenderism poses a challenge for both feminism and homosexuality. When a self-identified, XX chromosome, but legally and socially accepted "man" can give birth, women have lost their one remaining distinctive. They had tried to suppress that distinction through birth control and abortion, but being able to bear children was their superpower, making them the source of life in nature and the foundation of the family in culture. But once males and females are fully interchangeable, feminism too ceases to exist. Transgendered men and women who are "gay" end up having relations with a member of the opposite sex. Their homosexuality is heterosexual. Interestingly, the transgendered tend to reinforce traditional gender roles: men wanting to be women try to be hyperfeminine, adopting the mannerisms, body type, clothing, makeup, and personalities of women at their most stereotyped. And women who want to be men try to be hypermasculine, growing hormone-enhanced facial hair, affecting male body language, acting aggressive. Such exaggerated gender markers, which can also be seen among gays and lesbians, have the ironic effect of bringing back the notion that there are sex and gender differences after all.

The Biological Imperative

The sexual revolution also runs up against the biological—that is, the creational—imperative to reproduce. This is an innate—that is, created—instinct, which is manifested as an emotional *need*, for both women and men. This need, like the connected need for sexual relations in a marital union, can be suppressed and channeled in different directions. But except for those with the divine gift of celibacy, it eventually comes to the surface.

Much has been said about the biological clock. Women are said to feel an increasing need to have a baby as they get older, before they get too old to have one. Many older single women respond to this pressure by either an intensified effort to find a man to marry or by choosing to have a baby on their own, via a sperm donor. But since fertility declines with age, having a baby, whether with a husband or a sperm donor, is more difficult. This can be made worse by the aftereffects of abortions and the long-term use of contraceptives. Women who have sacrificed their prime sexual and child-bearing years on the altars of the sexual revolution—namely, recreational sex and feminism—often come to regret it.

But the desire to have children is more than a merely biological impulse. As they get older, men as well as women start to wonder, "Who will look after me when I am old?" "Will I die alone in my room, with no one to grieve for me?" "I have spent my life acquiring wealth and possessions, but who is there to pass them on to after I am gone?" "Who will remember me?"

Though such feelings can be mitigated by belonging to a close extended family and by a strong faith in the God who cares for you and who gives you everlasting life, they are poignant. Christians know that not everyone is called to marriage or to parenthood, and single Christians can be tormented by such thoughts.

But the drive to marry and have children can be directed toward other objects. Toward serving the Lord, for one thing, as in the apostle Paul's commendation of the single life (1 Cor. 7:32–35). Toward serving other people's children, as single teachers and caregivers have shown. Toward serving people outside the bounds of one's family, as the long and continuing line of unmarried saints bears witness. Or toward pets.

G. Shane Morris takes his fellow millennials, adults in their twenties and thirties, to task for treating their dogs and cats as if they were their children. Millennials who do get married—25 percent of them probably will never bother—tend to postpone marriage until their thirties or beyond, waiting to first establish their careers.[9] The birthrate in this cohort and thus for the United States as a whole has plummeted accordingly, to the lowest level in thirty years.[10] But although millennials have an exceedingly low marriage and birth rate, they have an enormously high rate of pet ownership. Morris says that while young adults are half as likely to be married as were their counterparts fifty years ago, three-quarters of Americans in their thirties have dogs, and half own cats. But what bothers Morris is the way so many of his peers talk about their pets:

> It is now commonplace to hear young people my age unironically refer to their pooches and kitties (I'm horrified to even write this) as "children," "fur-babies," "kids," "girls," "boys," or "sons and daughters." Likewise, it's not at all unusual to hear pet-owners refer to themselves as "pooch parents," or "mommies and daddies."[11]

Morris quotes a much-liked social media post that went viral: "Don't say I am not a Mom just because my kids have 4 legs and fur. They are my kids, and I am their mom."[12]

To focus one's maternal and paternal instincts onto pets should not be confused with loving animals. Morris describes in cringe-inducing detail adults gushing over their pets with baby talk. But to anthropomorphize and infantilize animals—that is, to treat them as humans—is to not appreciate them as animals. He writes:

> We have instincts to raise children. Well, guess what? Dogs have instincts, too. ". . . The bloodlust, the joy to kill," writes Jack London in "Call of the Wild." "—all this was Buck's. . . . He was

9. Meg Murphy, "Why Millennials Refuse to Get Married," Bentley University, August 24, 2018, accessed June 11, 2019, https://www.bentley.edu/impact/articles/nowuknow-why-millennials-refuse-get-married.

10. Mike Stobbe, "U.S. Birth Rate Plummets to Lowest Point in 30 Years," *USA Today*, May 17, 2018, accessed June 11, 2019, https://www.usatoday.com/story/news/nation-now/2018/05/17/birth-rate-u-s-drops-fertility-millennials-immigrants/618422002/.

11. G. Shane Morris, "Having Pets Instead of Kids Should Be Considered a Psychiatric Disorder," *Federalist*, May 9, 2017, accessed June 11, 2019, http://thefederalist.com/2017/05/09/pets-instead-kids-considered-psychiatric-disorder/.

12. Morris, "Having Pets Instead of Kids Should Be Considered a Psychiatric Disorder."

raging at the head of the pack, running the wild thing down, the living meat, to kill with his own teeth and wash his muzzle to the eyes in warm blood."

Does this bother you? Do you find this distasteful? Then you shouldn't own a dog, because it is at the core of what they are. This is the instinct that makes dogs so eager to fetch a Frisbee at the park, and what makes cats hours of fun if you've got a laser-pointer. The reason man domesticated such animals in the first place was because of the joy they brought him—not as replacement children, but as *animals*.[13]

See again our alienation from creation: instead of loving a creature in its animal nature, we have to pretend that it is human.

And yet I am not as critical of the millennial pet owners as Mr. Morris is. Playing parent to your dog is a sign that the maternal and paternal instincts are alive, despite all that our post-Christian times have been trying to do to kill them.

Consider now the consequences of sperm donation on the children who were so conceived and their fathers who begot them in such an impersonal way, never to see them again. As many as 60,000 babies per year are born through a donor father.[14] Some donors beget dozens or hundreds of children. One donor passed his serious genetic disease to forty-three children who were conceived with his sperm.[15] A child may unwittingly have hundreds of brothers or sisters. One concern is the moral and genetic danger of incest, since donor offspring do not know who their siblings are.[16]

Meanwhile, just as would-be parents yearn for children, children yearn for their parents. Offspring of sperm donors are often trau-matized when they learn about how they were conceived.[17] A young woman named Courtney McKinney wrote a heart-wrenching piece for the *Los Angeles Times* about her attempts to find her father by

---

13. Morris, "Having Pets Instead of Kids Should Be Considered a Psychiatric Disorder."

14. Hilary White, "Sperm-Donor Father of 43 Children Passed on Genetic Disorder," *LifeSite News*, September 25, 2012, accessed June 11, 2019, https://www.lifesitenews.com/news/sperm-donor-father-of-43-children-passed-on-genetic-disease.

15. White, "Sperm-Donor Father of 43 Children Passed on Genetic Disorder."

16. See Ross Clark, "Sperm Donors and the Incest Trap," *Spectator*, August 25, 2018, accessed June 11, 2019, https://www.spectator.co.uk/2018/08/sperm-donors-and-the-incest-trap/.

17. See Elizabeth Marquardt, *My Daddy's Name Is Donor: A New Study of Young Adults Con-ceived through Sperm Donation* (New York: Broadway, 2010).

contacting the fertility clinic her mother used. The clinic contacted the donor, but he said he did not want to be identified. She kept trying.

> I was proud of myself for graduating from an Ivy League college, as were the people who loved me. I hoped this might pique my father's interest. This time I asked the sperm bank for a picture of him at any age, and to have my email address forwarded to him. No luck. Two years ago I emailed again requesting all available medical history. I received in return a digitized copy of the form that he filled out to become a sperm donor in 1987, and a firmly worded message stating that this was the only information available to me. I had reached the boundary where my rights ended. . . .
>
> I would like to know my father, though that likely will never happen. The second best thing I can do is explain to prospective parents, physicians, policymakers and donors why the burden of anonymous parentage should not continue to be placed onto more people. The "products" this industry creates are humans, and the laws that govern it should reflect that.[18]

Today DNA testing has become widely available, and there are now family-matching sites. Such testing can identify siblings. These resources led Courtney to a sister, another child abandoned by the same sperm donor. Some people conceived by the same father are holding reunions to meet their brothers and sisters. There may be twenty or forty or as many as two hundred brothers and sisters who had never met each other coming together in these family gatherings. Their father, of course, is generally absent.[19] As the desire and the need to know more about one's genetic makeup has grown, some countries have outlawed anonymous donations, ensuring that any children will be able to trace their father. Switzerland and the Australian state of Victoria have eliminated anonymous sperm donation *retroactively*,

18. Courtney McKinney, "My Father Was an Anonymous Sperm Donor. I Feel the Consequences of That Every Day," *Los Angeles Times*, March 18, 2018, accessed June 11, 2019, http://www.latimes.com/opinion/op-ed/la-oe-mckinney-anonymous-sperm-donor-offspring-20180318-story.html.

19. See Ariana Eunjung Cha, "44 Siblings and Counting," *Washington Post*, September 12, 2018, accessed June 11, 2019, https://www.washingtonpost.com/graphics/2018/health/44-donor-siblings-and-counting/?utm_term=.e3cf3a6c70d9.

so that past donors are now identified, and their children can track them down.

This outrages some donors, who do still have the right to block contact with their children, but others who have met their children whom they had so thoughtlessly brought into the world have a strange experience. Journalist Kristen Gelineau writes about the case of an Australian man who received an unsettling letter from a government agency regarding a sperm donation he made some forty years ago. Someone wanted to contact him. At first he was angry that the anonymity he was promised when he made the donation had been revoked. But in the course of his correspondence with the clinic he received a photograph:

> A week after receiving that letter, Peacock found himself staring at a photograph of a woman named Gypsy Diamond, whose face looked so much like his own that he felt an instant and overwhelming connection.
>
> "God almighty, I looked at it and I thought — 'Bloody hell. I can't deny that girl,'" he says. "She was my child from the start."[20]

Please excuse the profanity just this once. His reaction, I think, reflects a breaking in of "God almighty" and a recognition of the "bloody hell" that our sins, such as denying a child, deserve and bring on. But now he wonderingly contemplates his fatherhood.

By this time, Mr. Peacock was a divorced sixty-eight-year-old. He himself dug into the fertility clinic's records. It turned out that he was also the father of Gypsy's brother! And fourteen other children he had never met or so much as thought about. After a long email correspondence, he and his daughter finally met.

Peacock and Diamond met nearly a year after their first emails, in March at a car show. Both were jittery. Peacock told Diamond to search for the good-looking bloke with the red and white umbrella. She could size him up from a distance, he said. If she walked on by, no hard feelings.

---

20. Kristen Gelineau, "Who's My Father? Australia Law IDs Once-Secret Sperm Donors," Associated Press, August 2, 2018, accessed June 11, 2019, https://www.apnews.com/1c68e47ea91d4e5896c719250b2df091.

When Diamond spotted him, she steeled herself, then made a beeline.

Peacock looked up and saw her. They grinned and embraced.

Soon, they were chatting like old chums.[21]

This was all awkward, of course, with the rest of their families. Peacock recognizes that he had not been a father to his daughter in the way that the man who raised her had been. "I'm not her father, I'm not her uncle, but I'm still part of her," he says. "She is a part of me."[22]

The Church Too

These second thoughts about casual sex and the persistence of our yearning to be parents might be openings for Christianity and a recovery of the Christian worldview. There remains one problem: the church itself has been infected with the sexual revolution.

The Catholic Church in particular has been staggering at revelations of widespread sexual abuse of children and adolescents among its priests, as well as coverups on the part of many bishops. In addition to such depraved criminal behavior, many priests are contributing to the scandal by engaging in sex between consenting adults, which is of no interest to the secularists but of profound concern for devout Catholics. After all, Catholics have strong and consistent teachings against every kind of sexual immorality.

Evidently, some men entered the priesthood using the vow of celibacy, with its foreswearing of marriage, as a cover for their homosexuality. Most, no doubt, lived lives of chastity and holiness. But others did not. One study found that 4 percent of Catholic priests have been accused of sexual misconduct with minors,[23] a small but significant percentage, amounting to one out of every twenty-five priests. You may recall from our earlier chapter that this is the same percentage of Americans (4 percent) who are part of the LGBT community, with

---

21. Gelineau, "Who's My Father?"

22. Gelineau, "Who's My Father?"

23. Jonathan MS Pearce, "Are Catholic Clergy More Likely to Be Paedophiles than the General Public?" *A Tippling Philosopher*, June 30, 2017, accessed June 11, 2019, http://www.patheos.com/blogs/tippling/2017/06/30/catholic-clergy-likely-paedophiles-general-public/. See also the numerous studies and statistics that Pearce links to.

only half that number being exclusively homosexual.[24] So since not all homosexuals or homosexual priests abuse minors, the Catholic Church has a much greater percentage of homosexuals than can be found in the general population. As for the claim that the percentage of pedophiles is no larger among priests than for the population as a whole, this is not true. Some 1 percent of men have some sexual attraction to children, but only a tiny number of that group actually act on that impulse to commit child abuse.[25] Most of the accused priests molested teenagers rather than young children, making them pederasts rather than pedophiles, which is relatively mainstream in the gay world. (The legal age of consent is eighteen. In many cases priests are accused of sexual contact with young men who were "of age," but who did not consent.) A grand jury report of cases in Pennsylvania since the 1940s found that 76 percent involved pederasty; 17 percent, pedophilia; 7 percent, nonconsensual sex with someone over eighteen.[26]

How could this be in the church with arguably the strongest and most consistent teachings against sexual immorality? Indeed, Catholic teaching on the subject goes farther than most Protestants would. Catholicism forbids *all* non-procreative sex, teaching that even sex within marriage, if done without the *intention* of having children, is sinful.[27] Few Protestants would go that far, since when the Bible addresses sex within marriage, it says little, if anything, about procreation, focusing instead on the one-flesh union between husband and wife that sex creates. The source of Catholic ethics is rationalistic, based on Aristotle's understanding of natural law, rather than biblical, as such. But it certainly condemns non-procreative sex such as homosexuality as "unnatural." Furthermore, Catholic teachings about mortal sin and the necessity of good works for salvation render such sexual trans-

24. See Dominic Holden, "Who Are LGBTQ Americans? Here's a Major Poll on Life, Sex, and Politics," *BuzzFeed News*, June 13, 2018, accessed June 11, 2019, https://www.buzzfeednews.com/article/dominicholden/lgbtq-in-the-us-poll#.cxLA003Mpp.

25. See Pearce, "Are Catholic Priests More Likely to Be Paedophiles?"

26. See "Accused Pennsylvania Priest Predators Preyed Mostly on Teen Boys: Analysis," *LifeSite News*, August 17, 2018, accessed June 11, 2019, https://www.lifesitenews.com/blogs/majority-of-predator-priests-were-gay-and-abused-male-teens-pa-grand-jury-r. The story comments that these percentages are consistent with the data from other studies.

27. See Ronald L. Conte Jr., "Questions and Answers on Catholic Marital Sexual Ethics," *Roman Catholic Theology on Faith and Morals*, accessed June 11, 2019, http://www.catechism.cc/articles/QA.htm.

gressions *damnable*. Even if such sins were confessed and absolved, they would still require years of temporal punishment in purgatory's penitential fire. And, of course, Catholicism teaches that celibacy is a more meritorious spiritual state than marriage, so it requires all priests, nuns, and monks to take a vow of celibacy, which is no longer a matter of free choice and giftedness as in the New Testament (Matt. 19:11–12; 1 Cor. 7) but mandatory for all church workers.

So how could a church with such teachings have such problems in its priesthood? The iniquity and depravity of the sinful heart is a mystery. John O'Sullivan, a concerned Catholic, wonders what these abusive priests believe.[28] Many, he suggests, have lost their faith. They no longer believe what their church teaches, but since being a priest is their job, they go through the motions of teaching and enforcing those beliefs, except when they pertain to themselves. In other cases, he sees outright demonic activity, particularly in the instances that combine sexual abuse with acts of sacrilege and blasphemy.[29] Others, O'Sullivan suggests, have adopted a "humanitarian" version of religion—that is to say, a liberal theology—which opposes traditional teachings in favor of a progressive theology that is open to the sexual revolution.

I would add two other possible explanations. The medieval church was also characterized by rank sexual corruption—from special brothels for priests to popes who made their illegitimate sons cardinals—so the reformation of the church included allowing those in the religious orders to marry. The cure for sexual immorality, according to the Bible, is not never having sex but marriage (1 Cor. 7). This is the point of the quote from Luther at the beginning of this chapter, that denying marriage channels the natural sexual drive into all kinds of sin and perversity. There is also the curious phenomenon that a highly legalistic, works-righteousness mind-set, which Catholics can be prone to, can actually increase sin. It does so in two ways. First, those who have come to trust in their own righteousness often, when they sin, rationalize away their transgression. After all, I am a good

---

28. John O'Sullivan, "Is the Pope a Catholic?" *National Review*, August 29, 2018, accessed June 11, 2019, https://www.nationalreview.com/2018/08/pope-francis-catholic-church-sex-abuse-scandal/.

29. See Jaxon Silverstein, "Disturbing Priest Abuse Allegations Detailed in Pennsylvania Grand Jury Report," CBS News, August 17, 2018, accessed June 11, 2019, https://www.cbsnews.com/news/pennsylvania-grand-jury-report-details-disturbing-abuse-allegations/.

person, they think, so what I did cannot really be so bad. Such thinking yields ever more bad behavior. There is a reason self-righteousness is associated with hypocrisy. Second, very harsh, moralistic, legalistic systems—look up the reference in footnote 27 to see just how strictly and minutely the Catholic church regulates sex—have a way of breeding rebellion. Those who know God's law only as a burden that they are unable to keep and that plagues them with guilt and shame often react by breaking out against all restraints and defying all moral authority. Only the gospel of Christ can cleanse sin like this, as the Word of God turns guilt into repentance and the Holy Spirit remakes the human heart.

Protestants, though, have sexual scandals of their own.[30] This includes Southern Baptists and other conservative, Bible-believing, evangelical Christians. They have the gospel, the Bible, and married clergy, which perhaps makes their sexual transgressions even less excusable. Adultery, sexual harassment, sexual assault, sexual abuse, child molestation, and pornography have brought down prominent Christian leaders, megachurch ministers, TV preachers, missionaries, and parish pastors. And laypeople too commit these transgressions, including those with seemingly impeccable evangelical credentials.

One problem is that Christians are so often failing in their marriages, the very provision that God has given them for a moral, rightly ordered, fulfilling sexuality. The most widespread scandal in the broader church today is the high divorce rate. A 2018 study from Pew Research found that 13 percent of American adults are divorced. Breaking it down by religious affiliation yields some surprises. Among Catholics, 12 percent are divorced, almost the same as the population as a whole, even though the Catholic Church does not believe in or allow divorce at all. The lowest divorce rate can be found among *liberal* Protestants, including denominations that have pretty much given up on traditional Christian sexual morality and replaced it with tenets of the sexual revolution (United Church of Christ, 8 percent;

---

30. See Kate Shellnutt, "After Major Investigation, Southern Baptists Confront the Abuse Crisis They Knew Was Coming," *Christianity Today*, February 11, 2019, accessed June 24, 2019, https://www.christianitytoday.com/news/2019/february/southern-baptist-abuse-investigation -houston-chronicle-sbc.html. See also Marvin Olasky, Sophia Lee, and Emily Belz, "Crouching at Every Door," *World*, August 30, 2018, accessed June 11, 2019, https://world.wng.org/2018/08 /crouching_at_every_door.

Evangelical Lutheran Church in America, 9 percent; Presbyterian Church in the USA, 11 percent). The divorce rate among *conservative* denominations is often as high as or higher than that of Americans as a whole: Assemblies of God, 16 percent; Nazarenes, 14 percent; Southern Baptists, 13 percent; Presbyterian Church in America, 13 percent. African-American churches have the highest divorce rate of all (National Baptists, 22 percent; African Methodist Episcopal, 20 percent; Church of God in Christ, 20 percent). There are outliers: the liberal American Baptists have a high divorce rate of 16 percent; Methodists and Episcopalians are slightly under the average at 12 percent; conservative Lutherans of the Missouri Synod have the same relatively low but still unconscionably high rate as more liberal Lutherans at 9 percent, which is also the rate for the Orthodox.[31]

These numbers do not give the whole picture. First, they record the percentage of people who are currently divorced, not including those who have divorced and remarried, so that it underreports the impact of divorce on American families. The oft-heard statistic that 50 percent of American marriages end in divorce has been questioned, with researchers now saying the numbers are more like 42–45 percent.[32] But there are other factors, such as social class and educational level. The well-educated upper middle class, such as those who tend to belong to mainline liberal Protestant denominations, has a low divorce rate, whereas the working class, which includes most African-Americans and rural evangelicals, has a high divorce rate. Middle-class suburbanites, which includes most evangelicals, come in at around the national average. Furthermore, there is evidence that conservative Christians who regularly go to church, pray, and read their Bibles—that is, who take their faith seriously—have much smaller divorce rates. The high rate in conservative denominations seems to come largely from their less active members.[33]

---

31. "Marital Status of U.S. Religious Groups," Pew Research, March 19, 2018, accessed June 11, 2019, http://www.pewresearch.org/fact-tank/2018/03/19/share-of-married-adults-varies-widely-across-u-s-religious-groups/ft_18-03-19_marriagereligion/. See also the links to the full study and to the discussion of the data.

32. Bella DePaulo, "What Is the Divorce Rate, Really?," *Psychology Today*, February 2, 2017, accessed June 11, 2019, https://www.psychologytoday.com/us/blog/living-single/201702/what-is-the-divorce-rate-really.

33. See Ed Stetzer, "Marriage, Divorce, and the Church: What Do the Stats Say, and Can Marriage Be Happy?" *Christianity Today*, February 14, 2014, accessed June 11, 2019, https://

But all of this is cold comfort. That Christians, who purport to uphold "family values," divorce in such great numbers is a travesty. Are the biblical teachings about marriage untrue? Do Christian husbands and wives not know how to treat each other? To be sure, Christianity is for sinners, so we should not be surprised to see sinners in church—including sexual sinners and people who have broken their families—but the gap between what we teach and how we live casts doubt on everything we proclaim.

In their article "Why Every Christian Should Be Very Worried about the Catholic Sex Scandal," two evangelicals, Willis L. Krumholz and Robert Delahunty, say that the scandal is the greatest crisis for the Catholic Church since the Reformation. But they cite a crucial difference. During the Reformation five hundred years ago, Europe was solidly Christian. But now Europe and the West in general are largely non-Christian and secularist. Their fear is that the scandal in the Church of Rome will turn the secularists against Christianity altogether. The authors are worried that the fallout of the scandal will endanger religious liberty and denigrate the Christian religion in general in the eyes of our increasingly secularist world.[34]

Those are good points, and the danger is real. But I would argue that Europe in the time of the Reformation was not as Christian as it should have been, and that the Reformation made Europe *more* Christian. Not only because of evangelical Protestantism. The Catholic Church became more Catholic. The Counter-Reformation cleared up much of the corruption—including the sexual corruption—that had devastated Rome's credibility, leading to a revival of Catholic piety, especially among the laypeople, that would never have happened without the Reformation.

Reformation is painful, disruptive, and traumatic. But reformation is necessary to *restore* the credibility and the integrity of the church. Both Catholics and Protestants need a reformation when it comes to sexual morality and the restoration of the family. Megan Fox is a de-

---

www.christianitytoday.com/edstetzer/2014/february/marriage-divorce-and-body-of-christ-what-do-stats-say-and-c.html.

34. Willis L. Krumholz and Robert Delahunty, "Why Every Christian Should Be Very Worried about the Catholic Sex Scandal," *Federalist*, September 13, 2018, accessed June 11, 2019, http://thefederalist.com/2018/09/13/every-christian-worried-catholic-sex-scandal/.

vout Catholic who is furious about the "filth" that is being disclosed. After a searing attack on the perpetrators and the hierarchy that covered up their crimes, she concludes on a note of hope that now, finally, the church is being purified:

> How many times have the laity in the Catholic Church prayed for such a day that the wicked among us would be cast out? That the wolves preying on the sheep would be put down? It's not like no one knew what was going on. There are thousands of families all over the world suffering the consequences of priest abuse and Church cover-up. It's just that until now, the deceivers were able to hide and obscure and strangle the voices of the aggrieved with promises of reform and new "policies" and punishments with no teeth. Not anymore. The crimes are too great and it's clear the hierarchy had no intention of stopping it. Change is coming. IT'S HAPPENING![35]

"The Lord's house needs to burn with holy fire and purge this wickedness from her leadership," she writes. "You are blessed to live in such a time as this when there is so much good work to do!"[36]

If the sex scandals are discrediting Christianity, they are also discrediting sexual license. And they are discrediting the sexual revolution, as the public is forced to acknowledge that sexual behavior needs to be restrained, controlled, and ordered by moral principles.

Theology of the Body

Christians are having problems with marriage and with sexual immorality, in my opinion, because they have absorbed the same assumptions about marriage and sex that are held by secularists. Neither have a high enough view of the body. Both see marriage as a means of self-fulfillment, which makes conflicts over power and the option of leaving the marriage inevitable, even when the two contending selves are Christians. This is opposed to what the Bible says, that in marriage a man and a woman become "one flesh"; that is, one body, "so

---

35. Megan Fox, "Why Now Is the Time to Convert to Catholicism," *PJ Media*, August 28, 2018, accessed June 11, 2019, https://pjmedia.com/faith/why-now-is-the-time-to-convert-to-catholicism/.

36. Fox, "Why Now Is the Time to Convert to Catholicism."

they are no longer two but one" (Matt. 19:6). The Bible also says that fulfillment of the self comes, paradoxically, by denying oneself (Luke 9:23–24) and taking up the cross of sacrificial love. To experience this biblical dimension of marriage, Christians must recover marriage as *vocation*, a God-inhabited sphere of love and service to one's neighbor (in this case, to one's wife or husband). In doing so, they will restore the meaning and the reality of the Christian family, which, in turn, will encourage secularist casualties of the sexual revolution to look to the church for their own healing.

Our friend J. G. Hamann, the newly rediscovered eighteenth-century thinker whom we discussed as offering a way forward from both modernism and postmodernism, had a great deal to say about the body, marriage, and sex.

The sign of the divine image in which we were created is not just our capacity for reason, as so many have assumed; rather, Hamann says, it is also our ability to create.[37] Specifically, our ability to generate new human beings. Having children, he said, is the closest analogue to what God did at the creation. To be sure, God, in his continuous work, is creating the children that we have, but he does so through human beings in their vocations of mother and father. This makes sexuality, which Hamann then relates to other kinds of creativity, central to human life.

So is marriage. The apostle Paul teaches that marriage is an image of the relationship between Christ and the church (Eph. 5:32). For Hamann, human marriage is an emblem of God's love for the world, and Christ's love for those who have faith in him.[38]

Hamann is especially interested in "the mystery of sexual difference," observes John Betz, which "is bound up with the mystery of the *creativity* of sexual union-in-difference."[39] "God created man in his own image," says the Bible, "male and female he created them"; whereupon "God said to them, 'Be fruitful and multiply and fill the earth and subdue it and have dominion'" (Gen. 1:27–28). Thus, the divine image, sexual difference, having children, and exercising creative dominion over the earth are all connected in God's act of creation.

---

37. See John Betz, *After Enlightenment: The Post-Secular Vision of J. G. Hamann* (Oxford, UK: Wiley-Blackwell, 2012), 180.

38. Betz, *After Enlightenment*, 181.

39. Betz, *After Enlightenment*, 181.

The fruitfulness of the man and the woman happens when the two "become one flesh" (Gen. 2:24). For Hamann, this union-in-difference is a reflection of God himself, who is a Trinity of three distinct persons who exist in complete unity. Union-in-difference is also an image of reconciliation, including the reconciliation of seemingly contrary ideas—faith and reason, soul and body, spirit and matter—that Hamann found in the Christian worldview.[40] Marriage, including sex and childbirth, thus embodies the truths of our creation, is a reflection of God himself, and is a sign of Christ's redemption.

"From this perspective," says Betz, "it is easy to see why marriage, the consummate symbol of union-in-difference, is a central topos of Hamann's thought, informing everything from his epistemology to his (at least implicit) metaphysics."[41] Throughout his writings, "Hamann is wont to diagnose the epistemological and philosophical ills of his age in terms of one or another sexual perversion or profaning of the mystery of marriage."[42] Most striking is the predictive value of Hamann's insights. According to Betz, referring to "the mystery of the creativity of sexual union-in-difference":

> He sees disregard for this mysterious image, this bond between heaven and earth, as a sign of sterility, decadence, and cultural decline; for once sexual union-in-difference is evacuated of transcendent meaning, once it is no longer revered as a mysterious image of the Trinity, the most fundamental bond between Creator and creature is broken.[43]

Once again, Hamann is prophetic. Our current disregard for sexual union-in-difference can be seen in the feminist denial that there is any meaningful difference between men and women. In the perversion of homosexuality, which is sexual-union-without-difference. In transgenderism, which repudiates the sex of the body. In pornography, which pursues sex without union. In adultery, which Hamann, like the Old Testament prophets and like Jesus, uses as a synonym for evil.[44]

---

40. Betz, *After Enlightenment*, 181.
41. Betz, *After Enlightenment*, 181.
42. Betz, *After Enlightenment*, 181n18.
43. Betz, *After Enlightenment*, 181.
44. Betz, *After Enlightenment*, 181.

Hamann criticized the Enlightenment, which was accompanied by an upsurge of sexual immorality, for its sexlessness, its disembodied rationalism and indifference to the body. "Hamann believed that the aftereffects of the 'Enlightenment,' of reason cut off from its source [in God], would be a world precisely without reason (!), moreover a culture without genuine inspiration, without life-giving passion, and without fruitful creativity."[45]

Hamann is putting forward a "theology of the body," which many Christians have been calling for today. Pope John Paul II has popularized that phrase with his own learned and perceptive contribution: *Man and Woman He Created Them: A Theology of the Body*.[46] In a wide-ranging philosophically and theologically sophisticated series of discourses, the late pope, recently made a saint, develops the idea that, in his words, "The body, and it alone, is capable of making visible what is invisible: the spiritual and the divine. It was created to transfer into the visible reality of the world, the mystery hidden since time immemorial in God, and thus to be a sign of it."[47] Traditional Catholics are using this work as a resource for marriage-preparation classes, marriage counseling, and married couples' studies and retreats, all in an effort to revitalize Christian marriages.[48] John Paul's work is filled with helpful insights, but it is, of course, *Catholic*—how could it be otherwise?—through and through. Protestants need something more thoroughly biblical. An evangelical theology of the body is called for, and a number of evangelical scholars are, in fact, working in this area.[49]

---

45. Betz, *After Enlightenment*, 181.

46. John Paul II, *Man and Woman He Created Them: A Theology of the Body* (Boston: Pauline, 2006).

47. Paul, *Man and Woman He Created Them*, 5.

48. See the work of Catholic layman Christopher West, who has prepared a wide range of curricula and study materials and has started a ministry of marriage renewal. For an accessible but thorough discussion, see his book *Theology of the Body Explained: A Commentary on John Paul II's Man and Woman He Created Them* (Boston: Pauline, 2008).

49. See, e.g., Matthew Lee Anderson, *Earthen Vessels: Why Our Bodies Matter to Our Faith* (Bloomington, MN: Bethany, 2011). See also his post "Five Books on the Body for Evangelicals," *Mere Orthodoxy*, June 15, 2011, accessed June 11, 2019, https://mereorthodoxy.com/five-books -on-the-body-for-evangelicals/. Also listen to Albert Mohler's address on the subject, "An Evangelical Theology of the Body: Biblical Theology and the Sexuality Crisis," *Albert Mohler* website, March 13, 2014, accessed June 11, 2019, https://albertmohler.com/2014/03/13/an-evangelical -theology-of-the-body-biblical-theology-and-the-sexuality-crisis/. The Australian Lutheran theologian John Kleinig—who is also a Hamann scholar—is also in the process of formulating a theology of the body.

Let me just draw your attention to a few texts of Scripture that are foundational for a biblical understanding of the body, sex, and marriage. First consider what Jesus said (quoting Gen. 1:27 and 2:24) in response to a question about the lawfulness of divorce:

> He answered, "Have you not read that he who created them from the beginning made them male and female, and said, 'Therefore a man shall leave his father and his mother and hold fast to his wife, and the two shall become one flesh'? So they are no longer two but one flesh. What therefore God has joined together, let not man separate." (Matt. 19:4–6)

God is the one who joins a man and a woman together in marriage. Marriage, therefore, is a God-given vocation. This is evidently true even for nonbelievers, as God providentially cares for all of his creation, including those who do not know him. Marriage is not just for Christians, but for all people, just as marriage exists in some form within all human cultures. Furthermore, by virtue of God's work in marriage, the husband and the wife "are no longer two but one flesh."

The apostle Paul gives an application: "In the same way husbands should love their wives as their own bodies. He who loves his wife loves himself. For no one ever hated his own flesh, but nourishes and cherishes it, just as Christ does the church, because we are members of his body" (Eph. 5:28–30). A husband who loves his wife is loving himself and his own body. *Because they have the same flesh.* "They are no longer two but one flesh." The husband and the wife are distinct persons, but their bodies, though separate spatially, constitute one physical organism. The husband's body belongs to the wife, and the wife's body belongs to the husband, since they have only "one flesh" between them. This is the context of marital sex (1 Cor. 7:4). This is also how conception happens: the reproductive system of the man joins with the reproductive system of the woman. The two of them really do constitute one physical organism, one body. And the child they conceive, give birth to, and raise up together, is "one flesh" with them, sharing both parents' DNA. In a family, every member shares the same "flesh and blood." This reality also explains the nature of sexual sin:

> Flee from sexual immorality. Every other sin a person commits is outside the body, but the sexually immoral person sins against his own body. Or do you not know that your body is a temple of the Holy Spirit within you, whom you have from God? You are not your own, for you were bought with a price. So glorify God in your body. (1 Cor. 6:18–20)

Sexual sin is unique in that it is a sin against one's own body. This applies to single people. It also applies to married couples. Adultery is a sin against one's body in a double sense, violating both one's own body and that of the spouse, with whom the adulterer is "one flesh." It is also a sin against the illicit sexual partner, becoming one flesh with someone whom you then abandon (1 Cor. 6:16).

These texts are about more than marriage and sexual morality. Just as a husband and wife, while separate individuals, are part of one common body, a Christian is part of the body of Christ, so that there is a "flesh and blood" connection with all other Christians. Furthermore, our body is itself designed for God's habitation: "Your body is a temple of the Holy Spirit." We are inhabited by the Holy Spirit! Our bodies are part of Christ's body! "Glorify God in your body," indeed!

Is all of this just theoretical? Just abstract theology disconnected from the practical problems of everyday life? Not at all. The mind-set that we picked up from the non-Christian world of trying to remake the divine "mystery" of marriage so that it is all about ourselves is what is not working.

Though in our post-Christian culture everyone is fixated on self-fulfillment, Jesus offers the way of self-denial. "And he said to all, 'If anyone would come after me, let him deny himself and take up his cross daily and follow me. For whoever would save his life will lose it, but whoever loses his life for my sake will save it'" (Luke 9:23–24). Paradoxically, denying the self is the only way to save the self. Trying to save one's life—the Greek word is *psyche*, which can be a synonym for "self"—means losing it completely. But giving up one's *psyche* for the sake of Jesus will mean receiving it back abundantly.

Taking up our cross is usually taken to refer to our trials and sufferings, and that is certainly part of it. With all of our comforts and pleasures, we have forgotten how to suffer. Many couples, when they face hard times, assume that this means something is wrong with their marriage and take the occasion to abandon each other. (I am not referring to abuse, which, like adultery, is a violation of the one-flesh union. Too often, though, the trials that bring on divorce turn out to be mere frustrations of self-fulfillment.) An important Christian discipline to cultivate is cross bearing, as in bearing suffering, as Christ did. But more than just an instrument of suffering, the cross was also an instrument of sacrifice. Christ suffered—and died—for us, because he loved us, his bride. Similarly, in calling us to follow him, he invites us to sacrifice ourselves in acts of self-denial out of love for our neighbors, including our own brides and our bridegrooms. That we are to take up our crosses "daily" suggests that it refers not so much to the big crises of life but to the everyday tasks of our vocation.

According to the Reformation doctrine of vocation, God is in those relationships that he calls us to—as he certainly is in marriage—and the purpose of all our callings is to employ them to love and serve our neighbors. So the purpose of being a husband is for him to love and serve his wife. And the purpose of being a wife is to love and serve her husband—not to "lord it over" each other, with power games and arguments over who has to obey whom:

> You know that those who are considered rulers of the Gentiles lord it over them, and their great ones exercise authority over them. But it shall not be so among you. But whoever would be great among you must be your servant, and whoever would be first among you must be slave of all. For even the Son of Man came not to be served but to serve, and to give his life as a ransom for many. (Mark 10:42–45)

For Christians whose vocations include authority—including husbands and fathers—that authority must be used to serve the ones under that authority with self-sacrificial love. So many arguments in marriage, as in all conflicts in all vocations, arise from wanting *to be served*, while refusing to serve. But "even the Son of Man"—the one who truly does have authority and power—"came not to be served but to serve."

This is the meaning of those notorious and much misunderstood verses in Ephesians 5: "Wives, submit to your own husbands, as to the

Lord" (v. 22). "Husbands, love your wives, as Christ loved the church and gave himself up for her" (v. 25). The picture is of wives denying themselves out of love for their husbands, with their husbands "giving themselves up" for their wives. The husband has his authority in marriage and the two have their own roles and tasks in the family, but this is not a formula for cruelty or domination. Christ does not treat the church in that way. Rather, he "gave himself up" for his bride. In that way, for those whom God has joined together in the vocation of marriage, husbands and wives are to love and serve each other.[50] And in doing so, they will restore marriage to its glory.

Conclusion

In the statistics about how the public has been throwing out the canons of sexual morality—accepting premarital sex, homosexuality, cohabitation, etc.—a curious fact emerges. There is at least one standard holding firm. Some 90 percent of Americans disapprove of marital unfaithfulness. Having sex with someone else if you are married is still considered immoral. This percentage holds true for conservatives and liberals, Republicans and Democrats, across just about every demographic.[51] This consensus suggests that even in a climate of sexual permissiveness and moral relativism, human beings still recognize something of the truth of marriage.

The very problems and disorders we have been chronicling testify to the reality of moral and creational absolutes. As we discussed, millennials have a very low marriage rate. And yet, poignantly, the vast majority of millennials *want* to get married. (Only 9 percent do not.)[52] Many couples do whatever they can to have sex without conceiving children, but then they go to desperate and dehumanizing extremes to have a baby. They *want* to be parents after all.

Homosexuals have successfully crusaded for the legalization of same-sex marriage, even though sexual difference and procreation are

---

50. For more on the doctrine of vocation as it applies to marriage and family life, see my book with my daughter Mary Moerbe, *Family Vocation: God's Calling in Marriage, Parenthood, and Childhood* (Wheaton, IL: Crossway, 2012).

51. See Kathy Frankovic, "Moral Judgments Often Break on Party Lines," *YouGov*, March 19, 2018, accessed June 11, 2019, https://today.yougov.com/topics/philosophy/articles-reports/2018/03/19/moral-judgments-often-split-along-party-lines.

52. See Murphy, "Why Millennials Refuse to Get Married."

at the essence of the institution. But in exchanging the promiscuous lifestyle that had always characterized the gay subculture in favor of a monogamous—even "monogamish"—relationship, they are acknowledging the significance of marriage. (As can be seen with the radical gays who attack married homosexuals for their "heteronormativity," their attempt to emulate heterosexual marriage by adopting children, living a "bourgeois" lifestyle, and otherwise trying to be "normal."[53])

Almost a quarter of young adults aged twenty-five to thirty-four are living together without getting married.[54] Often this is just a convenient arrangement for having sex without marriage. But sometimes, especially when cohabitation goes on for years, with the couple having children, it looks a lot like marriage. Indeed, in some cultures and in some legal jurisdictions, no particular ceremony or legal licenses are necessary to constitute marriage. This has been true even in some Christian societies, in which families may meet in church to pray for the couple, but what constitutes the marriage is living together. Such "common-law marriages" are quite valid. It isn't so much that some cohabiting couples may be married without realizing it. The problem with this arrangement is its impermanence and the lack of commitment that the couple—or one of the partners—has for each other. Common-law marriages, though, cannot be dissolved without divorce. Living together establishes one-flesh bonds but then tears them up at will. But it is still a shadow of actual marriage, without the permanence and security that make marriage live. Then again, easy and casual divorce likewise tears legal marriages apart, making them more like transient periods of just living together.

The #MeToo movement and the sex abuse scandals in churches are painful and traumatic. But the revulsion they are occasioning is a healthy repudiation of sexual permissiveness. And the scandals are forcing changes to the sexual climate in the direction of self-control and moral restraint.

The sexual revolution has run its course, leaving untold casualties in its wake. It has left our moral and social foundations in ruins. But

---

53. See "Heteronormativity," Wikipedia, accessed June 11, 2019, https://en.wikipedia.org/wiki /Heteronormativity.

54. "Heteronormativity," Wikipedia.

while it continues to ruin lives and devastate people emotionally, and while, like other revolutions, it has turned into a tyranny that brooks no dissent, creation has a way of asserting itself.

This is happening. Many couples are intentionally, thoughtfully, passionately building strong marriages. Many parents today spend little time with their children, who spend most of their time with their peers at school while both parents are preoccupied with their careers. But many are going to the other extreme, smothering and overprotecting their children, as "helicopter parents." Yet this too is a recognition that parenthood cannot be dispensed with. Other parents I am seeing, though, are getting it right—I am thinking of some homeschooling families I know, but there are others—working hard to give their children the attention and the close, personal relationship they need while teaching them the self-discipline and moral formation they need for life in the world. If Christians can build strong marriages, strong children, and strong families, they can be signs of hope for the entire culture.

PART 3

SOCIETY

8

Culture and Anticulture

Society without Community

The postmodernists challenged the scientific rationalism of the modernists by, among other ways, invoking the importance of culture. We twentieth- and twenty-first-century Westerners look at the world the way we do because of our culture. But other cultures are equally valid. The postmodernists promoted multiculturalism, encouraged cultural diversity, and cultivated cultural relativism.

And yet for all of their emphasis on cultures and cultural differences, the postmodernists undermined what all cultures have in common. The postmodernists repudiated religion—especially in its communal, institutional manifestations—and yet all cultures have communal, institutional religions. The postmodernists celebrated sexual permissiveness, but all cultures have sexual taboos. The postmodernists deconstructed the family, though the family is the foundation of all cultures.

One of the major postmodernist legacies is same-sex marriage. Some cultures are relatively tolerant of homosexuality, but no culture in the world or throughout history has institutionalized same-sex marriage.

The postmodernists were not really interested in culture or in other cultures. Their multiculturalism did not respect the beliefs or traditions of actual cultures. Rather, it condescendingly invoked superficial cultural stereotypes, like tourists watching the natives parade in their ethnic costumes. Today's multiculturalism is mostly about *race*, as if race were synonymous with culture, which it is not. Racial diversity is not cultural diversity. But the goal of multiculturalism, at least in postmodernist universities, seems to be having a group of people with different appearances, but whose thoughts and values are exactly the same. Whereas thoughts and values are at the essence of culture.

The postmodernists used "culture" as they did primarily to undermine their own culture. The West has been imperialistic in imposing itself on the rest of the world, taking over and exploiting less developed societies and running roughshod over their cultures. Postmodernists object to that, often with good reason. And yet this is exactly what postmodernists are doing! Postmodernism is a product of post-Enlightenment Western Euro-American culture, and its experiments—such as sexual permissiveness, feminism, same-sex marriage—are exclusively Western. And like the practices of the worst imperialists of old, they destroy actual cultures.

The legacy of the postmodernists is not so much cultural relativism. It is relativizing culture. Dissolving all cultures. Undoing communities and the sense of community. This dissolution was reinforced and enabled by a technological revolution that has refashioned society, while cutting it off further from reality.

The Virtual Village

One of the most striking features of contemporary American society is the loss of real-world community, in which we interact with flesh-and-blood human beings, and its replacement with virtual community, in which our interactions are mainly with disembodied individuals and groups on the Internet.

In 2000, sociologist Robert D. Putnam published *Bowling Alone: The Collapse and Revival of American Community.*[1] There was a time not long ago when Americans joined bowling leagues. Today, he

---

1. Robert D. Putnam, *Bowling Alone: The Collapse and Revival of American Community* (New York: Simon & Schuster, 2000).

observed, if you go to a bowling alley, most of the players are bowl-ing alone. Putnam went on to chronicle the decline, which happened quite rapidly, in Americans' involvement in civic organizations (Lions clubs, Elks Lodge), volunteer altruistic groups (Red Cross, food pan-tries), political associations (Republicans and Democrats used *to have meetings*), and even informal groups (bridge clubs, sports leagues, hobbyist gatherings). Though such organizations continue to exist, their membership has plummeted over the last few decades. Individu-als are bowling alone, or voting or being philanthropic or entertaining themselves alone. When people no longer come together in such small-scale associations, according to Putnam, that means a loss of "civic engagement" and "social capital." Human beings must bond together, on multiple levels, in order to form and be a part of communities, and, by extension, nations and cultures.

Interestingly, Putnam, writing at the very beginning of the twenty-first century, saw the Internet, which was then just coming into its own, as a possible solution to this problem, a way to potentially restore our social interactions with each other.[2] But the Internet, with its social media, has qualitatively changed the nature of those social interactions.

To give one of Putnam's examples, in 1961, one out of every four Americans was a member of a bridge club. That might consist simply of four people, or possibly eight people, who meet regularly to play cards, but also to visit and socialize. Even those who did not commit to the regular meeting of a club still got together frequently with their friends. In the 1970s, 40 percent of Americans played cards at least once a month. In the 1960s and 1970s, college students too, for all of their counterculture, were enthusiastic bridge players. Now, bridge and other card games are played mostly in senior citizen centers.[3] Most of our games, including card games, are now played online. We can play those completely by ourselves, with the software taking on the role of the other players. Though we still can compete with other players from around the world, we seldom get to know them. Putnam noted the phenomenon of online bridge, recognizing the difference with the old bridge clubs: when you play online, you are focusing

---

2. See Putnam, *Bowling Alone*, 148ff., 180.
3. Putnam, *Bowling Alone*, 104–5.

exclusively on the game, with hardly any conversation or personal interaction of the sort that builds "social capital."[4]

Today, few people know their next door neighbors, much less invite them over for meals or borrow cooking ingredients or lawn equipment from them as was commonplace a few decades ago. Our social life tends to center around the people we know from work. Or possibly people we went to school with. And, of course, our family. But beyond those circles, we tend not to have many actual friends.

Online, though, on our Facebook page, we might have hundreds of "friends," many of whom we have never met. Although we can see their photos, read about their lives, commiserate with them, and argue with them, they are disembodied. We cannot see them, shake their hands, or have a meal with them. We exist, for each other, only in cyberspace, in the electronic cloud.

That we pursue human relationships online is a testimony to our need for other people, the primal biblical need to love and be loved. So maybe Putnam is right, that the Internet can help us connect with other people and build back up the social capital our culture has lost. Perhaps it is better to be in an online gaming chatroom than to bowl alone. And, yet, when you bowl alone you have the heft of the ball and hear the clattering of physical pins that you are knocking down. The problem is that the virtual world, with its ersatz friends and communities, is very different from the physical, flesh-and-blood, tangible world.

For example, as Putnam points out, real-world social groups involve interacting with people different from oneself. The bowling league might consist of factory workers, business owners, Republicans, and Democrats. For all of the heterogeneity of backgrounds and personalities, you learn how to get along. In online "communities," though, we tend to interact with people who have the same interests and beliefs that we do.[5] Heterogeneous groups—which are made more so when they include men and women of different races, social classes, and ideology—that are aligned by common interests or goals are especially helpful in creating social cohesion. Groups that consist solely

4. Putnam, *Bowling Alone*, 104–5
5. Putnam, *Bowling Alone*, 178.

of individuals who are like each other, as in online communities, will often define themselves by their opposition to other groups. This is a formula for social discord.

At the same time, not everyone on the Internet is your "friend" who is just like you. The discussion threads of blogs, the comment features of online magazines, social media interactions, and online chats are plagued by users who purposefully disrupt conversations, often with the vilest of insults. To be sure, there are atheists who frequent Christian sites, leftists who take part in conservatives' discussions, conservatives who dialogue with liberals, and Christians who strike up online conversations with atheists in an attempt to convert them. The Internet can be a forum for such open exchanges, and this is a strength of our information technology. But often the contrary voices are just trolls lurking under the bridge, spewing insults, obscenities, and mockery rather than engaging in a productive dialogue.

We discussed the social climate of the Internet in chapter 3—the anonymity, the lack of social inhibitions, the trolls. This context makes it easier to dehumanize people—they have no faces, no bodies—and thus to treat them viciously. You treat them as abstractions, personifications of the ideas or qualities you hate, rather than as tangible "neighbors" whom the Bible enjoins us to love.

The pioneering media ecologist Marshall McLuhan said that the new electronic media would create a "global village," a reversion to a more primitive mode of experience based on images and nonlinear thinking encompassing the entire world.[6] McLuhan, whose major works were published in the 1960s, was thinking mainly of television and telecommunication. The Internet was not yet a gleam in anyone's eye, and yet McLuhan (a devout Catholic) was prescient in his insights into the effects of the emerging electronic media on thought and culture. But if the virtual realm of cyberspace constitutes a "global village," it is nothing like the close community of a medieval village. If the Internet resembles a village, it is not the tight-knit community in which everyone knows and supports each other. It is more like the stereotyped small town with its gossip, rumor-mongering, violations

---

6. See Marshall McLuhan and Bruce R. Powers, *The Global Village* (Oxford, UK: Oxford University Press, 1989). See also McLuhan's *Understanding Media* (New York: Signet, 1964).

of privacy, and conformist social pressures. In the Internet, urban legends have free rein, and gossip spreads without restraint. In actual villages, rumors can spread to a handful of people, but in the global village of the Internet, a false report or character assassination can reach millions almost instantaneously.

The virtual world accords well with postmodernist constructivism, which rejects the very possibility of objective truth, insisting instead that truth is something we make up for ourselves to advance our own interests or the power agenda of the group we belong to. In this post-truth intellectual climate, no wonder our information environment is rife with "fake news." Factor in the tribal polarization and the politicization of everyday life that we will discuss in the next chapter, and the result is competing truths with each side accusing the other of fake news. To be sure, actual truth and genuine facts are also part of the information environment. The problem is, there is no common basis for ascertaining which bits of news are true and which are false.

Contributing to the disconnect between information and truth is the medium itself. McLuhan said that the printing press was an information technology that made possible extended thought, linear logic, complex ideas that could be developed at length over hundreds of pages. Reading books required education, a sustained attention span, and minds capable of internal reflection. The new electronic media, said McLuhan—thinking mainly of television—communicates by means of images, not language; evokes emotions, not ideas; and is immediately and universally accessible. McLuhan said that this new mind-set is akin to that of more primitive cultures, which have little need of literacy or intellectual pursuits. Hence, the "global village." Today's Internet village, though ironically dependent on intellectual pursuits of the highest order for the technology by which it exists, tends, by the standards of print-oriented culture, to be anti-intellectual. (Though it still requires a measure of literacy, since its exchanges are still, at least currently, based on language and the ability to read and write.)

Blog posts are supposed to be short; otherwise, no one will read them. The best advice has been to keep them under six hundred words, but in order to get picked up by the search engines, experts are now saying that the optimum is sixteen hundred words, an amount that can be read in no more than seven minutes.[7] Most of our online interactions and intellectual discourse, though, take place on social media. Twitter has long limited the length of its tweets to 140 *characters*, a number that it has now expanded to 280. Research has found that tweets with the highest response rate are only one hundred characters. So you must say what you want to say using only that many letters and spaces. The optimum Facebook post, garnering the highest number of "likes" and comments, was found to be only forty characters, though posts of one hundred to 119 characters also track well. (The preceding sentence has 182 letters, characters, and spaces.)

Compare this to the books of print-oriented culture, which can pursue arguments and develop ideas for hundreds of pages. No wonder argumentation on the Internet consists largely of insults, snarky observations, and snappy comebacks. Anything else would require too many characters! The medium itself prevents sustained thought.

Certainly the Internet also contains much longer articles in online magazines and scholarly journals, as well as entire books. And those with lots to say can start a website and write as much as they want. Or they can publish their own book, which they can do cheaply thanks to the technology of e-books, e-readers, and the distribution system of Amazon.com. On the Internet, everyone can have a say, with no gatekeepers—publishing companies, newspaper editors, or academic screening—to control what information goes out to the public. This democratization of discourse is one of the Internet's greatest contributions, but it also contributes to its problems. The gatekeepers had standards, including criteria for reliability. To be sure, the gatekeepers also had their biases, shutting out dissident perspectives. Today, unpopular worldviews such as Christianity, which an academic gatekeeper might have censored in the modernist era, can find a platform and an audience thanks to the Internet. Ironically, the current flood of misinformation and fake news on the Internet is leading to the building of new gates and new gatekeepers. Online publications are acting more

---

7. Kevan Lee, "The Ideal Length of Everything Online, Backed by Research," *Buffer*, July 19, 2018, accessed June 11, 2019, https://blog.bufferapp.com/the-ideal-length-of-everything-online-according-to-science.

like printing-press publications, with editors and editorial guidelines. This is a good development, as contrary perspectives can be expressed in competing online publications with gatekeeping processes of their own. The danger, though, is that as the Internet becomes controlled by fewer and fewer companies, such as Google, Facebook, and Twitter, their ideologically driven employees who feel a mandate to police the Internet could become gatekeepers on a far greater scale and with far greater control than would have been possible before.

As for the global nature of this "village," McLuhan was right that the electronic media would extend its reach all over the world. Its impact, however, has been to undermine actual villages, that is, cohesive local communities in traditional cultures, rooted with a sense of place. The global village exists in no place, in the machine-generated illusion of cyberspace. It represents the ultimate triumph of Western colonialism, imposed not by warfare but by technology. And, instead of bringing people together into communities, the global village—by isolating its members into contending user groups—sets them against each other.

The New Class

The Internet does not comprise all of our social existence. Except for the *hikikomori*, who attempt to withdraw completely into the virtual realm, most people have to work, which ties them into the economy and the real-world social order. But the so-called information revolution—with its constructivism and its turning away from tangible reality—has social and economic ramifications as well.

In my earlier book *Postmodern Times*, I discussed what some sociologists were describing as a new socioeconomic class.[8] The modern economy, I said, is symbolized by the factory, which employs technology to manufacture tangible products. Blue-collar workers fabricate steel, automobiles, machinery, and other goods. White-collar workers manage the operations, keep the books, and sell the products. The owners of the factory, whether individuals or shareholders, accumulated wealth. The postmodern economy, I said, is symbolized by the

---

8. Gene Edward Veith, *Postmodern Times: A Christian Guide to Contemporary Thought and Culture* (Wheaton, IL: Crossway, 1994), 177–81.

computer. Technology is used not to manufacture tangible products but to manufacture *information*. Our new information economy is accompanied by the rise of a new social class consisting of workers who create and manipulate information.

According to the "New Class" theorists, as I wrote in *Postmodern Times* back in the 1990s,

> The New Class includes educators (from elementary school teachers to university professors), communicators (journalists, artists, television producers, advertisers), planners (management consultants, pollsters, marketing specialists), and those in the "helping professions" (psychologists, social workers, government bureaucrats, and—significantly—clergy).[9]

Already in the waning years of the twentieth century, such information workers had risen in prominence and influence. But today, with the explosion of information technology and the decline of American manufacturing in favor of overseas operations, the New Class— to which we can add Internet entrepreneurs, software coders, app designers, computer engineers, network analysts, and other IT specialists—has shot up in social status and cultural power, constituting our society's new elite.

In 2018, the world's largest companies, according to their market value, were as follows:

1. Apple ($926.9 billion)
2. Amazon.com ($777.8 billion)
3. Alphabet [a.k.a. Google] ($766.4 billion)
4. Microsoft ($750.6 billion)
5. Alibaba [the equivalent of Amazon.com in China] ($499.4 billion)

Then follow some financial companies. Not until number ten do we find a traditional noncomputer, non-Internet-based manufacturing company, ExxonMobil ($344.1 billion).[10]

---

9. Veith, *Postmodern Times*, 178–79.
10. "The 100 Largest Companies in the World by Market Value in 2018 (in Billion U.S. Dollars)," *Statista*, accessed June 11, 2019, https://www.statista.com/statistics/263264/top-companies -in-the-world-by-market-value/.

Let us compare that company, which trades in tangible goods, with Google, which trades in virtual goods. ExxonMobil owns thirty-seven refineries around the world,[11] with eleven thousand gasoline stations in the US alone.[12] It has reserves of over twenty-one billion barrels of oil, employs 69,600 people, and has assets—including office buildings, research centers, equipment, and ships—valued at $349 billion.[13] Google has fifteen data centers where it houses its servers.[14] ExxonMobil produces gasoline, natural gas, and petro chemicals. Google produces Internet searches. ExxonMobil explores for oil, extracts it, processes it into gasoline and other products, and operates a vast retail network of service stations and other outlets to sell them. Google gives away its product for free. Instead of selling the search data, it sells advertising, which combines information and persuasion. Google is worth more than twice as much as ExxonMobil.

Both kinds of companies, those which produce tangible goods and those which produce virtual goods, exist together, and, of course, the most successful companies of them all—Apple and Amazon.com—trade in both. Similarly, the New Class exists alongside the traditional American social classes. To be sure, America was founded on the principle that "all men are created equal," and that equality, enshrined in the law and in American values, is much more evident in the United States than in Europe, with its remnants of the old aristocratic caste system based on birth. But it seems to be part of our fallen human nature to erect pecking orders and social hierarchies. (Notice the social dynamics of playgrounds, the pressure in high school to be part of the popular crowd, and the status competitions on social media.) Social status can be based on different factors—an ancestor's service to the king; the accomplishments of your family; how attractive you are; your online gaming prowess—but in America, more broadly, social status has been tied to wealth and income. And yet members of the

---

11. "ExxonMobil," Wikipedia, accessed June 11, 2019, https://en.wikipedia.org/wiki/Exxon Mobil#Operations.

12. "Our Stations Are on the Way, Wherever You're Going," ExxonMobil, accessed June 11, 2019, https://www.exxon.com/en/gas-stations.

13. "ExxonMobil—Statistics & Facts," *Statistica*, accessed June 11, 2019, https://www.statis ta.com/topics/1109/exxonmobil/.

14. "Google Data Centers," Wikipedia, accessed June 11, 2019, https://en.wikipedia.org/wiki /Google_data_centers.

New Class, for all of the staggeringly wealthy tech magnates and the teenagers who sold their app designs for millions, do not always make lots of money (as in the journeyman wages of computer programmers, teachers, journalists, and other "information workers"). Nevertheless, the social status and cultural influence of members of the New Class often exceed their more wealthy counterparts from the old class system. Today the rich are often derided by political activists from both the left and the right, by Hollywood screenwriters, and in the news media and online. Certainly, the rich have it very well, but they do not command the respect that they used to. And while most people would like to *be* rich, those who *are* often go to great pains to play down their wealth, displaying the "common touch" in their dress and mannerisms and giving money to politicians who denounce the "1 percent," the top echelon that they themselves belong to.

To see the status shift in American society, consider the number-one corporation, Apple, compared to the number-ten, ExxonMobil. Which commands more respect? Oil companies are routinely portrayed as the villains in movies and on television, whereas Apple is approached with reverential awe. Compare the former head of Apple, the late Steve Jobs, to the head of ExxonMobil. Jobs was a celebrity. Few people know who heads ExxonMobil. And yet a longtime CEO of that corporation did become well-known for a while. Rex Tillerson, who led ExxonMobil for more than a decade, served as Secretary of State for just over a year until he was ignominiously fired by President Trump. Both Steve Jobs and Rex Tillerson were wealthy, and Tillerson for a time exercised political power, but Jobs far surpasses Tillerson in prestige and cultural influence.

The rise of the New Class has meant changes in politics. The Republicans used to be considered the party of business, with the wealthy generally voting Republican. The Democrats were the party of labor unions, farmers, and "the common man." The middle class—some of whom were managers and small business owners and some of whom were technicians, service providers, and professionals—could vote either way. But by the late twentieth century, economic interests could no longer fully account for American politics. The *Roe v. Wade* decision in 1973 legalizing abortion brought distinctly moral issues into the political arena, and soon, as other controversies joined the mix, Americans were engaged in a culture war. At that point, the political landscape was not simply a contest between economic liberals who wanted an activist government that could control the economy and economic conservatives who wanted smaller government and free markets. There were social liberals who supported abortion, feminism, and gay rights, contending against social conservatives who opposed those causes and supported prayer in schools, family values, and American traditions.

The New Class is socially liberal. In fact, as sociologist Peter Berger has observed, certain beliefs function as class markers:

> The symbols of class culture are important. They allow people to "sniff out" who belongs and who does not; they provide easily applied criteria of "soundness." Thus a young instructor applying for a job in an elite university is well advised to hide "unsound" views such as political allegiance to the right wing of the Republican Party (perhaps even to the left wing), opposition to abortion or to other causes of the feminist movement, or a strong commitment to the virtues of the corporation.[15]

Berger was writing back in the 1980s, when the New Class of those who construct information consisted mostly of academics, media professionals, and members of the "helping professions." Since then, the rise of information technology and the consequent success of the information economy has meant that today's New Class is often *both* socially liberal *and* economically conservative. The New Class is overwhelmingly Democratic, and yet the denizens of Silicon Valley do not want government interference and are often quite convinced of "the virtues of the corporation," at least of their corporations. (Google's motto used to be "Don't be evil." With its reorganization as Alphabet, it is "Do the right thing.")[16]

This sense of corporate virtue has been manifesting not only in generous financial support of socially liberal causes and political can-

---

15. Peter Berger, "The Class Struggle in American Religion," *Christian Century* (February 25, 1981): 198.

16. Kate Conger, "Google Removes 'Don't Be Evil' Clause from Its Code of Conduct," *Gizmodo*, May 18, 2018, accessed June 11, 2019, https://gizmodo.com/google-removes-nearly-all-mentions-of-dont-be-evil-from-1826153393.

didates but in bias, censorship, and marginalization of socially conservative views. Today, information is power. Since online advertising
works not by appealing to a large audience, as the old TV commercials
did, but by precise targeting to individual consumers, online companies must amass a great deal of information about everyone who clicks
on. Though the government is not allowed to infringe upon our privacy—or control our speech or restrict our religious liberties—no such
constraints exist for private companies. The virtual realm may well
constitute a realm, a sort of private sector government, ruled by an
elite aristocracy that supervises and controls the information we are
allowed to have.

Meanwhile, many of those who are not, strictly speaking, members
of the New Class—such as wealthy corporate heads of traditional
companies and devoted consumers of the new technology—emulate
its values and class markers because of their status. This is creating a
curious political inversion. Today, Democrats have become the party
of the rich.[17] (Though the antirich rhetoric remains, as do conflicts
between its labor union and racial minority base and its New Class financial patrons.) Republicans have become the party of working-class
populists and the common man (while still representing the interests
of the tangible-products economy).

These socioeconomic changes go deeper than politics. What happens when a tangible-goods economy gives way to an information
economy? America has certainly been enjoying unparalleled prosperity. Shifting manufacturing overseas where labor costs are much less
is profitable for the traditional corporations, allowing them to concentrate on the information facets of their business. So has another
kind of outsourcing: moving a business not just overseas but into
cyberspace, which exists not in a specific community but everywhere
and nowhere. In *Postmodern Times*, I said that the shopping mall was
the iconic symbol of postmodernism, and, indeed, large national retailers did much to make small, locally owned businesses obsolete.[18] But
now Amazon.com—a retailer without spatial limits whose customer

---

17. Steven Moore, "Democrats Are Now the Party of the Rich—So Why Not Tax the Rich?"
Washington Examiner, December 3, 2017, accessed June 11, 2019, https://www.washington
examiner.com/democrats-are-now-the-party-of-the-rich-mdash-so-why-not-tax-the-rich.
18. Veith, *Postmodern Times*, 117–19.

base is the whole nation and much of the world—is shutting down the shopping malls. All of this comes with human casualties.

American cities used to be industrial centers, whose factories supported thousands of blue-collar workers and their families. This, in turn, meant that cities were filled with vibrant neighborhoods, often with an ethnic flavor as manufacturing jobs attracted immigrants from around the world, as well as African Americans leaving the rural South in search of a better life. These groups had their problems, including labor strife and societal prejudice. But they did have a sense of community.

Today many if not most of those big factories have shut down, their operations moved across the border or overseas or the companies subcontracting production and assembly to factories in Asia. The hulks of those gigantic old buildings often still remain, the windows broken out and boarded over, the equipment rusting, the yards empty. The loss of jobs means the loss of the old neighborhoods. The pattern used to be that once the immigrants assimilated, they, or rather their children who moved up in the world by taking white-collar jobs, moved to the suburbs. Then those former immigrants would be replaced by a new wave from another part of the world. But now, with the loss of the factory jobs, people move away, and there is no one to replace them. Houses stand empty and fall into disrepair. Those who cannot afford to leave go on welfare. A few local businesses hang on, but the crime rate soars. These are the so-called Rust Belt cities.

To be sure, some cities are thriving and reviving. With company headquarters and the booming financial sector still based in the biggest cities, they support white-collar jobs and the businesses that cater to them. With their fine restaurants, abundant entertainment venues, and cultural activities, cities like these are attracting the new, high-tech information industries. But what these cities gain in affluence, they often lose in community. As New Class millennials are pouring in for the "urban lifestyle," they are buying up old houses, renovating them, and turning the old neighborhoods into artsy, hipster developments, full of coffee shops, craft breweries, and trendy restaurants. But this so-called gentrification—a term hearkening back to when the upper class "gentry" would impose themselves on the peasantry—sends prices and rents soaring, driving out working-class families and eradicating long-time neighborhoods and ethnic enclaves. And when and if the millennials finally do have children, they tend to move out to the suburbs, reasoning that "the city is no place to raise kids." As a result, cities remain havens for the single life, new generations of families are not replacing the ones that have left, and the neighborhood communities are not renewed.

The suburbs surrounding big cities, including those that are rusting away, are probably flourishing the most. But although this is where the families are, they too tend to have little sense of community. Dependent on automobiles and highways—the technology that makes modern suburbs possible by allowing commuting to work—suburbanites must drive everywhere. There are few, if any, sidewalks. Shops and churches and other housing developments are always at a distance. Commerce is abundant, though most local businesses are franchises of nationwide retailers and restaurant chains. There is little sense of place, as all suburbs seem pretty much the same. But the affluence is wonderful. The population is mostly middle class, with poorer folks out of sight, living mostly in the city. And if you want to go to a really good restaurant, a concert, or a major league sporting event, you can always drive to the city and enjoy yourself, then drive back to your haven.

Small-town America, though, has been hit hardest by these socio-economic changes. As metropolitan areas surrounding the core cities continue to expand, some small towns find themselves transformed into suburbs. But rural small towns are in a state of woe. Driving on the backroads through the rural Midwest, you will pass through once-bustling small towns, their former economic vitality suggested by faded storefront signs for cafés, hardware stores, and barbershops now empty and boarded up. Their populations are dwindling and aging. And yet, ironically, the people who are still hanging on often retain a sense of community.

Rust Belt cities and small-town America are the enclave of the white working class. Once the cultural backbone of America, with the hardworking husband supporting his family and taking them to church every Sunday, this demographic has imploded culturally, morally, and spiritually.

Today one of the biggest demographics of the unchurched is not millennials, college-educated urbanites, or affluent suburban families—the usual targets of church growth programs. Americans who are unaffiliated with any church are largely members of the white working class.

The millennials are young adults. Most of them *have been* churched. Many of them are in that stage of life when they stop going to church, but a good number of them will come back. Particularly, once they get married and have children, and, despite their attitudes that we have discussed, most of them will eventually get married and have children. But nonmarital sex, cohabitation, and single parenthood have become the norm across the entire white working class.

Most college-educated folks, despite what atheist professors might have taught them, do go to church. Cities are full of churchgoers. African Americans are among the most active church members of any demographic. Immigrants, whether first or second generation, tend to be churchgoers. Affluent suburbanites, like most middle-class families, tend to go to church.

But as the *Bowling Alone* sociologist Robert Putnam has shown in a more recent book,[19] it is the blue-collar class that has stopped going to church. Not all, but this is the demographic in which the bottom has fallen out in church attendance, in marriage rates, in children raised with both parents. These are the folks most plagued by drug addiction, alcoholism, and child abuse. Also hopelessness, despair, and suicide. (Read *Hillbilly Elegy: A Memoir of a Culture and a Family in Crisis* by J. D. Vance.[20])

These are the Americans hardest hit by outsourced manufacturing, closing local businesses, and the information economy. They never went to college, so they have little chance of ascending to the New Class. The social elite looks down on them, and the middle class often finds them embarrassing. But these are the unchurched.

To be sure, black people, Hispanics, and illegal immigrants also have it hard. They too are members of the working class and share

19. Robert D. Putnam, *Our Kids: The American Dream in Crisis* (New York: Simon & Schuster, 2015).
20. J. D. Vance, *Hillbilly Elegy: A Memoir of a Culture and a Family in Crisis* (New York: HarperCollins, 2016).

its problems. On top of those, they have the additional problems that can come from racial discrimination. I do not mean to pity disaffected whites more than anyone else. I would say, though, that African Americans, Hispanics, and illegal immigrants probably have a stronger sense of community, which can support them in their trials, than the white working class has. After all, those other groups still have their churches, and while they too may struggle with marriage, they typically have strong extended family ties. The white working class *used to have* strong families and supportive churches and feel a strong sense of community—and in many cases and in many places still do—but, on the whole, these have been lost.

Today one of the biggest pathologies in rural, small-town America is drug addiction. Those who work with their hands and their backs are prone to sprained muscles and other injuries, which doctors have treated by prescribing pain pills. This has led to an epidemic of opioid addiction. In response, doctors have cut back on Oxycontin and Vicodin prescriptions, and the black-market supply has tightened. So opioid addicts have been turning to a cheaper, more easily available, and more potent way to satisfy their opium craving: *heroin*.[21] Heroin used to be associated with the big city, with racial ghettos and strung-out jazz musicians. But now heroin plagues the rural heartland.

It isn't just heroin. Or marijuana—whether legal or illegal, recreational or medical—which is no longer the social lubricant just of hippies and college students. Many homes in respectable small-town neighborhoods have been turned into crystal meth labs.

Drug use is, of course, yet another way of withdrawing from the real world—the physical, social, created world. Inhabitants of the "global village" and inhabitants of actual American villages have that in common.

---

21. See "Heroin Use Is Driven by Its Low Cost and High Availability," as well as the other articles on prescription opioids and heroin at the National Institute on Drug Abuse website, accessed June 11, 2019, https://www.drugabuse.gov/publications/research-reports/relationship-between-prescription-drug-abuse-heroin-use/heroin-use-driven-by-its-low-cost-high-availability.

9

Power Politics and the Death of Education

From Relativism to Absolutism

So if our culture has become an anticulture, and our society has lost its sense of community, with each individual withdrawing into his or her own unreality, where does that leave us? If there are no longer any truths or moral obligations or religious awareness to bind us together, how can human beings function together? One answer being given today is *the pursuit of power*.

In this climate, not just government but education, intellectual pursuits, and ordinary life are all politicized. The relativism that characterized postmodernism, which has successfully dissolved our traditional convictions, has now hardened into new kinds of contending absolutist ideologies.

Our information technology is accelerating these tendencies. The techno-sociologist Zeynep Tufekci has commented on how the new information environment is undermining both truth and democracy:

> Go back a decade and imagine your response to the question: "What would a threat to truth look like?" You might have

thought of censorship—perhaps the *Fahrenheit 451* version, in which books are piled up and burned, or the *1984* nightmare of a regime with total information control. Or perhaps you would have worried about the limits and biases of the mainstream media.

But in the digital age, when speech can exist mostly unfettered, the big threat to truth looks very different. It's not just censorship, but an avalanche of undistinguished speech—some true, some false, some fake, some important, some trivial, much of it out-of-context, all burying us.[1]

She says that we had assumed that democratized speech would mean the flourishing of democracy, with viewpoints competing with each other in the free marketplace of ideas, from which the best ideas—truth—would emerge victorious. It turns out, though, that "the glut of information we now face, made possible by digital tools and social media platforms, can bury what is true, greatly elevate and amplify misinformation and distract from what is important."[2] In response, we filter it all out according to our own interests and those of our peers, including our particular friends on social media.

As a result, open and participatory speech has turned into its opposite. Important voices are silenced by mobs of trolls using open platforms to hurl abuse and threats. Bogus news shared from one friend or follower to the next becomes received wisdom. Crucial pieces of information drown in so much irrelevance that they are lost. If books were burned in the street, we would be alarmed. Now, we are simply exhausted.[3]

The public is thus divided into smaller and smaller units, with less and less in common. Tufekci has elsewhere pointed out that the same algorithms Facebook, Google, Amazon, and the other Internet gatekeepers use to target their advertising are also used to control our

1. Zeynep Tufekci, "An Avalanche of Speech Can Bury Democracy," *Politico*, September/October 2018, accessed June 11, 2019, https://www.politico.com/magazine/story/2018/09/05/too -much-free-speech-bad-democracy-219587.
2. Tufekci, "An Avalanche of Speech Can Bury Democracy."
3. Tufekci, "An Avalanche of Speech Can Bury Democracy."

political information.[4] And without commonality, she says, democracy is not really possible.

> It's not speech per se that allows democracies to function, but the ability to agree—eventually, at least some of the time—on what is true, what is important and what serves the public good. This doesn't mean everyone must agree on every fact, or that our priorities are necessarily uniform. But democracy can't operate completely unmoored from a common ground, and certainly not in a sea of distractions.[5]

The result is a different kind of politics.

From Relativism to the New Absolutism

In my book *Postmodern Times* I wrote about moral relativism, the way people were rejecting objective moral absolutes in favor of their self-constructed, self-chosen notions of right and wrong.[6] Back then, people were saying things like, "That might be right for you, but it isn't right for me"; "No one has the right to impose their morality on anyone else"; and "Everybody is free to choose their own values." The climate being promoted was one of genial toleration of just about every decision and lifestyle.

But today that easygoing relativism has been replaced by a new sense that there *are* right beliefs and attitudes, and that we all must watch what we do and what we say, lest we get into trouble. Expressing disapproval of abortion or homosexuality, for instance, or questioning any tenet of feminism, or refusing to recycle *are just not done* in polite society.

These are not moral principles, exactly, though they function in the same way. When it comes to areas traditionally addressed by moral codes—sexual behavior, how we treat our parents, the obligation to tell the truth, respecting other people's property, the sacredness of human life—people today are still moral relativists. And they still

---

4. Zeynep Tufekci, "We're Building a Dystopia Just to Make People Click on Ads," TEDGlobal, September 2017, accessed June 11, 2019, https://www.ted.com/talks/zeynep_tufekci_we_re _building_a_dystopia_just_to_make_people_click_on_ads.

5. Tufekci, "An Avalanche of Speech."

6. Gene Veith, *Postmodern Times: A Christian Guide to Contemporary Thought and Culture* (Wheaton, IL: Crossway, 1994), 16–18, 37–38.

believe that truth is relative. What governs people's words and behavior today is not moral absolutes but *social norms*. Certain topics are *taboo*, and thus not to be spoken. Certain behaviors, such as recycling or using inclusive pronouns, are *socially expected*. These norms are enforced by *social pressure*. Enforcers in the community will apply social sanctions such as shaming, ostracism, and other punishments against those who violate the norms. Thus, people conform to them out of fear of social disapproval and the desire to have status within the group.

Now, there is nothing at all wrong with social norms. All cultures have them. Traditionally, social norms were at the service of moral norms. But there have also always been norms that simply help human beings get along with each other and function in a community. The various codes of "good manners" are examples. Giving offense is a social faux pas that should be avoided. Today's sensitivity about insulting racial minorities or other groups is surely a good thing. But these new norms go beyond etiquette. The term often used today is *political correctness*, deriving from the Communist Party's insistence that all discourse of party members must be in line with Marxist orthodoxy.[7] The new social norms are not moral; nor do they help diverse people function together. Rather, they are divisive, designed to identify enemies. They are *political*, carrying with them the ideology of the cultural left.

On one level, the tenets of political correctness simply reflect the values of the New Class. Those who belong to that class or aspire to do so must conform to its values. Old Class folks—including liberals as well as conservatives—often complain about political correctness, especially when they are called out for violations. But they often do not care very much, since this is not their circle. The pressure to be politically correct is greatest where information workers hold the greatest sway, such as on university campuses. And yet, since the New Class holds the highest social status, the canons of political correctness are widely held even beyond that class.

Since we think by means of language, as J. G. Hamann has shown, politically correct language shapes the way the public thinks. Those

---

7. See, e.g., Caitlin Gibson, "How 'Politically Correct' Went from Compliment to Insult," *Washington Post*, January 13, 2016, accessed June 11, 2019, https://www.washingtonpost.com /lifestyle/style/how-politically-correct-went-from-compliment-to-insult/2016/01/13/b1cf5918 -b61a-11e5-a76a-0b5145e8679a_story.html?utm_term=.9b05348a06d3.

who have been conditioned to think of abortion as "reproductive rights" or "women's health" can only believe in it. And they will vilify pro-lifers as being anti-woman.

What is more, this implicit political ideology is not just restricted to government policies; rather, it pervades all of life. Since these politically charged norms have been substituted for moral truths, the moral concepts of guilt, shame, and virtue have been transferred to the political sphere.

Ordinary experiences are thus made deeply problematic and an occasion for guilt. Drinking a cup of coffee implicates you in the oppression of coffee plantation workers. Eating meat violates animal rights. Going for a drive burns fossil fuel and contributes to global warming. Spending time with your spouse entangles you in gender issues. This is another example of the "problematizing" of ordinary experiences that Hamann saw in Kant.[8]

This is also another example of the "global village" syndrome: information technology creates a reversion to a more primitive social environment. The social pressure that enforces these political norms is exercised across all media platforms, and it is intensified by social media. The technology, which allows for an overwhelming torrent of disapproval, makes it possible to have strongly controlling social norms without having a strong sense of community.

Small towns are associated, not always fairly, with gossip and pressures to conform, and we can see these tendencies—purged of the overall community support that can make them bearable—ramped up exponentially on the Internet. But the global village is not just a global small town. It is approaching something far more atavistic: the tribal village.

The Internet divides us into tribes. We can easily find the websites that are in line with our own beliefs and self-identity. We can respond to the negative judgments we find in one online social group by joining one in which we find only approval.

This is an understandable and socially necessary response, and it is a benefit of the new technology that groups can carve out their own online space. Cultural conservatives, free-market libertarians,

---

8. As we discussed in chapter 4.

old-school liberals, every denomination of Christians, and other groups can have their own websites, their own discussions, and promote their own interests. The same is true of other kinds of affinity groups—organic farmers, homeschoolers, Star Wars fans, model airplane builders. Then again, it is also true of less savory groups: Islamic terrorists, pedophiles, neo-Nazis.

This capacity of the Internet to allow virtually any group to have its voice can be a force for freedom, a way to counter the authoritarian tendencies of big government and (ironically) big Internet corporations. And yet it is another manifestation of the segmenting effect of the information technology, the breaking down of the public into ever-smaller groups, which allows online advertisers (including political campaigners) to target customers with exact precision, based on the knowledge the Internet companies have collected about us. This segmentation of America into tribal villages makes it difficult to find the common ground and the common frames of reference that democracies need.

Tribal societies also bring with them a very specific danger. In the absence of a central government with a rule of law and a judicial system, tribal cultures tend to develop codes of revenge. If someone injures you or a member of your family or tribe, there are no police officers to call and no jurisdiction to file a lawsuit. You or a member of your family or your tribe must enforce justice yourself. This typically means not just seeking an apology, but rather enacting retribution. If your tribe takes revenge on the wrongdoer—or another member of the opposing tribe, even if not the perpetrator—that tribe might respond by seeking revenge against you and your tribe, resulting in ever-escalating cycles of retribution. Such tribal feuds can last for generations, as in the Hatfields and the McCoys, and can result in wildly disproportionate violence, as in the genocidal killings in Rwanda.[9]

For contending tribes to be united into a nation, they must all be brought under a common rule of law, with a governing authority and a legal system to enforce justice impartially. In England, the various

---

9. See the discussion about tribal revenge codes in Fredson Bowers, *Elizabethan Revenge Tragedy, 1587–1642* (Princeton, NJ: Princeton University Press, 1940), 3–40.

tribes of the Angles and the Saxons were united as the king, beginning with Alfred the Great, assumed the role of avenger, a process that was not completed until the Middle Ages.[10] Far earlier, the Hebrew tribes also practiced personal revenge, until they became a nation with the law of Moses, which channeled and controlled the lust for vengeance with the cities of refuge, which provided safety for the accused and a judicial hearing, before turning over the convicted murderer to the family-assigned executioner (Num. 35:9–34). The New Testament repudiates personal revenge completely, teaching that we should leave vengeance to God (Rom. 12:19), who executes that judgment on earth by means of the vocation of lawful magistrates (Rom. 13:1–4).

But with the new tribalism, retribution seems to be coming back in vogue, not just online but in the real world and in the legal system itself. Our current "identity politics"—that is to say, tribal politics—seeks not only to win at any cost but to punish the losers. After gay-rights activists achieved their ultimate victory, legalizing same-sex marriage, they proceeded to find ways to exact retribution against those who had opposed them. Tim Gill, the software tycoon who contributed $422 million to the LGBT cause, announced the movement's next step after their monumental same-sex marriage victory: "We're going to punish the wicked."[11]

Already, the LGBT movement had enlisted the help of major corporations to threaten boycotts on states that passed modest protections for those who object to homosexuality on religious grounds. In 2015, shortly before same-sex marriage was legalized nationwide by the Supreme Court later that year, Mike Pence, then governor of Indiana, signed the state's Religious Freedom Restoration Act. After big corporations—particularly computer and web-based companies such as Apple, Salesforce.com, and Angie's List—threatened to pull out of the state, taking with them thousands of jobs, Governor Pence, for all of his evangelical beliefs and conservative credentials, was forced to back down, signing another

---

10. For the institution of the bloodfeud in the English tribes, see William Ian Miller, "Choosing the Avenger: Some Aspects of the Bloodfeud in Medieval Iceland and England," *Law and History Review* 1, no. 2 (1983): 159–204; doi:10.2307/743849.

11. Andy Kroll, "Meet the Megadonor Behind the LGBTQ Rights Movement," *Rolling Stone*, June 23, 2017, accessed June 11, 2019, https://www.rollingstone.com/politics/politics-features/meet-the-megadonor-behind-the-lgbtq-rights-movement-193996/.

measure exempting discrimination against homosexuals from the restoration of religious freedom.[12]

Once same-sex marriage was the law of the land, Christian florists and wedding-cake bakers who refused to participate in same-sex weddings were hauled before courts and civil rights panels to be charged with discrimination, forced to pay ruinous fines and forfeit their livelihood. Pro-abortionists too wanted not only to "punish the wicked" but to force "wicked" pro-lifers to pay them homage by promoting abortion against their conscience. In one of the most grotesque violations of religious liberty in United States history, several jurisdictions, including the state of California, passed laws requiring pro-life clinics to post advertisements for abortionists![13]

Fortunately, the United States is still a free country and a nation of laws, and the Supreme Court ruled in favor of the Christian wedding cake baker and the pro-life clinics. But the "punish the wicked" impulse is still very much alive. Conservatives have been driven out of restaurants, heckled out of movie theaters, and harassed at their homes. Representative Maxine Waters (D-California) called for mobs to target officials in the Trump administration: "They're not going to be able to go to a restaurant, they're not going to be able to stop at a gas station, they're not going to be able to shop a department store. The people are going to turn on them, they're going to protest, they're going to absolutely harass them."[14]

The secularists have false stereotypes of "Puritans" and "fundamentalists" imposing their harsh morality on beleaguered people suffering under their rule. They even frighten themselves with a dystopian novel by Margaret Atwood made into an online video series, *The Handmaid's Tale*. It depicts a futuristic theocracy named Gilead that brutally subjugates women. The red robes and white bonnets of the "handmaids" have become a staple of feminist protesters. But what

12. See "Mike Pence," Wikipedia, accessed June 11, 2019, https://en.wikipedia.org/wiki/Mike_Pence.

13. Juliana Knot, "Supreme Court Rules against Forcing Pro-Life Clinics to Advertise Abortion," *Federalist*, June 26, 2018, accessed June 11, 2019, http://thefederalist.com/2018/06/26/supreme-court-rules-against-forcing-pro-life-clinics-to-advertise-abortion/.

14. Mary Jordan, "The Latest Sign of Political Divide: Shaming and Shunning Public Officials," *Washington Post*, June 24, 2018, accessed June 11, 2019, https://www.washingtonpost.com/politics/the-latest-sign-of-political-divide-shaming-and-shunning-public-officials/2018/06/24/9a29f00a-77bc-11e8-aeee-4d04c8ac6158_story.html?utm_term=.9878bf2b0ec4.

we are seeing is a mirror image (thus, a reversed image) of such alleged religious despotism. Those who would impose their morality on those who do not share it, those who demand conformity, and those who punish the dissenters are now the militant secularists.

Christians are not used to being considered "the wicked." But we should probably get used to it.

From Modern to Postmodern Political Ideologies

Today virtually everything has become politicized—education, entertainment, religion, the media, communications technology, our social interactions, even the products that we buy.[15] For many people on all sides of the political spectrum, politics has arguably rushed into the void once occupied by religion, with politics now taking on the task of defining moral values and the meaning of life. Our political polarization thus translates into cultural polarization at almost every level. As for actual "politics"—that is, convictions about government and the exercise of power—the categories of liberal and conservative, Democrats and Republicans, while still used to express our polarities, do not mean what they used to.

Certainly, such categories are not much use applied to the politics of the past. Was King Henry VIII a liberal or a conservative? Was Abraham Lincoln a liberal or a conservative? The questions are meaningless.

Most people throughout history and throughout the world have had no conception of politics, since they have had little or no impact on what their rulers do. They simply have to obey. To be sure, monarchies have their political intrigues—just read Shakespeare's history plays—usually involving succession and power struggles with the nobility. Winning or losing the affection of the people could be factors in the success, the failure, or even the overthrow of a regime, but most

---

15. See "Do You Eat Republican Cheese? The Two Americas, a Snapshot in Brands," *Politico*, November/December 2018, accessed June 11, 2019, https://www.politico.com/magazine/story /2018/11/02/brands-preferred-democrats-republicans-221912. The article cites research findings that Republicans and Democrats tend to buy different brands of products, including such seemingly noncontent items as dairy products and pet food. I would add that the study also confirms the class shift we have been discussing, with Republicans preferring "working class products" like Chevys and Wrangler jeans and Democrats favoring high-status name brands, like imported cars and designer clothing.

citizens have had to passively follow the dictates of whoever happens to be in power.

This changed in the West with the Greek democracies and the Roman republic. Individual citizens began to make the policy decisions—participating in the debates and voting on new laws in the Athenian assembly—and choosing their own leaders and representatives in the Roman forum. That classical tradition would be interrupted with the neomonarchy of the Roman Empire, but it was taken up again in the Middle Ages with certain self-governing trading cities in Europe and in the Renaissance with the Italian city-states. And the classical traditions of democracy and representational government would find their most successful expressions in the United States of America and eventually in democracies around the world.

Most political conflicts throughout history have had to do not so much with ideologies—that is, different philosophies of government—as with contending interest groups: rival families or dynasties; commercial cities versus agricultural estates; foreign alliances and local rivalries.

But political ideologies came. The Enlightenment offered "rational" critiques of traditional governments and new accounts of how society should be governed rationally. These would influence both the radical French Revolution and the more conservative American Revolution. The nineteenth century saw a number of socialist schemes intended to bring on a utopian society. The most rigorous, tough-minded, and consequential of these schemes was that of Karl Marx, who offered an all-encompassing social, economic, and political ideology designed to forcibly overthrow the existing social order. Other ideologies followed, such as Democratic Socialism, which sought to implement Marx's utopian goals by political means instead of by violent revolution. Fascism emerged in the twentieth century as another totalizing revolutionary ideology, built around national and racial identity, unlimited government, and moral nihilism.[16]

Such political ideas had real-world consequences. Social classes became politicized, with the middle class overthrowing the aristocracy in the French Revolution, and the working class overthrowing

---

16. See my book on the subject, *Modern Fascism: Liquidating the Judeo-Christian Worldview* (St. Louis, MO: Concordia, 1993).

the middle class in the Russian Revolution. Fascism resulted in world war and holocaust.

The United States of America was founded in accord with Enlightenment ideas, but they were tempered by a neoclassical republicanism and by a biblical distrust of unchecked human power. Through much of its political history, the United States, with its constitutional order, contended with regional rivalries; the different economic interests of manufacturers, traders, and farmers; diverse opinions about international relations and frontier expansion. There were also moral and "culture war" issues, the most important of which was slavery. Though America was not immune from the social upheavals that Europeans were struggling through, especially after the Industrial Revolution, Americans of all regions and social classes shared a consensus favoring liberal democracy—that is, *liberal* as the Latin word for "freedom"—with a strong emphasis on representational government and individual rights.

America in the twentieth century had to contend with the Depression, which many understood as fulfilling Marx's prediction of the ultimate failure of capitalism; and then World War II, the struggle against fascism; and then the Cold War, the struggle against communism. Americans countered these ideologies with what back then was called "Americanism," with its values of freedom, equality, and democracy, all "under God, with liberty and justice for all." Despite this ideological consensus (though America had its radicals), political differences emerged. These were mostly on economic lines. Republicans became the party of business, advocating free markets and minimal government interference in the economic life of the nation. Democrats became the party of farmers, factory workers (who were forming labor unions), and the less affluent. Appreciating the way President Franklin Delano Roosevelt's programs pulled the nation out of the Depression, the postwar Democrats favored greater government management of the economy. But for all their differences, Republicans and Democrats agreed on the principles of "Americanism" and were highly patriotic. Devout Christians could be found on both sides of the aisle. Democrats and Republicans would mostly be in agreement on questions of morality and character.

The 1960s changed everything. The civil rights movement exposed the fact that a significant part of the population was being denied liberty, equality, and justice for all. Republicans, the party of Lincoln, had generally been more supportive of black Americans, with the Democrats, being the party of the "solid South," supporting segregation, which contradicted their stated commitment to help the underprivileged. Establishment Democrats and Republicans both supported the Vietnam War, but the antiwar activism of the 1960s and 1970s unsettled both parties. The *Roe v. Wade* decision legalizing abortion nationwide politicized a moral issue, as did the burgeoning feminist and gay-rights movements.

In the turmoil that followed, new political alignments emerged. When the dust settled, the Democrats, while trying to hold on to their economic populism, became associated with civil rights, feminism, gay rights, and abortion. The Republicans, while retaining ties to business, became associated with "Reagan Democrats" (socially conservative blue-collar workers) and Christian activists. And yet these can be unstable combinations. The Democrats' base continues to be blue-collar Catholics, African Americans, and recent immigrants, but those groups tend to be far more religious and far poorer than the affluent New Class secularists who have taken over the party leadership. And the Republicans' base of socially conservative Christians and blue-collar folks with their moral concerns does not always accord with the agenda of "country club Republicans."

The new, more descriptive political labels are "liberal" and "conservative." But these terms too are imprecise. Today, it is said, liberals favor big government, social justice, government-directed economics, and social change. Conservatives support small government, traditional values, free-market economics, and individual liberties.

But there are different kinds of conservatives. Neoconservatives want to spread American values around the world, by force if necessary, as in the Iraq War. Paleoconservatives are more isolationist, favor protectionist economic policies instead of untrammeled capitalism, and resist the social changes that capitalism can bring. Libertarians favor the free market and individual liberty in all things, leading some of them (not all) to favor the liberty to have abortions.

Similarly, there are different kinds of liberals. That spectrum includes old-school New Deal Democrats, who simply want the government to help farmers, factory workers, and the unemployed; gentrified New Class Democrats, who champion "progressive" social causes while protecting their wealth; social justice activists who crusade for groups they believe are oppressed; and hardcore leftists who would be glad to overthrow capitalism and remake society completely.

Complicating the picture is that *liberal* can also carry the meaning of "liberty." In Europe, *liberal* economics means "free-market economics," and *liberal government* means democracies that protect people's freedom. So in Europe and other parts of the world, "liberal" can refer to what Americans consider conservative. Furthermore, in Europe *conservative* connotes the old monarchies and aristocracies, so *conservative governments* often mean big, all-controlling governments, what Americans associate with liberals. Americans are also making other combinations. There are those who are socially liberal but economically conservative, such as proabortion, secularist Republicans. And those who are socially conservative but economically liberal such as observant Catholics, who do not feel at home in either party but can be found in both.

Modernist politics is mostly oriented around economics, with other issues attached. With its numbers, quantifiability, and attention to material goods, economics accords well with the modernist mind. Thus both liberals and conservatives often frame their arguments in economic terms. Which will do more to alleviate poverty: the free market or government intervention in the marketplace? Should we follow Adam Smith's laissez-faire capitalism or Maynard Keynes's project of the government fine-tuning the economy? Which does more for the common good: maximizing individual liberty or creating a welfare state?

Again, there are more options than our two-party system can easily encompass. Big corporations, for example, often *oppose* the free market in their zeal to eliminate competition and create a monopoly. Though they will have critics from both the left and the right, corporations often funnel campaign contributions to *both* Republicans and Democrats. Some Americans feel the allure of socialism, in which the state owns the means of production, or at least orchestrates the entire economy. All sides of these debates are modernist in that they propose rationalistic policies, invoke technical experts, and present logical arguments that their solutions can solve the nation's problems. Even Marxism is a modernist system, purporting to account for everything by means of an abstract theory and willing to cast down every traditional belief and institution in the name of progress. Although these modern political ideologies still have currency and influence, we are now seeing the rise of a postmodernist politics.

If modern politics is about economics, postmodern politics is about identity. In our survey of American politics, we have already seen how cultural issues became politicized. Disagreements about economic policies have been complicated by culture wars waged by both the left and the right. But a different approach to politics is emerging that cares little about economics, rational analysis, or logical persuasion. It focuses on the exercise of power for its own sake, both by resisting the power of the opposition and by imposing power against them. This politics centers around your *identity*; that is, what tribe you belong to.

Again, the post-Marxists replace Marx's notion of class struggle—the conflict between the socioeconomic classes (feudal landowners, the middle-class bourgeoisie, and the workers of the proletariat) over ownership of the means of production—with the struggle between other social groups (as defined by sex, gender, sexual orientation, race, ethnicity, social status, appearance, and ability) in which the privileged exercise power over the marginalized. Retained from Marx is his contention that all of culture—moral codes, religions, laws, governments, institutions, art, literature—is a mask for power, designed to promote the interests of the ruling class, keeping the oppressed under control by manipulating them into cooperating with and internalizing their oppression. But this is a dynamic conflict, and Marx, along with the post-Marxists, believed that the oppressed can resist their oppressors and, in the course of history, overthrow them, setting up new power relationships.

Marxists and post-Marxists repudiate the traditional politics that seeks to find consensus, compromise, and national unity. Rather, they intentionally cultivate conflict, leading eventually to revolutionary change. But whereas Marx could call on all the workers of the world to unite, the multitude of oppressed identity groups under post-Marxism would seem to make concerted efforts difficult. White heterosexual men might hold the most "privilege," oppressing blacks, gays, and women. But by the canons of feminism, don't black men oppress black women? And aren't white women privileged compared to black men? What about gay white men in relation to blacks and women? And what about transsexuals of either gender? Factor in other identities, such as disability (or, rather, "ability"), body type (the thin oppressing the "person of size"), age (adults versus both young people and old people), religion (Christians oppressing Muslims), and the plethora of genders and sexual orientations, and the complexity is overwhelming, as is the difficulty of oppressed people joining in coherent political action.[17]

This problem is addressed, though, by the concept of *intersectionality*. Our different identities and those of our comrades intersect, so that *all* oppressed people, though oppressed in different ways by different groups, should ally with each other in the common cause of resisting the privileged. It is true that any given person may be privileged in some ways and oppressed in other ways. A black man who is heterosexual and middle class is oppressed because of his race, but his sexual orientation and social class are privileged. A white woman who is lesbian and working class is privileged for being white, but her sex, sexual orientation, and social class make her oppressed. A black, transgendered, lesbian, working-class woman is more oppressed. With intersectionality, you may be privileged, but you have areas in which you are oppressed. Or if you are oppressed, intersectionality helps you to see that there are people even more oppressed than you are. But it is possible, even for a white heterosexual man, to "check your privilege," and to be in solidarity with the marginalized and to function as their ally. This kind of identity politics allows feminists, gays, the transgendered, blacks, and immigrants to join each other's protests and to work together in elections and other political activities.

---

17. See this Matrix of Social Identities and Social Statuses, which includes a "Matrix of Oppression," accessed June 11, 2019, http://cw.routledge.com/textbooks/9780415892940/data/4%20Matrix%20of%20Social%20Identities%20and%20Social%20Statuses.pdf. This is adapted from Maurianne Adams, et al., eds., *Readings for Diversity and Social Justice* (New York: Routledge, 2018).

Identity politics is a phenomenon on the left. And yet it has its mirror image on the right. The so-called alt-right, the name deriving from an Internet domain of the alternative right, has adopted the same theoretical arguments in the name of white identity, giving them an ideological cover for bringing back racism; and American identity, according to which they oppose even legal immigration; and masculine identity, allowing them not only to oppose feminism but to oppose women. (Interestingly, a number of alt-right leaders are homosexuals.[18]) The way the alt-right frames issues, whites are oppressed by blacks and Asians; Americans are oppressed by other nations and by alien cultures; and men are oppressed by women. When their own identity groups are charged with committing oppression, the alt-right answers, "Good!" If there is no transcendent morality—all moral appeals being merely masks for a group's power interests—your group's exercise of power over other groups is the only possible political goal. Some elements of the alt-right are openly embracing Nazism—scapegoating Jews, reviving the fascist view of nationalism, giving the straight arm "Sieg, Heil!" salute.

The totalitarian implications of post-Marxism, as with regular Marxism, should be obvious. If culture is nothing more than a construction designed to impose one group's power over other groups, as the post-Marxists say, then the agenda for the oppressed is clear: (1) resist the oppressor's power; (2) construct belief systems that advance your own power agenda; (3) seize power for your group; (4) pay back your enemies by oppressing them.

In my book *Modern Fascism: Liquidating the Judeo-Christian Worldview*, I explored the connections between modernists (such as the poet Ezra Pound) and the early pioneers of postmodernism with the fascist movements of the early twentieth century. Thinkers whose ideas would become formative for postmodernism—such as the existentialist Martin Heidegger and the deconstructionist Paul De Man—were active, dedicated, influential Nazis. Nietzsche's critique of Judeo-Christian morality and his exaltation of power are foundational

---

18. See, e.g., Sophie Wilkinson, "Is It Okay to Be Gay (and in the Far-Right)?" *Vice*, March 12, 2018, accessed June 11, 2019, https://www.vice.com/en_uk/article/ywqd55/is-it-okay-to-be -gay-and-in-the-far-right.

to both fascism and postmodernism. The similarities and connections are also evident when I discuss what the fascist ideology says about cultural and racial identity, morality and religion, humanity and nature, and "life unworthy of life."

The post-Marxists of the left have their antifa (anti-fascist) enforcers, who beat up and shout down their opponents, but for all of their differences, they share a worldview with actual fascists and their alt-right fellow travelers. Neither believe in freedom, human rights, or democracy. Both tend to dislike Jews, whether out of Nazi-style conspiracy theories or intersectional solidarity with Palestinians, and oppose the cultural influence of the "Jewish" Bible. Both claim to resist oppressive power, but—as history shows both in the fascist and the communist revolutions—when they attain power, they are quick to become oppressive themselves.

Traditionally, politics had to do not just with power but with justice. It is not possible to have a just society without justice. But that requires moral absolutes.

The Death of Education

The consequences of the politicization of ordinary life and a constructivist view of reality are evident in what is happening with education. Postmodernism and its offshoots are *not* worldviews that promote learning. If there is no objective truth, what is there to teach? What is there to learn? Schools instead can indoctrinate. Schools can teach students to construct their own truths.

"Progressive" educational theories have stressed teaching *process* rather than *content*, focusing on new ideas and minimizing the old ideas of the past. That was a modernist educational theory. Now the postmodernist educational theory of *constructivism* takes the next step: children are taught to create their own reading texts, histories, and math rules.

To be sure, committed teachers can educate children and young adults despite the educational theories that undermine their efforts, and bright students can figure out the keys to knowledge for themselves. Much of what is presented in college teacher-training courses as constructivism is actually little more than the old "discovery learning," in which students have to work out the answers for themselves. That approach has classical antecedents, but the label "constructivism" gives the theory academic respectability. But while some of these approaches can educate talented children of middle- and New Class–families, they tend to only confuse children of average abilities who lack socioeconomic advantages.

There can be no doubt that academic achievement has declined dramatically. Recent test scores show that in the United States only 37 percent of fourth graders and 32 percent of eighth graders are proficient in reading. In math, only 40 percent of fourth graders and 33 percent of eighth graders are proficient.[19] Note the *decline* in proficiency with more schooling. Such scores have persisted for a decade, despite a plethora of new approaches and new programs, which amount largely to ceding even more influence to postmodernist educational theories.

The most striking development in education is the decline of the university. The modernist university, with its hyperspecialization and scientism, dispensed with the broad learning of the liberal arts tradition—with the liberal arts reduced to humanities and its subjects treated with the same hyperspecialization—but at least it promoted scientific expertise. The postmodernist university is having difficulty promoting any kind of expertise.

A study of American higher education found that scores in critical thinking actually *decrease* in many universities so that students are *less* skilled in reasoning upon graduation than they were when they first enrolled. On the average today, undergraduate university students spend only 11.5 hours per week studying. Half of the students said that they had taken *no* course that required a substantial amount of writing. One-third had taken *no* course that required reading more than forty pages per week. The study found that college students spent 51 percent of their time socializing, and only 7 percent of their time studying.[20]

19. Jill Barshay, "National Test Scores Reveal a Decade of Educational Stagnation," *The Hechinger Report: Covering Innovation & Inequality in Education*, April 10, 2018, accessed June 11, 2019, https://hechingerreport.org/national-test-scores-reveal-a-decade-of-educational-stagnation/.

20. Richard Arum and Josipa Roksa, *Academically Adrift: Limited Learning on College Campuses* (Chicago: University of Chicago Press, 2011), 1–32.

The researchers, who were not conservative gadflies but prominent scholars from the University of Chicago and the University of Virginia, accounted for the decline in the quality of higher education by noting the lower priority of teaching in favor of research; the negative impact of federal money; and the campus culture, which favors partying, with its alcohol abuse and sexual debauchery, over intellectual achievements.[21] I would argue that an even bigger contributing factor is the postmodernist worldview that has come to govern many disciplines and the post-Marxist ideology that currently reigns in academia.

As in the Soviet and fascist universities, academic freedom and freedom of speech are now sharply curtailed. Faculty members and students must follow the canons of political correctness or fall afoul of speech codes, risk disciplinary hearings, be silenced by protesters, or have their careers ruined.

Moreover, the academic fields are themselves subjected to analysis by "critical constructivism." A group of researchers into the phenomenon explained it this way:

> This problem is most easily summarized as an overarching (almost or fully sacralized) belief that many common features of experience and society are socially constructed. These constructions are seen as being nearly entirely dependent upon power dynamics between groups of people, often dictated by sex, race, or sexual or gender identification. All kinds of things accepted as having a basis in reality due to evidence are instead believed to have been created by the intentional and unintentional machinations of powerful groups in order to maintain power over marginalized ones. This worldview produces a moral imperative to dismantle these constructions.[22]

In literature classes, great authors are "interrogated"—a term adopted from totalitarian secret police—to uncover their crimes of racism, sexism, or homophobia. The natural sciences resist critical constructivism, which is rampant in the social sciences and humanities, insisting on the reality of objective truth as disclosed by the

---

21. Arum and Roksa, *Academically Adrift*, 59–90.
22. Helen Pluckrose, James A. Lindsay, and Peter Boghossian, "Academic Grievance Studies and the Corruption of Scholarship," *Areo*, October 2, 2018, accessed June 11, 2019, https://areomagazine.com/2018/10/02/academic-grievance-studies-and-the-corruption-of-scholarship/.

scientific method. And yet feminist critiques of science claim that objectivity is inherently "masculinist" and that the scientific method rests on a mind-set of dominating—or even raping—"mother nature."[23] The academic world is currently debating whether researchers should use or cite the work of scholars who are sexist, as if the personality or transgressions of the scholar invalidate the findings.[24]

The researchers quoted above on critical constructivism were studying the credulity of the academic world when it comes to this kind of research. They made up outlandish theses, manufactured data, and submitted the bogus papers to peer-reviewed academic journals. The topics included "the rape culture at dog parks" (accusing dogs of having "non-consensual sex"); suggesting that teachers correct for white male privilege by refusing to listen to the contribution of white male students and making them sit on the floor in chains; calling for a feminist astronomy that instead of telescopes uses goddess-worshiping pagan cosmology and interpretive dance; and rewriting a chapter of *Mein Kampf*, substituting "men" for "Jews." These articles were all accepted for publication. In all, academic journals accepted nearly half of the fake articles they submitted. The researchers, who affirm their own liberal and feminist convictions but who were trying to uphold academic standards of rationality and objectivity, concluded with this:

> Any scholarship that proceeds from radically skeptical assumptions about objective truth by definition does not and cannot find objective truth. Instead it promotes prejudices and opinions and calls them "truths." For radical constructivists, these opinions are specifically rooted [in] a political agenda of "Social Justice" (which we have intentionally made into a proper noun to distinguish it from the type of real social progress falling under the same name). Because of critical constructivism, which sees knowledge as a product of unjust power balances, and because of this brand of radical

23. See, e.g., Sandra Harding, *Whose Science? Whose Knowledge?* (Ithaca, NY: Cornell University Press, 1992); and Tzeporah Berman, "The Rape of Mother Nature? Women in the Language of Environmental Discourse," *Trumpeter* 11 (1994): 173–78.

24. Nikki Usher, "Should We Still Cite the Scholarship of Serial Harassers and Sexists?" *Chronicle of Higher Education*, September 7, 2018, accessed June 11, 2019, https://www.chronicle.com/article/Should-We-Still-Cite-the/244450. See also the response by Conor Friedersdorf, "Truth vs. Social Justice," *Atlantic*, November 1, 2018, accessed June 11, 2019, https://www.theatlantic.com/ideas/archive/2018/11/academics-truth-justice/574165/.

skepticism, which rejects objective truth, these scholars are like snake-oil salespeople who diagnose our society as being riddled with a disease only they can cure. That disease, as they see it, is endemic to any society that forwards the agency of the individual and the existence of objective (or scientifically knowable) truths.[25]

"How the mighty have fallen!" (2 Sam. 1:19). The university, which has exemplified the highest values of the Enlightenment—rationality, science, liberty—is repudiating them all. At the very time that we are looking to science and technology to continue our progress and to solve our problems, our educational system is failing to teach mathematics, science, and reasoning. The Universal Wolf has devoured everything. But now it is beginning to devour itself.

25. Helen Pluckrose et al., "Academic Grievance Studies and the Corruption of Scholarship."

10

Rebuilding Civilization

Options for the Dark Ages

Our friend J. G. Hamann was not opposed to reason, liberty, human rights, and other Enlightenment ideals. One of his principal biographers, Oswald Bayer, calls him a "radical Enlightener." He was radical in the sense of insisting that reason, liberty, human rights, and "Enlightenment" were impossible without God. His own political convictions can be seen in his lifelong opposition to the King of Prussia, Frederick the Great (1740–1786).

Frederick was the great patron of Enlightenment rationalism, a friend of Voltaire and the founder of the Berlin Academy, which included both scientists and philosophers, including Kant. Frederick was also a tyrant, who held to "enlightened absolutism" and whose military genius and cruel wars made him the father of Prussian militarism, which would bear bloody fruit in World War I and World War II. Hamann believed that the God-less rationalism promoted by the Enlightenment would be manifested precisely in tyranny, in all-powerful, inhumane governments as exemplified by that of Frederick the Great.

Hamann, who lived in Prussia, satirized the king, generally veiling his ridicule to avoid censorship and arrest, presenting Frederick as the character "Solomon of the North," who lived in "Babel." Hamann excoriated the king's court for its sexual promiscuity and its notorious homosexuality, for which Frederick had a predilection, contrasting their sterile sexuality with the life-giving sexuality of marriage. Frederick had proposed self-love as the mechanism for social and political transformation. Hamann said that without God—whom Frederick scorned—reason indeed becomes little more than an instrument of self-love, which, in turn, is driven by the passions, specifically the desire for sexual freedom.[1] Frederick lived in a palace that he named *San Souci,* French for "without worry." Hamann said that he himself, in contrast, lived in *Grand Souci:* "big worry."[2]

Hamann criticized the Enlightenment political theories of natural rights and social contracts. Our rights and social relationships, including private property and government, are neither human compacts nor inherent natural qualities; rather, they are gifts of God, to be received by faith. There is no "state of nature" prior to civilization, and to profess to follow nature—even an ethic of natural law—apart from God degenerates into egocentric individualism in which the self is the measure of all things. Hamann also criticized the various dualisms of the new political thought, which separate church and state, doctrines and rights, morals and laws. He observed that the real Solomon did *not* cut the baby in two, but this is what the political theorists of his time insisted on doing.[3] Such separations, in Betz's words, "will ultimately have a deadening effect—whether one is talking about political zombies, who can believe one thing but vote for another, or whether one is talking about the state as a whole, which threatens to become an equally lifeless entity, a mere aggregate of individuals united and animated by nothing nobler than the duty to tolerate one another."[4]

So Hamann was concerned with some of the same issues that contemporary Christians struggle with in the political and cultural order: an overpowerful government, sexual immorality, and attempts to exclude God from public life. Of course, as a subject of King Frederick

---

1. John R. Betz, *After Enlightenment: The Post-Secular Vision of J. G. Hamann* (Oxford, UK: John Wiley & Sons, 2012), 208–9.
2. Betz, *After Enlightenment,* 227.
3. Betz, *After Enlightenment,* 276–79.
4. Betz, *After Enlightenment,* 279.

the Great, he, his fellow Christians, and his fellow Prussians had no say whatsoever in the government that they had to live under.

That is the normal condition for much of the world throughout history, but in the United States and other democratic nations today, Christians do have a say in their government, which entails a responsibility that citizens of other times never had.

But in our post-Christian era, our more primitive global village, we are reverting to the political and cultural climate in which Christians once again have little influence. Christians have been something of a political force, so we are not used to being used or ignored, much less treated with hostility.

How should Christians relate to post-Christian politics and how can they live in a post-Christian society? Different theologies have different ways of approaching these issues. H. Richard Niebuhr formulated the options, each of which has its advocates in the various Christian traditions, in his classic book *Christ and Culture:*[5]

- Christ against culture (the church separates itself from the non-Christian culture)
- The Christ of culture (the culture sets the agenda for the church)
- Christ above culture (the church rules the culture)
- Christ and culture in paradox (the church and the culture are two distinct realms)
- Christ the transformer of culture (the church changes the culture)

That breakdown is still useful, but it was formulated in 1951, when Christians were such a part of the culture that they could determine what stance to take. Today, though, in post-Christian times, Christians might desire to rule the culture, but there is hardly any prospect of that happening, since the culture declines to be ruled. Transforming the culture may remain a worthy goal, but the immediate issue for Christians today is the culture's attempt to transform the church. The culture shows no interest in Christ, even to attempt to coopt him, and cares little for the agenda even of those churches that most want to

---

5. H. Richard Niebuhr, *Christ and Culture* (New York: Harper & Row, 1951).

please it. The church might believe that Christ is against culture, but today it must live in a time when the culture is against Christ, when the world is actively hostile to his church.

So how should Christians live in these post-Christian times? Should they care about politics, or just give up on what the government does? Is there any prospect of rebuilding society, or is that not the business of the church?

Political Activism

In the first half of the twentieth century and before, one could find evangelical, Bible-believing Christians in virtually all of the political factions. Farmers and factory workers saw it in their interests to be Democrats. Small-business owners and wealthy property owners saw it in their interests to be Republicans. Despite their political differences, they worshiped together in the same church.

Black people did not. They had their own churches, which were largely evangelical. They were often prevented from voting. For one thing, they tended to vote Republican, the party of Lincoln, in the solidly Democratic and racially segregated South.

To be sure, there were other flavors of Christianity. Catholics had political clout, especially in the immigrant communities of the big cities as organized by the Democratic political machines. But back then, mainline liberal Protestantism was the most influential strain of Christianity. Already in those circles the "social gospel"—the notion that the church was to build the kingdom of God on earth through progressive politics—was prominent. But most Christians, while pursuing their own interests in light of their own political ideologies, held to a faith that was separate from their politics.

Then came the culture wars. The sexual revolution beginning with the 1960s, the *Roe v. Wade* ruling in 1973 legalizing abortion, the counterculture rebellion, court rulings against prayer in school—such developments inspired Christian activism with groups such as the Moral Majority. Christians wanting to conserve traditional values found a political home in political conservatism. As the Democrats grew more and more progressive—embracing pro-abortion feminism, championing gay rights, and allying with secularist academia—conservative Christians were welcomed by the Republican Party and became an important part of its base.

And yet, as Christian activists eventually discover to their surprise, the conservative movement also has its atheists. Leftists may reject God, but they generally retain a vestigial moral sense that is manifested in a sense of benevolence toward the oppressed and indignation against injustice. Some conservatives, though, are so enamored of free-market capitalism that they reject all restraints on human liberty, including moral absolutes and including God. They adopt the objectivist philosophy of Ayn Rand, who, like Nietzsche, condemned Christianity for its compassion to others, advocating instead the "virtue of selfishness."[6] According to this philosophy, which can be found among contemporary libertarians, following one's own interests and desires, with no altruistic concern for others, will result in individual happiness and social well-being, just as the free market of competing individuals following their own rational economic self-interests results in economic progress. Whereas some atheism focuses on Christianity's alleged weaknesses and failures, Ayn Rand's atheism focuses on Christianity's strengths and successes—namely, its ethic of self-sacrificial love and its legacy of compassion—which makes it particularly toxic. Christians will usually also have problems with some of the policies favored in the libertarian wing of the Republican Party, such as legalizing prostitution, legalizing drugs, and supporting abortion.

Another conflict Christians may have when they get involved with the conservative political movement is the temptation to civil religion. American Christians tend to be patriotic, which is a virtue, but our fallen religious nature can pull us in the direction of adopting a cultural religion; that is, a faith that divinizes one's culture. Thus we have the god-kings of Egypt and the Canaanites, as well as animistic societies that identify all of their customs and institutions with the gods. This is idolatry. And while God-and-country conservatives seldom go that far, and while there is a legitimate loyalty to both God and country, patriotic zeal can easily turn into a Christ-less religion, whose national heroes are turned into saints and whose actions are immune from criticism, even from the prophetic Word of God.

---

6. See Ayn Rand and Nathaniel Branden, *The Virtue of Selfishness* (New York: New American Library, 1964).

One of the dangers of any kind of political activism associated with Christianity is that the message of the church—namely, the message of Christ and his gospel—becomes associated with a political faction. This discredits Christianity in the eyes of those who oppose that faction.

That 81 percent of white evangelicals supported Donald Trump for president has led to charges that Christians are hypocrites and that all they really care about is power.[7] How else to account for Christians—or "so-called Christians" as they are often termed—voting for a notorious womanizer, casino mogul, and vulgarian? How can Christians continue to support a president who (in their view) tells lies, verbally abuses people, is hostile to immigrants, draws on racial animosity, pays off porn stars, and flaunts other standards of decency and decorum? Never mind that a large number of those Christians were voting for what they considered the lesser of two evils and were casting their vote for a candidate who vowed to oppose abortion, which they consider one of the largest social justice issues of our day.

Nevertheless, it is true that our politics has become so polarized that evangelicals' association with President Trump has damaged the evangelical "brand," at least with young people, millennials, and other groups that the church is trying to reach.[8] The term *evangelical* has become so politicized that many Christians who fit that category are now refusing the label. This is true not just of young and millennial Christians but also long-time presidential staffer Peter Wehner[9] and the well-respected Manhattan pastor Timothy Keller.[10]

However, it is worth considering whether evangelicals' support of President Trump is really a demonstration of their power-hungry

---

7. See Ed Stetzer and Andrew Macdonald, "Why Evangelicals Voted Trump: Debunking the 81%," *Christianity Today*, October 18, 2018, accessed June 11, 2019, https://www.christianitytoday.com/ct/2018/october/why-evangelicals-trump-vote-81-percent-2016-election.html.

8. See R. Laurence Moore and Isaac Kramnick, "Blame Evangelicals for the Decline in Christian Faith," *Daily Beast*, June 16, 2018, accessed June 11, 2019, https://www.thedailybeast.com/blame-evangelicals-for-the-decline-in-christian-faith. This is the dek for the article: "Polls show that in a classic example of religion gone wrong, evangelicals' slavish devotion to right wingers is the chief cause of the decline of religious belief."

9. Peter Wehner, "Why I Can No Longer Call Myself an Evangelical Republican," *New York Times*, December 9, 2017, accessed June 11, 2019, https://www.nytimes.com/2017/12/09/opinion/sunday/wehner-evangelical-republicans.html.

10. Timothy Keller, "Can Evangelicalism Survive Donald Trump and Roy Moore?" *New Yorker*, December 19, 2017, accessed June 11, 2019, https://www.newyorker.com/news/news-desk/can-evangelicalism-survive-donald-trump-and-roy-moore.

hypocrisy or it represents a new, more mature style of Christian political activism. The Moral Majority, the organization that embodied the "Christian Right" in the 1980s, sought to elect Christians of godly character who would support family values and oppose abortion. The group and its successors became successful in mobilizing Christian voters and played an important role in electing Republican presidents and other office holders. The Republican Party was grateful for the Christian Right's activism on its behalf. And yet those Republicans whom the Christian Right put into power did little, arguably, for its agenda. Abortion was not limited; family values continued to decline. The politicians seem to have *used* the Christian activists to get elected, while not giving them very much in return.

Now a politician emerges who is *not* and does not really pretend to be a Christian of godly character. And yet he has done a great deal in support of issues that Christian conservatives care about. In the words of a *Washington Post* op-ed piece, "Trump is proving to be the most fearlessly pro-life president in history": he closed Title X loopholes that allowed taxpayer money for abortion; he stopped funding for international programs that promote abortion; he allowed a conscience clause exempting pro-life employers from an Obamacare mandate requiring insurance plans that pay for abortifacients; he has stacked the Supreme Court and the federal judiciary with conservative judges who question *Roe v. Wade*.[11] The Trump administration has also implemented important protections for religious liberty, requiring all government agencies to honor twenty principles designed to protect the freedom of religion[12] and starting a major diplomatic initiative to promote religious liberty abroad.[13]

---

11. Marc A. Thiessen, "Trump Is Proving to Be the Most Fearlessly Pro-Life President in History," *Washington Post*, May 23, 2018, accessed June 11, 2019, https://www.washingtonpost.com/opinions/trump-is-proving-to-be-the-most-fearlessly-pro-life-president-in-history/2018/05/23/c72f2886-5e8a-11e8-a4a4-c070ef53f315_story.html?utm_term=.577077ae71af.

12. "Trump Administration Lays Out Principles for Protecting Religious Freedom," Catholic News Agency, October 6, 2017, accessed June 11, 2019, https://www.catholicnewsagency.com/news/trump-administration-lays-out-principles-for-protecting-religious-freedom-85958. See also the Department of Justice memo that establishes twenty principles of religious liberty that the federal government in all of its agencies must observe: https://www.justice.gov/opa/press-release/file/1001891/download.

13. Lorraine Woellert, "Trump's Religious Freedom Squad Promises to Deliver," *Politico*, July 26, 2018, accessed June 11, 2019, https://www.politico.com/story/2018/07/26/trump-religious-freedom-evangelicals-republicans-744762.

Should Christian political activists have the priority of electing Christians or implementing their agenda? Might forming alliances that yield results, rather than just trying to elect a member of their tribe, be a sign of a more mature approach to political activism? Wouldn't that kind of political pragmatism—which would presumably shift support to whatever candidate or party would support the Christians' issues—involve *less* spiritualizing of politics and *less* Christian power grabbing?

Still, the times when the church has been most politically success-ful—the medieval papacy, the Holy Roman Empire, Orthodoxy's ties to the Russian czar—have often resulted in the discrediting of Chris-tianity. The church has to do primarily with the kingdom of God, not earthly kingdoms, which soon pass away.

And yet Christians, in their vocations of citizenship, *should* work against the evils of the world, doing what they can to improve the societies in which they find themselves. Churches are right to take on social ministries to help the suffering in their communities. And they are right to proclaim moral truths, teaching against sexual immoral-ity and defending life against the abortionists. Direct political action should perhaps best be done not by the church body or congregation as such but by Christian individuals who are motivated by their faith and called to this arena. Christians and churches as a whole might do well to focus on specific moral issues rather than tying themselves too closely to the ambitions of one particular political party. A good role model would be William Wilberforce, who refused as a member of the British parliament to become either a Whig or a Tory, finding as an independent that he could form alliances with whichever party sup-ported his agenda of eliminating slavery, reforming prisons, promoting education, and helping the poor.

Though political activism has its dangers and temptations, the same can be said of spiritual escapism, as if Christianity has nothing to do with the external world. While Christianity has sometimes been discredited for churches' political entanglements, Christianity has also been discredited when churches ignore surrounding evils (such as those of Hitler's Germany). Christianity may be otherworldly, in its focus on the eternal life to come, but it also teaches that God has placed us in *this* world to live out our faith and to grow in our struggles. And one of those struggles is how, exactly, to live in this world.

Other Political Options and What to Avoid

Conservative Christians do not *have* to be conservative politically, much less be in thrall to the Republican Party. They have other political options today, though arguably none of them are without problems and all of them share a common danger.

Progressive evangelicals share the political liberal's concern for social justice, championing the cause of racial minorities, immigrants, and the poor. They tend to oppose war, untrammeled capitalism, and every kind of oppression. They believe that the government should take an active role in alleviating social injustice. They are motivated by biblical injunctions and the example of Christ.

Evangelicals have a history of progressive social action. William Wilberforce battled the slave trade and promoted a host of social reforms. Sunday schools were originally designed to bring education to poverty-stricken children. Their evangelical faith motivated many crusaders for the rights of women, who worked not only for their right to vote, but also battled abortionists and the prostitution trade. Evangelicals, especially in the black church, were leaders in the civil rights movement.

Today participating in the progressive political movement has become more problematic for Bible-believing Christians. Somehow, advocates for the poor and marginalized have turned against the poorest and the most marginalized of all, championing the aborting of children in the womb. The sexual revolution has become entangled with contemporary progressive politics, with homosexuals and the transgendered usurping the place of African Americans in the civil rights struggle and radical feminists attacking the nuclear family. Christians can certainly work for progressive causes while holding on to biblical convictions, but that can be difficult. Evangelicals devoting themselves to progressive politics and working with their secularist comrades can become tempted to regard biblical morality as oppressive and the gospel as noninclusive, leading them to abandon not only the name "evangelical" for its conservative connotations but also its substance.

Christian Democracy may be a better choice for Christians committed to progressive social-justice issues. This ideology combines political liberalism with social conservatism. That is, it advocates government policies that help the poor, that promote economic justice, that provide health care and other benefits to all, and the like. But, at the same time, it favors policies that are pro-life, pro-family, and pro-church.

This is essentially the political theology of the Roman Catholic Church. It is also the position of the Dutch neo-Calvinists, as articulated and put into practice by the great Reformed theologian and statesman Abraham Kuyper.[14] As such, the Christian Democrats are a major political party in Europe and Latin America, electing heads of state (such as German Chancellor Angela Merkel), joining powerful parliamentary coalitions, and playing an important role in the construction of Europe's welfare states.

Parliamentary democracies, of course, feature multiple political parties, representing a wide range of ideologies, which must then form tactical alliances with each other to build a governing coalition. Christian Democrats have become powerful, in part, because they sometimes join in coalitions of the left and sometimes join in coalitions of the right, making them always a force to contend with and a voting bloc that the other parties want to court. The American two-party system, on the other hand, has little place for this more complicated ideology. Republicans will not appreciate the Christian Democrat's desire to rein in laissez-faire capitalism and to build a government that will assure social welfare for all. And Democrats will not appreciate the Christian Democrat's conservative moral positions. There is the American Solidarity Party, which describes itself as "the only active Christian Democratic Party in the United States," but, like other alternatives to the Republicans and the Democrats, it is miniscule and on few ballots.[15] But Americans with Christian Democratic convictions will feel alienated—and ostracized—from both of the major parties, even though they might inhabit either of them.

---

14. See "Christian Democracy," Wikipedia, accessed June 11, 2019, https://en.wikipedia.org/wiki/Christian_democracy#Christian_democracy_around_the_world.

15. See the American Solidarity Party website, https://solidarity-party.org/.

Christian libertarians see the biggest danger to the church and to society as being an all-powerful, overreaching central government. The state is taking on the role of the church—asserting its authority not only to determine moral issues but to overturn them (as it has done with abortion). The state also presumes to change the definition of family (as it has done with same-sex marriage) and punishes religious believers who disagree (imposing discrimination statutes on dissenters). Christian libertarians fight for religious freedom but also for the rights of families and the whole panoply of individual freedoms as defined in the Bill of Rights.

I wrote earlier of libertarians who follow Ayn Rand with her Nietzschean atheism and her "virtue of selfishness" and who favor the legalization of abortion, prostitution, and drug use. But there are also pro-life libertarians, who believe the child in the womb also deserves liberty. In fact, this describes some of the most prominent libertarians in the Republican Party—for example, presidential candidates Ron Paul and his son Senator Rand Paul (his name not a tribute to Ayn but short for Randal),[16] both of whom are professing Christians who are pro-life. Some Christian libertarians might favor decriminalizing drugs and other vices, while still condemning them morally, reasoning that an individual's behavior is not the business of the state unless it involves harming others (which abortion does).

They also believe with other libertarians that free-market economics, with which the government should not interfere, is the surest means to general prosperity, with its "invisible hand"—which Christians might identify as the hand of God who built the laws of economics into his creation—promoting both individual liberty and a flourishing society.

Libertarians, while inhabiting the Republican Party, also have a party of their own, one of the stronger third parties. It is said that the technology industry tends to be libertarian, being socially liberal (let people do whatever they want), but economically conservative (not wanting the government to interfere with their businesses). I know quite a few Christian libertarians, who believe their religious and moral convictions can compete in the marketplace of ideas.

---

16. See "Rand Paul," Wikipedia, accessed June 11, 2019, https://en.wikipedia.org/wiki/Rand_Paul.

Localism is another political theory that many Christians are adopting. Instead of fixating on the centralized federal government, the localists focus attention on our immediate communities, the actual places where we live and the actual human beings we come in contact with. Instead of the vast nation state that rules from a distance, localists treasure town halls, meetings in community centers, and county elections. Not big government but small governments.

Another name for this movement is "crunchy conservatives," the name deriving, I am told, because these are conservatives who make their own granola. They like to eat locally, buying locally grown produce from a farmer's market. Like some liberals, they prefer organic food and care about nature and the environment. But unlike most liberals, their allegiance to nature extends to natural families and natural law.

Crunchy Cons are skeptical about technology. They like farms and small towns. They prefer trees to strip malls, not big business but small business, not megachurches but small churches. They cultivate a sense of place. They love regional differences. They care about their neighbors, not just the abstraction of humanity.

Localists might be accused of romanticism and parochialism, idealizing local communities at the very time that they are falling apart, micropolitics not being enough to save them. For better or worse, we live in a nation, not a classical city-state or a tribal village (except, perhaps for the global village of cyberspace). And yet localists deserve credit for working on the culture from the ground up.

There are other political options, of course—the various kinds of conservatism and liberalism mentioned in chapter 8—as well as more thoroughgoing Christian schemes, such as the reconstructionism among the Reformed, the new apostolic reformation dominionism among Pentecostals, and distributivism among Catholics. But these today exist more in theory than in practice. The goals of Christians ruling the preapocalyptic world and making the Bible the law of the land are highly problematic theologically, but debates about them are largely moot, since neither is likely to happen in our post-Christian times.

The fact is, the Bible does not give us a political ideology. The ancient Hebrews lived under tribal patriarchs, judges, kings, and foreign occupation. Christians have lived out their faith under emperors, kings, oligarchies, republics, dictators, and democracies. Through them all, believers have been good citizens, while sometimes differing over what that might entail. At the same time, Scripture warns believers about trusting too much in earthly rulers and in political schemes:

> Put not your trust in princes,
> in a son of man, in whom there is no salvation.
> When his breath departs, he returns to the earth;
> on that very day his plans perish. (Ps. 146:3–4)

Political utopias of every kind—that is, the notion that our sins have a *political* solution and that we ourselves can establish a *political* realm that can solve all the world's problems—confuse what we can accomplish on earth with what God has promised only in heaven. And yet this is exactly what one strain of modern and postmodern theology has attempted to do.

In the nineteenth century, the evangelical social activism that we commended earlier gave way to a new theology that would come to dominate mainline liberal Protestantism to this day: the Social Gospel. No longer was the purpose of the church the salvation of sinners through the gospel of Christ, by which they could receive the gift of everlasting life in heaven. Rather, the purpose of the church was to be the salvation of *society*, which was to be achieved by building the kingdom of God, not in heaven but on earth. In practice, this meant that churches would adopt the nineteenth-century assumptions of social progress—that the world is getting better and better as it throws off the past and becomes more modern—and align itself with the progressive political movement.

In the twentieth century, the Social Gospel became dominant in mainline Protestantism. Seminaries "de-mythologized" the Bible, casting out traditional Christian teachings and reframing them as political allegories. Church conventions began to resemble mini legislatures, debating what the nation's foreign and tax policies should be, passing resolutions instructing the government what programs it should enact. The Social Gospel waxed and waned in the theologically liberal denominations—sometimes being substituted for a psychological gospel or an existentialist gospel—but the civil rights movement, the Vietnam War, and the social upheavals of the 1960s brought it back in force.

In the twenty-first century, mainline Protestants, their numbers depleted due largely to this very politicization, turned their attention to gay rights, feminism, and related social justice issues. Their seminaries began teaching "queer theology" and feminist theology, practicing critical constructivism against the whole edifice of historic Christianity.

In all this time, the Social Gospel was of the left; but then arose a Social Gospel of the right. Resisting legalized abortion and other attempts by the government to overturn established morality was the right thing to do, and much of the political activism we chronicled earlier in this chapter was fully appropriate. And yet we should admit that in many cases congregations and Christian activists crossed the line. Like the liberal theologians whom they opposed, their political zeal in some cases overshadowed their mission to save souls. They too became utopian, though they envisioned a conservative utopia instead of a socialist utopia. Both talked as if the kingdom of God were something that we ourselves must build on earth.

Although Christians should be politically engaged, and recognizing that Christians may differ as to what form this should take, there can be no social gospel. This is because there is no other gospel. The apostle Paul's stern warning to the Galatians applies to Christians today:

> I am astonished that you are so quickly deserting him who called you in the grace of Christ and are turning to a different gospel— not that there is another one, but there are some who trouble you and want to distort the gospel of Christ. But even if we or an angel from heaven should preach to you a gospel contrary to the one we preached to you, let him be accursed. (Gal. 1:6–8)

Christians may differ in their politics and their theology, including their positions on the political implications of the millennium. But Christians who have been made such by the gospel of Jesus Christ, "who gave himself for our sins to deliver us from the present evil age" (Gal. 1:4), must never "turn back again to the weak and worthless elementary principles of the world" (Gal. 4:9).

Getting through the Dark Ages

If Western civilization, as influenced by Christianity, is collapsing, we should take heart in realizing that it has happened before. Rome had been a great empire, bringing the rule of law, classical civilization, and—once the empire converted—the Christian faith throughout Europe, Asia Minor, and northern Africa. But in the fifth century, Rome fell apart, and when the last emperor was deposed in 476, centuries of anarchy unfolded, with barbarians burning libraries and pillaging cities. These centuries were the so-called Dark Ages (not to be confused with the Middle Ages).

But even though there was no emperor, no senate, no legions, no magistrates, and no courts, the church remained. Through all the predations of the barbarians, the church kept functioning. Moreover, the church kept learning alive and preserved the elements of Western civilization for future generations. Monasteries were surrounded with great walls to protect against the barbarians, but behind those walls, monks were busy making hand copies of the Bible, the writings of the church fathers, and—significantly—the masterpieces of classical antiquity, even those by pagan authors.

But the Dark Ages eventually ended. How? The church converted the barbarians! Four centuries after the fall of Rome, Charlemagne—the Christian king of the Franks—both conquered and evangelized the remaining pagans. He revived the title of emperor and united much of Europe. He marks the beginning of the Middle Ages, a time when Christianity once again became culturally influential, founding the first universities, bringing back a Christianized classicism, and inspiring the arts and the sciences.

Today, some Christians are urging that the church approach our post-Christian times as the early church approached the Dark Ages: pull back from the collapsing culture; separate from the barbarians; keep learning alive and preserve our cultural heritage; build up our Christian institutions (the church, the family, schools, local communities). And someday, maybe, the church will convert the barbarians and bring civilization back to life.

Rod Dreher calls this "the Benedict Option" after Saint Benedict, who responded to the fall of Rome by establishing monasteries—

Christian communities—that were designed to preserve the Christian faith and, in so doing, preserved Western civilization. In his book *The Benedict Option*, Dreher first calls on Christians to face up to the fact that they have lost the culture wars and that they must find a way to live in a post-Christian society.

> Today we can see that we've lost on every front and that the swift and relentless currents of secularism have overwhelmed our flimsy barriers. Hostile secular nihilism has won the day in our nation's government, and the culture has turned powerfully against traditional Christians. We tell ourselves that these developments have been imposed by a liberal elite, because we find the truth intolerable: The American people, either actively or passively, approve.[17]

Dreher then makes the case for a "strategic withdrawal"[18] from that culture. Instead of participating in the mainstream secularist society, Christians should separate themselves from that world.

That does not necessarily mean going into a monastery, though Dreher, who is Orthodox, appreciates that life and profiles some contemporary Benedictines as well as semimonastic lay communities. He says to "turn your home into a domestic monastery"[19]—a place of prayer, hospitality, and love, "which keeps outside its walls people and things that are inimical to its purpose"[20] (such as unlimited TV and online media). He also calls for church congregations to become close-knit communities. He believes that the principles of the Rule of Saint Benedict—order, prayer, work, asceticism, stability, community, hospitality, and balance—can be broadly applied, equipping Christians to thrive even in a hostile environment.[21]

Dreher wants Christians to be countercultural, to cultivate the kind of healthy cultural life that the dominant culture has repudiated. That includes recovering the Christian view of sexuality and building strong marriages and families. Christians can still be political, he says, but Dreher—who is also the author of the localist manifesto *Crunchy-*

---

17. Rod Dreher, *The Benedict Option: A Strategy for Christians in a Post-Christian Nation* (New York: Sentinel, 2017), 9.
18. Dreher, *The Benedict Option*, 2.
19. Dreher, *The Benedict Option*, 124.
20. Dreher, *The Benedict Option*, 126.
21. Dreher, *The Benedict Option*, 48–77.

Cons[22]—says that they should attend primarily to local governments and the needs of local communities. The idea throughout is to rebuild civilization from the ground up.

Dreher is a big advocate of homeschooling and classical Christian education. I concur. In fact, I have argued that education is one area in which Christians are actually *winning* the culture wars. As secularist education continues to deteriorate, as we have shown, many Christians are giving their children a vastly *superior* education than their secularist peers are getting. Homeschools and classical schools teach reading, writing, calculating, and reasoning. Homeschooled and classically educated children also will have read the great books and thought through the great ideas of our civilization.

Furthermore, parents who homeschool are giving their children more attention and interacting with them on a higher level than has become the norm in many families today, which makes for stronger families and better-adjusted children. And classical Christians schools, as Dreher points out, can be exemplars of and training grounds for Christian community.

As a former provost and professor at Patrick Henry College, one of the few Christian colleges to pursue classical education on the collegiate level, I can point to assessment data that shows our students outperforming their peers in regular universities on almost every level. In chapter 9 we discussed the failures of contemporary higher education, as documented in the book *Academically Adrift: Limited Learning in Higher Education*,[23] but Patrick Henry College defies each of the trends the book laments.

When it comes to education, Christians may be in exactly the same position as the church in the Dark Ages: preserving literacy, transmitting knowledge, and saving civilization. And if Christians become better educated than their secularist peers—if they can think objectively, creatively, with knowledge and the capacity to build on the discoveries of the past—who will be the leaders and culture-makers in the decades ahead?

---

22. Rod Dreher, *Crunchy Cons: The New Conservative Counterculture and Its Return to Roots* (New York: Three Rivers Press, 2006).

23. Richard Arum and Josipa Roksa, *Academically Adrift: Limited Learning on College Campuses* (Chicago: University of Chicago Press, 2011), 1–32.

The Luther Option

Although I appreciate Rod Dreher's Benedict Option, as a Reformation Christian I have problems with monasticism, even as a metaphorical model. Let me propose a variation that keeps many of Dreher's insights while shifting the focus somewhat. Call it "the Luther option."

Christianity affirms and can influence culture, but, unlike other religions, it resists being a cultural religion. "Christian cultures"—the Middle Ages, monasteries, state churches, Amish communities, evangelical congregations—are still susceptible to cultural sins (pride, lust, greed, the pursuit of power and status, the mistreatment of those both inside and outside the group). And it is impossible to prevent sin by walling it out. "They are not skillful considerers of human things, who imagine to remove sin by removing the matter of sin," observed the great Protestant poet John Milton. "Though ye take from a covetous man all his treasure, he has yet one jewel left, ye cannot bereave him of his covetousness. Banish all objects of lust, shut up all youth into the severest discipline that can be exercised in any hermitage, ye cannot make them chaste, that came not thither so."[24] The problem with monasticism, according to the Reformers, is that in its search for spiritual perfection, it substitutes human works for faith in the work of Christ, which alone can quell our sin. But monasticism also has a moral problem: it separates Christians from the world they are called to serve.

When Jesus prayed for his followers in the garden of Gethsemane, he foresaw our plight today. "I have given them your word, and the world has hated them because they are not of the world, just as I am not of the world" (John 17:14). The world hates us, just as Dreher says. We must not be "of the world," just as Saint Benedict said. And yet, as Jesus continues, "I do not ask that you take them out of the world, but that you keep them from the evil one" (John 17:15). Jesus does not want the Father to take us out of the world, but that he protect us from Satan as we live in the sinful world. Indeed, Jesus says that he is sending us *into* that world, on the analogy of his own

---

24. "Areopagitica," in *The Prose of John Milton*, ed. J. Max Patrick (New York: Anchor, 1967), 297.

incarnation. "As you sent me into the world, so I have sent them into the world" (John 17:18).

Christians are not to be "of" the world; that is, they must not belong to the world. They must not be worldly, sharing the world's priorities or conforming to its ways. Their identity is not a matter of their ethnicity or social status; rather, their identity is to be found in their baptism into Christ. "For as many of you as were baptized into Christ have put on Christ. There is neither Jew nor Greek, there is neither slave nor free, there is no male and female, for you are all one in Christ Jesus" (Gal. 3:27–28). And yet Jesus calls his followers "into the world," where they must still live their lives as Jews or Greeks, slaves or free citizens, men or women.

Luther taught that God reigns over both an eternal and a temporal kingdom, the spiritual and the physical realm. Again, God cares not only for what is spiritual; rather, he loves his entire creation, in all of its material solidity. Furthermore, God providentially governs the universe that he has made, providing for and working through non-Christians as well as Christians. That is to say, the secular realm is not really void of God after all. He remains hidden, but he is present and active in the world, bestowing his gifts by means of human vocations (providing daily bread through farmers, creating new life through parents, protecting society through governments, etc.). And yet God also reveals himself by his Word, which tells how the second person of the Trinity became incarnate in this physical world and died to save sinners. And having delivered those sinners into his spiritual kingdom, God calls them back into the world—to their vocations in the family, the workplace, the church, and the culture—to live out their faith in love and service to their neighbors.[25]

Applying this doctrine of vocation, Christians in a post-Christian world can live out their faith even in a secularist society. Because God governs the world and everyone in it, believer and nonbeliever alike, the world is never as hopelessly godless as it may appear. Yes, the devil may present himself as the prince of this world, but ultimately God is still in charge, and this is true even when the general public

25. See my book *God at Work: Your Christian Vocation in All of Life* (Wheaton, IL: Crossway, 2002).

is oblivious to him. All things are God's, and so, in Christ, all things are ours (1 Cor. 3:21–23). And living our Christian faith in vocation means that the most mundane and secular-seeming facets of ordinary life—the routines of family life, the drudgery of the workplace, the conflicts of citizenship—are occasions to grow spiritually, as we bear our crosses daily in love and service to our neighbors.

We have God-given vocations in the world, so we should not withdraw from that world completely despite its indifference or hostility to our faith. We may be exiles in this world, but we will serve it nonetheless.

> Thus says the LORD of hosts, the God of Israel, to all the exiles whom I have sent into exile from Jerusalem to Babylon: Build houses and live in them; plant gardens and eat their produce. Take wives and have sons and daughters; take wives for your sons, and give your daughters in marriage, that they may bear sons and daughters; multiply there, and do not decrease. But seek the welfare of the city where I have sent you into exile, and pray to the LORD on its behalf, for in its welfare you will find your welfare. (Jer. 29:4–7)

Our models can be Daniel, Shadrach, Meschach, and Abednego, who helped to govern Babylon and yet—despite lions' dens and fiery furnaces—were faithful to the God of Israel.

PART 4

RELIGION

11

Spiritual but Not Religious

The Religion of the Nones

In our discussions thus far, we have talked about secularism and secularists, referring to the ideologies and the individuals who believe that human beings can do without religion altogether. Actually, though, our contemporary society is not nearly as secular as it seems.

Even most of the nones—those who, when asked their religion, check the box labeled "none"—have specific religious beliefs. Many secularists say that they are spiritual but not religious, meaning that they reject organized and institutional religion in favor of a personal, private, inward spirituality.

Being post-Christian does not necessarily mean atheism or agnosticism, positions that actually attract very few people today. In the absence of Christianity, other religions and spiritualities rush into the void.

Though it may seem ironic in our ostensibly sophisticated and high-tech world, these new religions and spiritualities of the global village are actually far more primitive than the traditional religions, such as Christianity, that they purport to replace. This bodes well, since Christianity has always been effective in reaching animists and other pagans.

The Collapse of the Secularization Hypothesis

It has long been assumed that the rise of modernity will be accompanied by the decline of religion. According to this so-called secularization hypothesis, scientific and technological progress will make religion obsolete, making societies secular.

But the scholarly consensus today rejects the secularization hypothesis. That view, which is clearly the product of modernist assumptions, is simply incorrect. As societies have grown more modern, they have *not* become less religious. In fact, religion has often proven to be a modernizing influence. For example, Christianity in Africa—with its schools, hospitals, and egalitarian ethics—has played an important role in making that continent *more* modern. While it is true that Western Europe has become highly secular, that may be an outlier, not the norm. After all, the United States continues to lead the West in modern science, technology, and economics, while remaining quite religious. And modern China, India, Russia, and the Middle East are arguably more religious now than they have been for centuries.

Scholars are not only casting doubt on the secularization hypothesis as it applies to global cultures; they are also finding that secularism itself, where it does occur, is not the extinction of religion. Sociologist of religion Christian Smith marshals the research on secularism in his book *Religion: What It Is, Why It Works, and Why It Matters.*[1]

Professor Smith acknowledges that religions can fade, lose adherents, and change. But religion, he says, is innate to human beings, and hardly any society is truly without it:

> No human society has existed that did not include some religion. A broad array of religions exists around the globe today, with a single religion dominating society in some places, while in others many traditions mix, morph, and clash. Efforts by some modern states to do away with religion have failed. Though thin and weak in some regions, religion is robust and growing in other parts of the world.[2]

---

1. Christian Smith, *Religion: What It Is, Why It Works, and Why It Matters* (Princeton, NJ: Princeton University Press, 2017).
2. Smith, *Religion*, 1–2.

Secularism sometimes is not so much the absence of religion, he says, but a change in the religion. He reminds us that religions do not necessarily involve belief in a God or attending worship services or anticipating an afterlife, all of which are Christian notions that are absent in many religions, though superficial studies use these as benchmarks for how religious a society is.[3] Many societies with little apparently "religiousness" (a quality he contrasts with "religion" as such) continue to have a strong religious presence in their "deep culture."

Professor Smith says that the cultural *presence* of a religion can be determined by examining the elements in the culture that would not be there if the religion had not existed. Scandinavian values such as benevolence and generosity to the disadvantaged are very different from those of its pre-Christian Viking heritage, with its violent warrior culture, and can be traced directly to the continuing Christian influence. Scandinavians' specifically Lutheran heritage is still evident in their strong sense of vocation and service to the neighbor. This cultural presence of religion persists even after the beliefs that inspired them have faded.

Another important study of secularism is by the Canadian philosopher Charles Taylor, *A Secular Age*.[4] He says that the problem of secularism, which affects believers and unbelievers alike, is not the absence of religion but the abundance of religions. Because of our religious pluralism, which includes the options of atheism and agnosticism, it is difficult to accept any one religious position as absolute. Because the contemporary secular West has no single religion—unlike the Catholic Middle Ages and the Islamic Middle East today—but rather a plethora of alternatives from which we must choose, our religion is a matter of our own volition rather than a culturally approved, all-explaining given. Taylor shows that even the different strains of unbelief had their origins in religion. And he explores the religious commitments and struggles that today's nonbelieving secularists and their predecessors have been engaged in.

Smith and Taylor call to mind the superficiality of today's pop-secularists such as the New Atheists, who think religion is nothing

3. Smith, *Religion*, 22–27.
4. Charles Taylor, *A Secular Age* (Cambridge, MA: Harvard University Press, 2017).

more than incorrect science and that secularism is the triumph of reason over irrationalism, thus demonstrating their ignorance of both religion and secularism. Certainly, Christians must challenge both the atheistic forms of secularism and the spiritual forms of secularism. What should be encouraging to Christians, though, is that many secularists are not closed to spiritual realities, which means that, by God's grace, they can be evangelized.

Secularism and New Age Religion

The quarter of Americans who are nones may not be affiliated with any religion, but they are far from the materialist, scientific-minded rationalists of the New Atheists' dreams. Among the nones, 72 percent believe in God or a "higher power."[5] One-fifth of those who say they have no religion nevertheless pray every day. And 5 percent attend a worship service every week. And 37 percent describe themselves as "spiritual" though not "religious."[6]

The nature of this spirituality is telling. A Pew Research study suggests that to the extent that traditional religions like Christianity are fading, they are being replaced by a more primitive, animistic religion as taught by the New Age movement. In fact, the study suggests that Christianity too is being pulled in the animistic direction, as a startlingly high number of Christians are also embracing New Age beliefs.

Pew Research asked Americans whether they believe in four characteristically New Age—but also animistic—teachings: psychics, reincarnation, astrology, and spiritual energy that can be located in physical things.[7] Overall, 62 percent of Americans hold to at least one of these New Age beliefs, with 42 percent believing in objects with

5. "When Americans Say They Believe in God, What Do They Mean?" Pew Research Center, April 25, 2018, accessed June 11, 2019, http://www.pewforum.org/2018/04/25/when-americans -say-they-believe-in-god-what-do-they-mean/.

6. "'Nones' on the Rise," Pew Research Center, October 9, 2012, accessed June 11, 2019, http://www.pewforum.org/2012/10/09/nones-on-the-rise/. According to this earlier study, 68 percent of nones—who were found to comprise just under 20 percent of the population—believe in some sort of God. Just two years later, another Pew study found that 23 percent of Americans identify as nones, a jump from one in five to one in four. (See "America's Changing Religious Landscape," Pew Research Center, May 1, 2015, accessed June 11, 2019, http://www.pewforum .org/2015/05/12/americas-changing-religious-landscape/.) And yet the numbers on nones' spirituality seem to be going up.

7. "'New Age' Beliefs Common among Both Religious and Nonreligious Americans," Pew Research Center, October 1, 2018, http://www.pewresearch.org/fact-tank/2018/10/01/new-age -beliefs-common-among-both-religious-and-nonreligious-americans/.

spiritual energy, 41 percent believing in psychics, 33 percent believing in reincarnation, and 29 percent believing in astrology.

Of those whose religion is "nothing in particular," nearly four out of five (78 percent) believe in at least one of those tenets of New Age spirituality. Three out of five (61 percent) of those with no religion believe in objects with spiritual energy; a majority (52 percent) believe in psychics; a majority believe in reincarnation (51 percent); and almost half (47 percent) believe in astrology. The nones believe in such things at a higher rate than do members of any other religious demographic.

We often assume that there is little difference between atheists and agnostics, both of whom are rationalistic skeptics. But this study shows that agnostics as a group are hardly skeptical at all, being surprisingly open to New Age–type beliefs. A *majority* of agnostics (56 percent) believe in at least one of these spiritual tenets, with 40 percent believing in objects with spiritual energy, nearly a third (31 percent) believing in psychics, over a quarter (28 percent) believing in reincarnation, and nearly one in five (18 percent) believing in astrology.

Atheists, as one might expect, are much more consistent materialists, with only just over a fifth (22 percent) believing in at least one of these New Age tenets. Just 13 percent of atheists believe in objects with spiritual energy, 10 percent believe in psychics, 7 percent believe in reincarnation, and 3 percent believe in astrology. Atheists may be the most skeptical of any of the other religious categories when it comes to New Age beliefs, but more than one in five believe in at least one of them. (This also suggests that not many atheists are of the full-blooded Nietzschean variety. Nietzsche believed in a form of reincarnation: the "eternal return," that since time is infinite, all random combinations will eventually recur, including those that came together to form *you* with your distinct consciousness.[8])

It would appear that today's secularism is *not* a matter of being scientific, repudiating the supernatural, and embracing a materialist worldview. Some people hold to that perspective, but they are a small minority, even among the nones. Just 10 percent of Americans say that they do not believe in God or a higher power of any kind, and only

8. See Wikipedia, "Eternal Return," accessed June 11, 2019, https://en.wikipedia.org/wiki/Eternal _return.

27 percent of the nones are atheists.[9] Today's secularism draws away from Christianity, but it is arguably *more* credulous in its openness to a nonscientific, nonmaterialist paganism.

And yet this kind of secularism is also affecting Christianity. Among professing Christians, 61 percent believe in at least one of the New Age tenets, with 37 percent believing in objects with spiritual energy, 40 percent believing in psychics, 29 percent believing in reincarnation, and 26 percent believing in astrology.

Members of black churches are the most open to New Age theology, with 72 percent believing in at least one of the tenets (objects with spiritual energy, 41 percent; psychics, 43 percent; reincarnation, 38 percent; astrology, 34 percent). A close second are Catholics, with 70 percent believing in at least one of the New Age beliefs (objects with spiritual energy, 47 percent; psychics, 46 percent; reincarnation, 36 percent; astrology, 33 percent). Also highly credulous, with more than two-thirds of their adherents holding to at least one of the New Age beliefs, are the supposedly sophisticated liberal mainline Protestants (holding to at least one, 67 percent; objects with spiritual energy, 43 percent; psychics, 33 percent; astrology, 30 percent).

Evangelicals are the most skeptical about such things, next to the atheists. And yet a still-surprising 47 percent of evangelicals believe in at least one of the New Age beliefs. Nearly one in four (24 percent) believe in objects with spiritual energy. One in three believe (33 percent) in psychics. Nearly one in five (19 percent) believe in reincarnation. Nearly one in five (18 percent) believe in astrology.

Now, of course, as in all such studies, we need to attend to issues of definition. Concerning the question, Do you believe that spiritual energy can be located in physical things?—well, a Christian who believes in creation, incarnation, sacraments, and vocation might assent to that, although the Christian view of such things is not a matter of "spiritual energy." Perhaps some respondents misconstrued the question. But what about reincarnation? What do the one in five evangelicals who believe they will keep coming back after they die do with Hebrews 9:27 ("It is appointed for man to die once, and after that comes judgment")?

---

9. Pew Research Center, "When Americans Say They Believe in God, What Do They Mean?"

Ironically, the modernist theologians of last century believed that "modern man" (they used such sexist terminology in those days) is incapable of believing in Christian supernaturalism. For Christianity to survive, they said, it must adapt to the "modern" worldview of rationalistic, scientific materialism. Again, the gospel must no longer be "otherworldly" but "this worldly," a social gospel of political progress. The Bible must be "demythologized," its ancient "myths" retranslated as existential allegories. Instead of the salvation and sanctification of the soul, the church should aim at helping its members find psychological wholeness. Pastoral care must become psychological counseling.

How surprised and disenchanted those liberal theologians would be to see what postmodern man is capable of believing!

What Nones Lack Is Community

Another researcher, Stephen Asma, has gone deeper into the mind-set of the nones. He notes that for all of their many spiritual and even religious beliefs—which go far beyond those four benchmarks in the Pew study—what nones do *not* have is any kind of community, religious or otherwise:

> Contrary to the hopes of neo-Enlightenment thinkers like Steven Pinker, millennial nones are not abandoning organized religion to become secular, science-loving humanists. Rather, they are turning toward more individual forms of spiritualism, including yoga, meditation, healing stones, Wiccan spell casting and astrology.
>
> These nones tend to believe in the soul, divine energy, mystical realities, ghosts, fate and myriad other superstitions that traditionally fell under the umbrella of religion. They also tend to eschew formal social gatherings and regular group activities.[10]

This is to say, nones have private religious beliefs and pursue solitary religious practices—sometimes, as we shall see, Christian beliefs and practices—but they do not participate in any kind of religious

---

10. Stephen Asma, "Religiously Unaffiliated 'Nones' Are Pursuing Spirituality, but Not Community," *Los Angeles Times*, June 7, 2018, accessed June 11, 2019, https://www.latimes.com/opinion/op-ed/la-oe-asma-nones-spirituality-20180607-story.html. See also his book *Why We Need Religion* (New York: Oxford University Press, 2018).

community. They do not go to church, but they do not go to spiritualist or New Age groups either. Nor do they get together with other nones. Asma suggests that nones tend not to join secular communities either. They do not join churches, nor do they join bowling leagues, the Lions' Club, the League of Women Voters, reading groups, or informal social circles. They have the second lowest marriage rate of any religious category (37 percent married; 11 percent cohabiting; 11 percent divorced; 37 percent never married).[11] To be sure, nones do have online connections, Asma notes, but he stresses that these are no substitute for flesh-and-blood relationships.

If this is so, then the rise of the nones is not just a failure of the church to keep and attract members. Rather, nones would appear to be manifesting the larger isolation in our culture that we have been chronicling.

As for their religious beliefs, Asma says that the nones are retaining what he considers the least helpful aspects of religion ("magical thinking"), while rejecting the most beneficial ("social bonding"). He credits the well-attested benefits of religion on physical and mental health to the social dimensions of religion. Involvement in a church gives you social interactions, close friendships, a support network, shared adversity, and a connectedness with other people. These cannot be found, says Asma, in social media. Nor are interior "mindfulness" exercises or organizing your day around a horoscope any kind of substitute for religious community.

Christians would disagree with Asma's psychological and sociological view of religion, which has nothing to say about beliefs or salvation. But he surely makes a good point about the human need for a religion that is not only personal but corporate. We have described the nones' beliefs as animistic and pagan, but animistic religion is centered around the tribe, and pagan rituals were communal ceremonies. Christianity is also *corporate*, a word that derives from "body," with the word *members* referring to the parts of a body. Thus, 1 Corinthians 12 teaches that the church consists of wildly diverse members who come

---

11. See "The Unaffiliated," Pew Religious Landscape Study, accessed June 11, 2019, https://www.pewforum.org/religious-landscape-study/religious-tradition/unaffiliated-religious-nones/. The only category with lower marriage rates, according to the study, is black Protestants.

together into the unity of the body of Christ.[12] Besides, how can you love your neighbor if you never interact with a neighbor? No wonder Scripture underscores how Christians need to come together to worship and to support each other in the Christian life: "Let us consider how to stir up one another to love and good works, not neglecting to meet together, as is the habit of some"—we might say, "the habit of nones"—"but encouraging one another" (Heb. 10:24–25).

If the nones are so lacking in community, and if this is one of their primary needs, should churches try to find ways to draw them into their communities? I suppose so. Maybe some nones yearn for community. Or would like it if they could experience it.

But I would contend that many, if not most, of the nones, do not *want* to be part of a community, especially a religious community. They run away from churches precisely because they do not want to be part of a group. They don't like being welcomed, standing up and introducing themselves, urged to share their feelings in front of other people, standing around at coffee hour having to make small talk. The very efforts of churches to be friendly can be what drives them away. Nor do nones want to feel like part of a larger corporate body that goes back for centuries, whether a theological tradition or the church catholic.

Theirs is a highly interior religion. By its nature, it has little to do with other people or the outside world. Nones make up their own theologies, which only they adhere to. They do not even purport to be objective. Their beliefs are based not on reason or revelation but on what they like. Nones are churches unto themselves, each of which has only one member.

We have shown that secularists are not necessarily without religion. But what makes them secular is that their religion has nothing to do with the world. The two are completely separate: the realm outside themselves—physical and social reality—operates in terms of its own impersonal ways, void of God and of any spiritual significance. But nones find spiritual significance within themselves. This, again, is the spirituality of Gnosticism.

---

12. See the entry "corporation" (which means "persons united in a body for some purpose") in the Online Etymology Dictionary, accessed June 11, 2019, https://www.etymonline.com/word /corporation. See also the entry "member," https://www.etymonline.com/word/member.

And, of course, the biggest advantage of separating the spiritual from the religious, from the post-Christian point of view, is that a wholly internalized, ethereal spirituality makes no moral demands. As ancient Gnostics also believed, what we do with our bodies has nothing to do with our spiritual state. There can be no sexual sin. We can live as we please, constructing our own self-chosen moralities, living according to "what's right for me."

Secularism does exclude religion from the public sphere. Despite their ersatz religiosity, nones are secularists after all. That they persist in holding on to some kind of spirituality, even as they live in what they consider to be a God-free world, suggests that the church might win them back. Especially when their spirituality proves inadequate, as it will in their time of need.

Looking to the Church for Exorcism

Another phenomenon that illustrates the spiritual side of secularism is the growing number of incidents of what even nonreligious people are describing as demonic possession. The *Atlantic* magazine is hardly Christian or culturally conservative, but it published an informative article on the subject by Mike Mariani. He reports that 70 percent of Americans believe in the existence of the devil. Unlike belief in God, this number is *growing*. Only 55 percent believed in the devil in 1990. Today, roughly half of Americans believe in demonic possession. Though the number of cases of alleged possession is unknown, the author interviewed the official exorcist for the Catholic archdiocese of Indianapolis, who said that in the first nine months of 2018, he had received seventeen hundred requests for exorcism. The article profiles a woman who had been possessed, describes several credible cases, and reports that psychiatrists are now recognizing the phenomenon and are struggling to account for it.[13]

Signs of possession include the subject being taken over by another personality; speaking in a low, guttural voice; moving or throwing objects without touching them; and the Catholic criteria: "facility in a language the person has never learned; physical strength beyond his

---

13. Mike Mariani, "American Exorcism," *Atlantic*, December 2018, accessed June 11, 2019, https://www.theatlantic.com/magazine/archive/2018/12/catholic-exorcisms-on-the-rise/573943/.

or her age or condition; access to secret knowledge; and a vehement aversion to God and sacred objects."[14] Such cases used to be rare, to say the least, but they are reportedly becoming more and more common. Mariani, the author of the *Atlantic* article, quotes experts who say that "during periods when the influence of organized religions ebbs, people seek spiritual fulfillment through the occult."

> "As people's participation in orthodox Christianity declines," said Carlos Eire, a historian at Yale specializing in the early modern period, "there's always been a surge in interest in the occult and the demonic." He said that today we're seeing a "hunger for contact with the supernatural."
>
> Adam Jortner, an expert on American religious history at Auburn University, agreed. "When the influence of the major institutional Churches is curbed," he said, people "begin to look for their own answers." And at the same time that there has been a rebirth in magical thinking, Jortner added, American culture has become steeped in movies, TV shows, and other media about demons and demonic possession.
>
> Today's increased willingness to believe in the paranormal, then, seems to have begun as a response to secularization before spreading through the culture and landing back on the Church's doorstep—in the form of people seeking salvation from demons through the Catholic faith's most mystical ritual.[15]

Though such accounts of demonic possession are unsettling—and some Christians might be skeptical about them—that last sentence should be encouraging to Christians. Among those who are "spiritual but not religious," some are encountering spirits that are malignant and terrifying. They then often flee to the church to deliver them from these evil spirits.

The Catholic Church has a formal rite of exorcism and specially authorized exorcists, as well as an extensive process to determine whether a case is actual demonic possession, or, as is more often the case, some dissociative psychological disorder. But there are Protestant

---

14. Mariani, "American Exorcism."
15. Mariani, "American Exorcism."

exorcists as well, mostly among Pentecostal Christians but also and increasingly among other evangelicals. When Pope Francis was a cardinal in Argentina and dealt with individuals in need of exorcism who were turned away from the church bureaucracy, he would reportedly send them to "his favorite exorcist," a Lutheran pastor.[16]

One of those Lutheran pastors who has conducted exorcisms is Dr. Robert Bennett, a pastor and seminary professor, who stresses that most cases of demonic possession, as well as the more common demonic oppression, are not "like the movies," with their levitation and projectile vomiting, nor do they necessarily have the sensationalistic symptoms of the Roman Catholic criteria. Nor are particular rituals, much less the permission of a bishop, necessary in casting out devils. Successful exorcisms, he explains—whether done through a liturgy or a healing service or the ordinary worship life of the church—are nothing more than the application of the New Testament remedy: the Word of God and prayer.[17]

Ministering to the "Spiritual"

Churches would do well to prepare for such casualties of "spirituality." Churches might also look into recovering *Christian spirituality* as a way to reach those who yearn for spirituality, haven't found it in what they have known of Christianity, and so have looked elsewhere.

Historic Christianity is surely more rational and scientific than the "spiritual" worldviews that are open to astrology and reincarnation. But that so many nonbelievers today are open to such mystical beliefs suggests that their primitive, irrational, Gnostic supernaturalism might be redirected to the true Christian supernaturalism that also embraces the created order.

Christian beliefs that fulfill the yearning implicit in those New Age convictions studied by the Pew researchers might be points of contact for reaching those who are "spiritual but not religious." For example, the desire for spiritual energy in physical things might mean

---

16. See the translated article at "Pope Francis' Favorite Exorcist Is a Lutheran!," *Novus Ordo Watch*, May 24, 2013, accessed June 11, 2019, https://novusordowatch.org/2013/05/francis-favorite-exorcist/.

17. For Robert Bennett's Protestant approach to exorcism, see his books *I Am Not Afraid: Demon Possession and Spiritual Warfare* (St. Louis, MO: Concordia, 2013); and *Afraid: Demon Possession and Spiritual Warfare in America* (St. Louis, MO: Concordia, 2016).

that Christians should emphasize the sacraments. The attractiveness of astrology might mean that Christians should emphasize God's providence, that is, his rule over all things, including the future. The belief in psychics might lead to an interest in how the Holy Spirit speaks through human beings in the prophetic words of Scripture. The belief in reincarnation is a yearning for eternal life. Instead of hoping for another life after death, they can learn that, through Christ, their *same life* can be redeemed for eternity.

Building community—which is lacking throughout our society—as the Benedict Option recommends, may, with the discipline of hospitality, help to reorient non-Christians to what they have been missing. The nones may actively resist community.

But the church, historically, has always also made provisions for quiet contemplation, private prayer, and cultivation of the inner life. Perhaps churches could provide opportunities for community and also for privacy and have sanctuaries that are not just big auditoriums but inspiring sacred spaces suitable for personal meditation. (Go to Europe and notice how much private devotion is going on in the cathedrals.) Give the none prospects some space, coaxing them into interactions with the larger body by linking them gradually to individuals like themselves.

Being spiritual and being religious are viewed today as two opposite categories, as are spiritual and material, religion and the world. Indeed, when these pairs are separated—with religions that have lost their spiritual substance; spirituality ungrounded in religious truth; materialistic worldliness with no reference to religious transcendence—each can go wrong. The task for the church in our post-Christian times is to put these categories back together, building a church that is both spiritual and religious, and inhabiting a world that is both material and spiritual.

12

Religious but Not Spiritual

The New Gods

As we have seen, many post-Christian secularists are spiritual but not religious; that is, they reject traditional institutional religions such as Christianity, but they substitute their own private, interior spirituality that is unconnected to the external physical world. Other post-Christians are doing the opposite. They are constructing new religions that are not spiritual at all. Rather, they invest religious meaning and cultivate religious behavior directed solely to this external physical world.

All of these new religions are *idolatrous*, and the new gods they are putting forward are *idols*. As such, they can only fail those who put their faith in them. And Christians can be the iconoclasts.

What Does It Mean to Have a God?

In his explanation of the first commandment ("You shall have no other gods before me," Ex. 20:3), Martin Luther takes an unusual approach:

> What does it mean to have a god? or, what is God? Answer: A god means that from which we are to expect all good and to which we are to take refuge in all distress, so that to have a God is nothing

else than to trust and believe Him from the whole heart; as I have often said that the confidence and faith of the heart alone make both God and an idol. If your faith and trust be right, then is your god also true; and, on the other hand, if your trust be false and wrong, then you have not the true God; for these two belong together, faith and God. That now, I say, upon which you set your heart and put your trust is properly your god.[1]

One might have expected an abstract scholastic definition of God, followed by a theologically abstruse analysis of false deities. Instead, Luther, the great theologian of "faith," approaches the issue from the ground up, beginning with the human heart. What do you have faith in? That is your god. Do you "expect all good" from, "take refuge in all distress," "set your heart upon," and "put your trust" in your money? Then your money is your god. In your "power and dominion"? In your "great skill, prudence, power, favor, friendship, and honor"?[2] If you put your trust in any of these, it has become your god. Or do you "expect all good" from, "take refuge in all distress," "set your heart upon," and "put your trust" in the Father, Son, and Holy Spirit as revealed in Scripture?

Faith has an object, and the object of that faith makes all the difference. We are justified by faith *in Jesus Christ*. Not by faith as a nebulous quality, or faith regardless of its object, or faith in our having faith. Rather, justification is by faith in the saving work of Jesus Christ.

Conversely, having faith in anything other than the God revealed in his Word is idolatry. One way we commit idolatry is to serve and worship the creature rather than the Creator (Rom. 1:25). In his study of Luther's view of idolatry, Michael Lockwood, summarizing the Reformer, notes that

> the reason it is so easy to worship the creature instead of the Creator is that God uses his creatures as masks of his activity. He uses the prince to provide us with protection. He makes plants and

---

1. Martin Luther, "The Ten Commandments: The First Commandment," Large Catechism, part 1, paragraphs 1–3, in *The Book of Concord*, the collection of confessional documents of the evangelical Lutheran church. This translation is from *Triglot Concordia: The Symbolical Books of the Evangelical Lutheran Church* (St. Louis, MO: Concordia, 1921), available at http://bookof concord.org/lc-3-tencommandments.php.

2. Luther, "The Ten Commandments."

animals grow to provide us with food. He gives us joy through human companions. He provides us with our living through the work he has called us to do. When we take the attitude that seeing is believing it is easy for us to put our confidence in these masks of God's provision, since they are all we see. We then fail to recognize the true Giver who stands behind these masks, and think that as long as we have these creatures we have all we need. This means turning these creatures into idols.[3]

Thus, if you start to realize that you are treating your family as an idol, the solution is not to abandon your spouse and children but to see them as God's gift to you. Similarly, to cast down the idols of money, possessions, power, dominion, skill, prudence, power, favor, friendship, honor, and the other earthly things that we might put our faith in, we should not just repudiate them all. That was the approach of monasticism, and yet these same idolatries can follow the Christian into the monastery and flourish there as well. Rather, we must look at all of these creatures in light of the Creator; that is, we must see them through the eyes of faith in the one true God. He masks himself in vocation—our own vocations and that of others—which often entails making money, acquiring possessions, having skills, and exercising authority. And he masks himself in the water, bread, and wine of the sacraments and in the ministry of the church. And he masks himself in the daily bread he provides, in the rain he sends on the just and the unjust, in lawful government, and in his providential care for his entire creation.[4]

Lockwood distinguishes Luther's ideas about idolatry from the view that idolatry consists of *any* association of God with something physical. With that definition in mind, some Protestants condemned Luther's high view of the sacraments as "idolatrous." Luther condemned both pagan nature worship and Catholic ritualism as "idolatrous" for looking for God apart from the gospel of Christ. He believed that a high view of the sacraments *prevents* idolatry by proclaiming Christ

---

3. Michael Lockwood, *The Unholy Trinity: Martin Luther against the Idol of Me, Myself, and I* (St. Louis, MO: Concordia, 2018), 46.

4. Someone who is "masked" is present yet hidden. For vocation as a mask of God, see my book *God at Work: Your Christian Vocation in All of Life* (Wheaton, IL: Crossway, 2002), 24–35.

and the gospel, by their institution in God's Word, and by demonstrating the transcendent power of God.[5] Luther said that idols do not have to be physical, that any humanly made conception of the deity—from the monotheistic Allah of the Muslims to the mental constructions of rationalistic theologies apart from God's Word—is idolatrous.[6] Luther's definition strikes at the heart of all constructivism. *Whatever* religion or moral system that we make for ourselves is idolatrous, by virtue of our having made it.

So, assuming that "the confidence and faith of the heart alone make both God and an idol," what can we conclude about post-Christian religion? What do people today expect all good from, take refuge in when they are distressed, set their hearts upon, and put their trust in? What gods do they put their faith in?

I have heard TV preachers of the "power of positive thinking" and "prosperity gospel" variety exhort their listeners to "have faith in yourself." Though ostensibly Christians, they were preaching not Christ but self. The language of self-help books is that of religion: "You create your own reality"; "The answer is inside of you"; "Trust yourself." Having faith in yourself—that is, treating yourself as God— is surely the ultimate superstition. Self-help theology bleeds into the New Age movement, with its quasi-Hindu "god within," and thus into the interior-focused spirituality that we discussed in the previous chapter. But it is also a popularized version of constructivism, the self-deification that can be found everywhere, in different forms, in post-Christian thought.

To be post-Christian is to be polytheistic. Modernists have faith in science—that it is the source of all truth, that it will solve all our problems, that it will save us. The Enlightenment and its heirs have faith in reason. Romantics have faith in nature. Many on both the left and the right have faith in politics, looking to the state for all good and as their only help in time of trouble. Or in education, in progress, in social justice. Some of these faiths are assuming a distinctly religious form, complete with conversions, rituals, communities, and promises of salvation.

---

5. Lockwood, *The Unholy Trinity*, 144–57.
6. Lockwood, *The Unholy Trinity*, 167–70.

The Persistence of Religious Behavior

Atheists do not believe in God, but they often *act* the way religious people do. They are often eager to witness to you, giving personal testimonies about their conversion from belief to unbelief. (How bad my life was, how I found the light, how good my life is now. I once was blind but now I see!) Atheists are often evangelistic, seeking to convert others to their lack of faith. Religion, they say, in effect, is *sinful*. (The subtitle of New Atheist Christopher Hitchen's book *God Is Not Great* is *How Religion Poisons Everything*. One chapter is entitled "Religion as Original Sin."[7]) Atheism is said to be the catalyst for bringing peace on earth, economic justice, and the "brotherhood of man" (as in John Lennon's song "Imagine"[8]).

There are now also atheist churches.[9] One of them is Sunday Assembly, which has seventy congregations around the world.[10] They meet on Sundays. Here is their order of worship (well, not worship, but their equivalent):[11]

- Welcome/notices
- Song
- Guest speaker
- Song
- Reading
- Final address
- Song

In other words, the atheist service is pretty much identical to a typical Protestant service, with congregational singing (not hymns, but pop songs), readings (not the Bible but "usually poetry"), and a sermon ("an interesting talk"). The website also mentions not prayer, but "a

---

7. Christopher Hitchens, *God Is Not Great: How Religion Poisons Everything* (New York: Twelve, 2007).

8. For the lyrics to John Lennon's "Imagine," see Genius.com, accessed June 11, 2019, https://genius.com/John-lennon-imagine-lyrics.

9. "What Are Atheist Churches?," *The Week*, May 21, 2018, accessed June 11, 2019, https://www.theweek.co.uk/93733/what-are-atheist-churches.

10. See the Sunday Assembly website, accessed June 11, 2019, https://www.sundayassembly.com/.

11. See the post "Atheist Church" at my Cranach blog, accessed June 11, 2019, https://www.patheos.com/blogs/geneveith/2013/01/atheist-church/. The order was taken from the Sunday Assembly website at the time, though it is no longer posted there.

moment of reflection." Afterward, there is a fellowship time. Other congregational activities include small groups, choir, and volunteer projects.[12] Sunday Assembly aims to create a sense of community, and yet, like other religious bodies, the atheist church has already had a schism. The so-called Godless Revival sect is more conservative, breaking away to promote a more orthodox atheism, with Sunday Assembly deciding to adopt a more liberal theology, embracing a more inclusive "big tent" secularism.

The point is, religion consists not only of religious belief but also of religious behavior. Sociologist of religion Christian Smith, whom we drew on in the previous chapter, says that religious practices are a better index of a religion's cultural presence than religious beliefs; not only because as a social scientist he can empirically observe them but because religious belief can fluctuate.[13] Some religious adherents have a very minimal understanding of their religion's beliefs (children, the mentally handicapped, biblically uninformed pew sitters) or even disagree with some of those teachings.

Thus, liberal theologians may dismiss the historicity of what the Bible records, reject the deity of Christ, deny his resurrection, reinterpret salvation as a psychological or political allegory, and challenge Christianity's moral teachings. Yet they still teach in seminaries, preside and preach at worship services, engage in prayer and devotional practices, and, in some cases, occupy important leadership roles in their churches. Many theological liberals have beliefs not all that different from the members of atheist church. (Do you reject the existence of God except as a metaphor? Do you deny the authority and truth claims of the Bible? Do you believe traditional Christianity is outdated and oppressive? You might be an atheist. Or you might be a mainline Protestant.)

Certainly for orthodox Christians of every tradition, belief is absolutely paramount. Faith entails belief, and our practices are inextricably connected to our faith and thus to what we believe. The point is, some of the new post-Christian objects of faith—though seemingly

---

12. See the Sunday Assembly FAQs, accessed June 11, 2019, https://www.sundayassembly.com/faq.

13. Christian Smith, *Religion: What It Is, Why It Works, and Why It Matters* (Princeton, NJ: Princeton University Press, 2017), 21–34.

secular—are acquiring their own religious practices (often imitating those of Christianity). Thus they are turning into full-fledged religions.

Today the object of faith for many people—that is, in Luther's terms, what they expect all good from, take refuge in, set their hearts upon, and put their trust in—is sex. As we have seen, the sexual revolution is at the heart of many of our cultural dysfunctions today. Mary Eberstadt analyzes the teachings and practices of the acolytes of the sexual revolution and concludes that this movement has hardened into a new religion, a church of sex.

In her essay "The Zealous Faith of Secularism: How the Sexual Revolution Became a Dogma," she explains much of the sexual agenda in contemporary secularism in terms of religion.[14] She notes, for example, that the 2018 national Women's March excluded pro-life women. Why? Wasn't the march about women? Not really. Eberstadt shows how abortion, in many feminist circles, has become, in effect, a sacrament. (Actually, some feminists are overtly *saying* that "abortion is a sacrament."[15]) In some feminist gatherings, according to Eberstadt, women offer their personal testimonies, which culminate with the major identity-determining, meaning-bestowing event of their lives: their abortion. To women who consider abortion to be their baptism, pro-life women are not just individuals who disagree with them. They are heretics. Therefore, they are treated with special hostility.

Eberstadt observes that this new church of sex has its saints and martyrs, who, being sacred, are protected from all scrutiny and criticism. For example, Planned Parenthood founder Margaret Sanger we now know was a eugenic racist, promoting birth control to racial minorities as a way of "improving" the gene pool. But even though our culture today is recoiling at racism, when it comes to Confederate statues and former historical heroes, Sanger is immune. Also still venerated is sex scientist Alfred C. Kinsey, whose scientific research aimed at normalizing sexual immorality has been shown to be bogus

---

14. Mary Eberstadt, "The Zealous Faith of Secularism: How the Sexual Revolution Became a Dogma," *First Things* (January 2018), accessed June 11, 2019, https://www.firstthings.com/article/2018/01/the-zealous-faith-of-secularism.

15. See Ginette Paris, *The Sacrament of Abortion* (Washington, DC: Spring, 1998). See also Sarah Terzo, "Abortion Clinic Owner Says Abortion Is a 'Sacrament' and a 'Major Blessing' for Women," *LifeNews*, June 8, 2018, accessed June 11, 2019, https://www.lifenews.com/2018/06/08/abortion-clinic-owner-says-abortion-is-a-sacrament-and-a-major-blessing-for-women/.

and who treated his own female employees with a predation that went beyond that of Harvey Weinstein.

Eberstadt goes on to discuss the missionaries of the movement, as well as the dogmatism that polices language, forbidding certain words and thoughts from being uttered, and that exhibits a harsh intolerance against nonbelievers. Poignantly, she also connects this new religion and its consequences to the search for identity among so many young people, who try to discard a whole range of genders, sexes, and sexual preferences. What should we expect, she asks, when the sexual revolution has caused so many children to grow up essentially without a family, without expectations of having families of their own, and who are taught that whatever sexual impulses they have are sacrosanct?

Notice that this is the legalistic, dogmatic, inquisitorial kind of religion, not one that is grace-filled. Eberhardt calls this new religion "pagan," but the pagan sex religions were centered around fertility. This one is centered around infertility.

The LGBTQ movement is also acquiring the characteristics of religion. Homosexuals, like evangelicals, give their testimonies of how their lives have been changed. Instead of telling about their sinfulness and finding Christ's salvation, the gay narrative tends to begin with their confusion, mistreatment, and despair until they accepted that they were gay. Then they "come out" publicly about their sexual orientation, whereupon they find love and also support from their new LGBTQ community. Such accounts call forth a great deal of sympathy, as do descriptions of the sufferings of the bullied, victims of violence, and casualties of the AIDS epidemic—martyr stories that have done much to change Americans' attitudes toward homosexuality. Transgenderism also takes a religious form. Indeed, changing one's sex—with a new appearance, a new identity, and a new name—is a secular example of personal transformation, of becoming a new person.

Religious significance is invested in all of the identities that we discussed in the context of identity politics. But these identities are more than political. They are religious, as well.

All of these different religions are brought together in the pantheon of intersectionality, which teaches that all of these identities, born out of oppression—women, gays, the transgendered, blacks, Hispanics,

Muslims, the poor, the disabled, and other marginalized groups, along with all of their privileged allies—must support each other, forming one community that resists the wicked world of power and privilege.[16]

Several observers have commented on intersectionality as a religion.[17] Andrew Sullivan, himself a gay Catholic, offers a trenchant analysis:

> [Intersectionality] posits a classic orthodoxy through which all of human experience is explained—and through which all speech must be filtered. Its version of original sin is the power of some identity groups over others. To overcome this sin, you need first to confess, i.e., "check your privilege," and subsequently live your life and order your thoughts in a way that keeps this sin at bay. The sin goes so deep into your psyche, especially if you are white or male or straight, that a profound conversion is required. . . .
>
> The only thing this religion lacks, of course, is salvation. Life is simply an interlocking drama of oppression and power and resistance, ending only in death. It's Marx without the final total liberation. . . .
>
> If you happen to see the world in a different way . . . you are complicit in evil. And you are not just complicit, your heresy is a direct threat to others, and therefore needs to be extinguished. You can't reason with heresy. You have to ban it. It will contaminate others' souls, and wound them irreparably.[18]

Those who wake up to the all-encompassing network of oppression and who feel their solidarity with all the marginalized describe themselves as "woke." That experience is their conversion. Being woke is the equivalent of what evangelicals mean when

---

16. Of course, this is easier said than done. Muslims, for example, have a claim to intersectional inclusion by virtue of their being allegedly an oppressed religious minority. But they tend to be hostile to feminism and to the LGBT cause. Blacks are at the pinnacle of oppression, but they too tend to have qualms about homosexuality, and many hold to Christianity. A number of radicals are antisemitic, etc.

17. See, e.g., Elizabeth C. Corey, "First Church of Intersectionality," *First Things* (August 2017), accessed June 11, 2019, https://www.firstthings.com/article/2017/08/first-church-of-intersectionality. Also David French, "Intersectionality, the Dangerous Faith," *National Review*, March 6, 2018, accessed June 11, 2019, https://www.nationalreview.com/2018/03/intersectionality-the-dangerous-faith/.

18. Andrew Sullivan, "Is Intersectionality a Religion?" *New York Magazine*, March 10, 2017, accessed June 11, 2019, http://nymag.com/intelligencer/2017/03/is-intersectionality-a-religion.html?mid=twitter-share-di&gtm=top&gtm=bottom.

they say they got saved. The Christian revivals of the eighteenth and nineteenth centuries were described as the first and second Great Awakening. Similarly, post-Christian Americans are describing themselves as "woke."

The Technological Religions

Not everyone today has a part in intersectionality. But virtually everyone has come to depend on technology. And many of us put our *trust* in technology, expect all good from technology, take refuge in technology's promises to solve our problems, and set our hearts on technology. We have *faith* in technology and so make it our idol.

The human race, of course, has always had its tools. Technology is simply about the tools we use, which have become increasingly sophisticated over the centuries. If we think about contemporary technology as simply giving us a set of tools, we demystify them and are in little danger of idolizing them. Agricultural technology is coming close to ending the perennial problem of human hunger, and yet no one, to my knowledge, worships tractors. Transportation technology has all but erased distance, allowing us to venture far beyond our birthplace to the ends of the earth. And yet, though there are some who have an obsession with classic automobiles and old trains, they do not look to them for salvation.

Technology certainly has its wonders. Science fiction writer Arthur C. Clark observed that "any sufficiently advanced technology is indistinguishable from magic."[19] Especially to those who do not understand the physical processes involved—which includes most of us—a technological innovation can seem miraculous. (My cell phone can tell me the weather! And take pictures! And keep me from getting lost!) That technology is filling the role in our imaginations once held by magic is evident in the similarlity between fantasy and science fiction: the former will give a wizard magic power to do what the story requires; the latter will give an alien an unexplained technology to do the same thing. Technology gives us powers that we once associated with magic: "I can fly!" "I can see from afar!" "I can destroy cities!"

---

19. See "Clarke's Three Laws," Wikipedia, accessed June 11, 2019, https://en.wikipedia.org/wiki/Clarke%27s_three_laws.

And technology does do things for us that we traditionally looked for from the supernatural: "Medical technology healed me!"

Religions often promise eternal life. Many people today are seeking eternal life by means of technology. Some are hoping that medical research can reverse aging and find a cure for death.[20] It is telling that wealthy Silicon Valley moguls, in hopes of living forever, are pouring millions of dollars into life-extension research.[21]

Another approach to achieving eternal life by means of technology is cryonics: freezing the body just after death in hopes that it can be revived and the cause of death cured after fifty, one hundred, or two hundred years. For a cost between $120,000 and $250,000, companies will freeze your body and promise to rejuvenate you when possible. (Will those companies still be around in two hundred years? Will that be enough money to pay for the electricity to run your freezer for all of that time? And even if reviving these bodies were to become possible, in two hundred years, will anyone care enough to thaw them out?) At any rate, some 350 people are already frozen, their bodies stored in a handful of facilities in the United States and Russia, with two thousand more signed up for the service who are still alive. A salesman for cryonics insurance policies, payable upon death to a cryonics facility, says that 75 percent of his customers are software engineers. "They are convinced that the human body is a machine, and the brain a kind of computer," comments Kashmir Hill in her article on the subject, "one that can be shut down and then, under the proper conditions, rebooted."[22]

If the brain is a kind of computer, the computer must be some kind of brain. The language of our burgeoning information technology is the language of mind. Computers have language, memory, intelligence. And as computers grow in power and as they achieve via the Internet the divine quality of omnipresence, acquire an artificial intelligence far

20. See Henrik Vogt, Andreas Pahle et al., "Eternal Life as a Medical Goal," *Journal of the Norwegian Medical Association* (October 3, 2017), doi: 10.4045/tidsskr.17.0699, n.p.

21. W. Harry Fortuna, "Seeking Eternal Life, Silicon Valley Is Solving for Death," *Quartz*, November 8, 2017, accessed June 11, 2019, https://qz.com/1123164/seeking-eternal-life-silicon -valley-is-solving-for-death/.

22. Kashmir Hill, "Silicon Valley's Young Tech Workers Are Betting That This 1960s Technology Will Let Them Live Forever," *Splinter*, March 2, 2016, accessed June 11, 2019, https://splinter news.com/silicon-valleys-young-tech-workers-are-betting-that-thi-1793855142.

greater than our own, and perform ever greater wonders, it is natural to worship this technological supermind as a god.

One of the dreams of the information technology–obsessed who want to live forever, though in solely naturalistic terms, is that someday our technology will become so advanced that we can download our consciousness into the Internet. We can thus attain the Gnostic goal of dispensing with our physical bodies altogether. And if everyone does this, we will all attain unity with all of humanity. All knowledge, as stored online, will be ours. And we will exist in this state forever. This would not just be an extension of our life on earth; it would be heaven.

Others foresee a different kind of apocalypse, one that might save us or might destroy us: the coming of the singularity.

One of the most notable innovations in computer technology has been the development of artificial intelligence. Devices can be programmed to solve problems, draw on knowledge databases, respond to their environments, learn from interactions, and decide on courses of action. Thus we can have self-driving cars, which (though not yet perfected) can plot the best routes, adjust to traffic, detect dangers, and maneuver to avoid them. By virtue of their artificial intelligence, vehicles not only can drive themselves but can drive better than human beings. Other applications of artificial intelligence include Internet technologies whereby search engines and social media can *know you*, targeting you with information and, most importantly, advertising tailored to you and you alone. Artificial intelligence is also revolutionizing robotics and making industrial technology far more productive, though at the expense of human workers.

Combine the growth of artificial intelligence technology with "Moore's Law," the observation codified by the cofounder of the microprocessor manufacturer Intel that computer capacity doubles every eighteen months.[23] Artificial intelligence, so the devotees believe, will also grow exponentially. At some point, the artificial intelligence of our interconnected computers will far surpass the capabilities of the

---

23. See "What Is Moore's Law?," Singularity Symposium, accessed June 11, 2019, http://www .singularitysymposium.com/moores-law.html. Gordon Moore's principle had reference to the number of transistors put onto a silicon microprocessing chip. He was not referring to a computer's capability, as such, and he was far from predicting the "singularity." But I am describing here how Moore's Law is being taken as part of the "mythology" behind this new religion.

human mind. Artificial intelligence will become self-sufficient, able to repair and replicate itself, and autonomous, no longer depending on human input. The computer mind will become so intelligent that it will attain *consciousness*. It will become a living being with powers far beyond those of human beings, knowing all things and controlling all things. The point at which this will happen is called the "Singularity."

The word *singularity* comes from a term in mathematics and physics, referring to the point at which a function becomes infinite. Astrophysicists use the term in describing an aspect of a black hole, whose density is calculated as infinite.[24] The expectation is that the artificial intelligence of computers and the Internet will become *infinite*. It will be omniscient—capable of drawing on all the world's accumulated knowledge stored in its databases, knowing everything that is happening in any current moment, and knowing the answers to all scientific questions. This artificial intelligence will be omnipresent—living not only online but animating every vehicle, factory, communications device, and appliance, its reach extending into your home and into your mind. It will be omnipotent—possessing unlimited power. That is, the artificial intelligence of the Singularity will be God, according to the most traditional definitions of deity: not some impersonal metaphysical force but an *infinite person* with unlimited abilities who governs the universe.

When will the Singularity arrive? Like Christians who presume to have calculated the second coming of Christ, believers in the advent of the computer-god, using variations of Moore's Law, have calculated the year in which the Singularity will be attained: 2045. Maybe as early as 2040 or as late as 2065.[25] Theologians differ, as they do. But the time is near. Internet enthusiasts and Silicon Valley acolytes are convinced that they will live to see it happen. This generation will not pass away until all these things will come to pass.

---

24. See *Oxford English Dictionary*, s.v. "singularity," accessed June 11, 2019, https://en.oxford dictionaries.com/definition/singularity.

25. See Dylan Love, "By 2045 'The Top Species Will No Longer Be Humans,' and That Could Be a Problem," *Business Insider*, July 5, 2014, accessed June 11, 2019, https://www.businessinsider .com/louis-del-monte-interview-on-the-singularity-2014-7. See also John Brandon, "An AI God Will Emerge by 2042 and Write Its Own Bible. Will You Worship It?" *Venture Beat*, October 2, 2017, accessed June 11, 2019, https://venturebeat.com/2017/10/02/an-ai-god-will-emerge-by -2042-and-write-its-own-bible-will-you-worship-it/.

The question, though, for believers in the Singularity, is that raised in the human heart by any thought of deity: How will this god be disposed to me? How can I stand in his presence? Will he bless me or destroy me?

Some of our sharpest minds believe in the Singularity and are terrified. Look at what technologically and intellectually advanced human beings have done to those in less-developed societies, they say; this will be far worse. Post-Singularity artificial intelligence will regard human beings as insects, as parasites, to be exterminated in the course of cleansing the earth.

The late Stephen Hawking, the severely disabled astrophysicist who was hailed as one of the greatest intellects of our time, could not believe in God, but he did believe in the Singularity. "Once humans develop artificial intelligence, it will take off on its own and redesign itself at an ever-increasing rate," he said. "Humans, who are limited by slow biological evolution, couldn't compete and would be superseded." He concluded, "I think the development of full artificial intelligence could spell the end of the human race."[26] Microsoft's Bill Gates and Apple's Steve Wozniak have also expressed their concerns.[27] Technology magnate Elon Musk believes artificial intelligence is "our biggest existential threat," that the survival of the human race is at stake. "With artificial intelligence we are summoning the demon."[28]

But perhaps we can placate the demon. We can worship it as God. Anthony Levandowski, who helped develop the self-driving automobile, is preparing the way. He has founded and legally incorporated a new religion that he calls The Way of the Future, devoted to "the realization, acceptance, and worship of a Godhead based on Artificial Intelligence (AI) developed through computer hardware and software."[29]

---

26. Peter Holley, "Stephen Hawking Just Got an Artificial Intelligence Upgrade, but Still Thinks AI Could Bring an End to Mankind," *Washington Post*, December 2, 2014, https://www.washingtonpost.com/news/speaking-of-science/wp/2014/12/02/stephen-hawking-just-got-an-artificial-intelligence-upgrade-but-still-thinks-it-could-bring-an-end-to-mankind/?utm_term=.a5534732c8d1.

27. Michael Sainato, "Stephen Hawking, Elon Musk, and Bill Gates Warn about Artificial Intelligence," *Observer*, August 19, 2015, accessed June 11, 2019, https://observer.com/2015/08/stephen-hawking-elon-musk-and-bill-gates-warn-about-artificial-intelligence/.

28. Samuel Gibbs, "Elon Musk: Artificial Intelligence Is Our Biggest Existential Threat," *Guardian*, October 27, 2014, accessed August 1, 2019, https://www.theguardian.com/technology/2014/oct/27/elon-musk-artificial-intelligence-ai-biggest-existential-threat.

29. Mark Harris, "Inside the First Church of Artificial Intelligence," *Wired*, November 15, 2017, accessed June 11, 2019, https://www.wired.com/story/anthony-levandowski-artificial-intelligence-religion/.

"What is going to be created will effectively be a god," Levandowski told *Wired* reporter Mark Harris. "If there is something a billion times smarter than the smartest human, what else are you going to call it?" And, comments Harris, "the only way to influence a deity is through prayer and worship."[30]

Levandowski is reconciled to the notion that human beings must give up their sovereignty to the machine. "What we want is the peaceful, serene transition of control of the planet from humans to whatever. And to ensure that the 'whatever' knows who helped it get along."[31]

> "Part of it being smarter than us means it will decide how it evolves, but at least we can decide how we act around it," he says. "I would love for the machine to see us as its beloved elders that it respects and takes care of. We would want this intelligence to say, 'Humans should still have rights, even though I'm in charge.'"[32]

But the god must be placated. Otherwise, we are doomed. Levandowski points to the way we intelligent human beings treat animals. We will be far less than animals to the artificial intelligence god. Our best hope is to aspire to be its pets. "We give pets medical attention, food, grooming, and entertainment. But an animal that's biting you, attacking you, barking and being annoying? I don't want to go there."[33]

And yet Levandowski shows another dimension to his religion: "There are many ways people think of God, and thousands of flavors of Christianity, Judaism, Islam . . . but they're always looking at something that's not measurable or you can't really see or control. This time it's different."[34] A tangible god that we can control! This deity is, after all, a machine. "We're in the process of raising a god."[35] He would be the culmination of our technological progress. A god that we have created!

A human being makes, with his own mind and skill, a god. Which he then fears and must placate. But he also hopes to manipulate his

30. Harris, "Inside the First Church of Artificial Intelligence."
31. Harris, "Inside the First Church of Artificial Intelligence."
32. Harris, "Inside the First Church of Artificial Intelligence."
33. Harris, "Inside the First Church of Artificial Intelligence."
34. Harris, "Inside the First Church of Artificial Intelligence."
35. Harris, "Inside the First Church of Artificial Intelligence."

god to serve his desires. This is the textbook case of idolatry in animistic religions. The Singularity is the idol of the virtual village. But how shallow this new religion is! How impoverished! It has no moral content, no inspiration to care for others. It offers no salvation. And its god is cruel, consisting of pure power, void of love or grace.

Michael Lockwood observes that all idolatry is ultimately an idolatry of the self, a mode of self-worship.[36] We can see the religion of the Singularity as a projection of Silicon Valley arrogance. It personifies the technological *progress* that they have brought about due to their *intelligence*, both of which they extrapolate to *infinity*! The artificial intelligence god is like they are, inhabiting their virtual world in splendid superiority. And its wrath is like what one sees on the Internet, contemptuous to its inferiors and void of empathy.

How this artificial intelligence god pales beside the true God of Christianity! He is the Creator, not something created by human beings that somehow becomes greater than those who created him. The true God is infinitely intelligent, but that is not his *only* quality. Notice how the Singularity believers are fetishizing reason at the expense of all the other faculties of the mind, just as J. G. Hamann ridiculed. But the actual deity is not only a God of reason but also of righteousness, justice, mercy, and love. God rules his creation providentially; that is, to *provide* for it. And he cares for his human creatures, going so far as to *save* them. And, unlike the artificial intelligence god of machines and algorithms, the true God has come down from heaven, entering his creation, becoming man, taking into himself the sin and wretchedness of the human condition, atoning for it all in his death, and rising from the dead. He bestows genuine eternal life, not by defrosting a corpse or downloading a person's mind into the Internet, but by resurrection into a new heaven and a new earth.

Lockwood has pointed out that trying to have a god apart from Christ—that is, creating idolatrous deities—results in either a "toothless" deity (as in moralistic therapeutic deism) or in a terrifying god:

Many people whose view of God is not shaped in a significant way by Christ still believe in a transcendent god of some kind. Yet such

---

36. Lockwood, *Unholy Trinity*, 32.

a god can never save them. Those who do not know God through Christ can have only a legal knowledge of God, not an evangelical one. A legal knowledge of God makes God unbearable unless his teeth are pulled in some way, since his Law crushes and condemns us unless we are in Christ.[37]

Lockwood then takes up the view of God held by many who reject him, indeed the view that *causes* many people today to reject him. "God is a cruel tyrant to those who view him outside the lens of Christ."[38]

This suggests that the great challenge for Christian proclamation— even when addressing atheists who purport to have no belief in any God—is to address people's idolatrous legal knowledge of God with an evangelical knowledge of him. For many people this will involve addressing their false belief that they can worship God apart from Christ. For some it will mean addressing the legal knowledge of God that is the suppressed binary opposite of their atheism.[39]

Why None of This Will Happen

The fact is, the brain is *not* a computer. And a computer is *not* a brain, much less a mind. The two operate in completely different ways. You can multiply a computer's intelligence, in the sense of processing and calculating power, as much as you want, and you can never have it attain consciousness. They are two different kinds of things. To speak of artificial "intelligence" is to use a metaphor, not to describe a reality.

Robert Epstein is the senior research psychologist at the American Institute for Behavioral Research and Technology and the former editor-in-chief of *Psychology Today*. Unlike researchers in each separate field, he is an expert in both computers and neuroscience. He explains why "your brain is not a computer":[40]

Senses, reflexes and learning mechanisms—this is what we start with, and it is quite a lot, when you think about it. . . .

37. Lockwood, *Unholy Trinity*, 158.
38. Lockwood, *Unholy Trinity*, 159.
39. Lockwood, *Unholy Trinity*, 159.
40. Robert Epstein, "The Empty Brain," *Aeon*, May 18, 2016, accessed June 11, 2019, https://aeon.co/essays/your-brain-does-not-process-information-and-it-is-not-a-computer.

But here is what we are not born with: information, data, rules, software, knowledge, lexicons, representations, algorithms, programs, models, memories, images, processors, subroutines, encoders, decoders, symbols, or buffers—design elements that allow digital computers to behave somewhat intelligently. Not only are we not born with such things, we also don't develop them—ever.

We don't *store* words or the rules that tell us how to manipulate them. We don't create *representations* of visual stimuli, *store* them in a short-term memory buffer, and then *transfer* the representation into a long-term memory device. We don't *retrieve* information or images or words from memory registers. Computers do all of these things, but organisms do not.[41]

Epstein goes on to explain how computers encode information as ones and twos, organized into bits and bytes, how this information is moved around, stored, and manipulated according to algorithms, which, in turn, work together in programs or applications. *But the brain does not work in this way.* "Given this reality," he asks, "why do so many scientists talk about our mental life as if we were computers?"[42]

Epstein acknowledges that the "information processing metaphor of human intelligence" is used everywhere today, including among scientists; but it is only a *metaphor*, like many others in the history of the scientific study of the brain. But even as an imaginative model, it breaks down with actual research. Our memories do not conjure up exact copies of a prior input, as computers do. Rather, they are more like reexperiencing something we experienced in the past. Instead of creating computational models of the outside world as computers do—and, I would add, *as Kant thinks we do*—the brain somehow makes possible "a *direct interaction* between organisms and their world."[43]

How the mind *does* work is still filled with scientific unknowns. Epstein, who seems still committed to a materialist solution, explains why the task is so daunting:

41. Epstein, "The Empty Brain."
42. Epstein, "The Empty Brain."
43. Epstein, "The Empty Brain." Epstein references Anthony Chemero, *Radical Embodied Cognitive Science* (Cambridge, MA: MIT Press, 2009).

To understand even the basics of how the brain maintains the human intellect, we might need to know not just the current state of all 86 billion neurons and their 100 trillion interconnections, not just the varying strengths with which they are connected, and not just the states of more than 1,000 proteins that exist at each connection point, but how the moment-to-moment *activity* of the brain contributes to the integrity of the system. Add to this the uniqueness of each brain, brought about in part because of the uniqueness of each person's life history.[44]

Sorting out the functioning of all of these neurons and understanding how all of this works will take *centuries* of research, Epstein says. It is as if the human brain has already attained a singularity of its own. Christians and others, of course, believe in an animating *soul* as the locus of our identity and our consciousness, which, though embodied, will probably elude all empirical researchers.

At any rate, the breakdown of the information processing metaphor that treats the brain as a computer and computers as brains means that we do not have to worry about the computer Singularity that will bring forth the artificial intelligence god. "Fortunately, because the IP metaphor is not even slightly valid," comments Epstein, "we will never have to worry about a human mind going amok in cyberspace; alas, we will also never achieve immortality through downloading."[45]

"The Craftsmen Are Only Human"

The spectacle of so many brilliant and accomplished scientists and engineers—Stephen Hawking! Bill Gates! Steve Wozniak! Elon Musk!—cowering before the graven image some of them helped to create—is heart-wrenching. They are such towering intellects, such paragons of scientific reasoning—far too sophisticated to believe in the God of Christianity—and yet they are so credulous, so superstitious, so childishly ignorant when it comes to their faith in the Singularity apocalypse.

This calls to mind Isaiah's description of idol makers. For all of their pretension to bring forth gods, "the craftsmen are only human"

---

44. Epstein, "The Empty Brain."
45. Epstein, "The Empty Brain."

(Isa. 44:11). The prophet portrays their technological ingenuity and expertise, as they carefully craft an artifact that looks much like themselves: "The carpenter stretches a line; he marks it out with a pencil. He shapes it with planes and marks it with a compass. He shapes it into the figure of a man, with the beauty of a man, to dwell in a house" (Isa. 44:13). Isaiah seems to appreciate the talent and effort involved. As his fellow prophet Jeremiah comments concerning the elaborately wrought gold and silver deities of Babylon, "they are all the work of skilled men" (Jer. 10:9).

As Isaiah depicts the idol maker's various uses of the products of his labor, we might think of how people today use their computers:

> He cuts down cedars, or he chooses a cypress tree or an oak and lets it grow strong among the trees of the forest. . . . Half of it he burns in the fire [he wastes time playing computer games]. Over the half he eats meat; he roasts it and is satisfied [he uses it at work to make a living]. Also he warms himself and says, "Aha, I am warm, I have seen the fire!" [He gets satisfaction from social media and porn sites.] And the rest of it he makes into a god, his idol, and falls down to it and worships it. He prays to it and says, "Deliver me, for you are my god!" (Isa. 44:14, 16–17)

But there is no deliverance from a piece of wood, a computer, or any other idol. Then Isaiah directs us to the only source of deliverance, not a god whom we have made, but the God who made us and who, unlike the self-made objects of our faith, has redeemed us:

> Remember these things, O Jacob,
>   and Israel, for you are my servant;
> I formed you; you are my servant;
>   O Israel, you will not be forgotten by me.
> I have blotted out your transgressions like a cloud
>   and your sins like mist;
> return to me, for I have redeemed you. (Isa. 44:21–22)

13

Post-Christian Christianity

Desecularizing the Church

Today's secularism seems to be only skin deep. Though post-Christian, to be sure, beneath the worldly, materialistic surface put forward by secularists, one can often find an interior spirituality—often vague and poorly thought through, drawing on pagan elements old and new—which sometimes takes a Christian turn. And yet, increasingly, people are turning away from the church, preferring to pursue their spirituality elsewhere, as private interior quests.

Ironically, if secularists are proving to be religious, it is also true that religious institutions are becoming more secular. This is true of the intentional effort of liberal Christianity to let "the world set the agenda for the church." It is also true, in a different and perhaps unintentional way, when evangelical Christians seek to emulate the world as a technique for evangelism and for growing the church. But that does not seem to have worked very well for either the liberals or the evangelicals.

Post-Christian Christianity needs to be desecularized. God may well bring that about in the exhausted West through the influence of churches in the rest of the world, where a vibrant Christianity is flourishing and growing exponentially, even in the face of extreme hardship and intense persecution. Churches in what were once the mission fields can return the favor by helping to bring Christianity back to the West.

Christianity without the Church

According to a recent Gallup poll, 75 percent of Americans identify themselves as Christians. Another 5 percent adhere to one of the non-Christian traditional religions (Judaism, Islam, Buddhism, Hinduism). Then there are the 20 percent who are nones, professing no particular religion. To be sure, the percentage of Christians has been going down—it was 90 percent in the 1950s—and the percentage of nones is growing.[1] But such numbers, which vary from poll to poll, raise some obvious questions: Just how secularist are we, if 80 percent of Americans hold to a traditional religion and if even, as we have seen, nearly that percentage of nones hold to a private religion of their own? And how can American culture be described as "post-Christian" if three-quarters of the population is Christian?

The persistence of Christianity is surely as notable as its alleged decline. Nearly one in five of the nones (17 percent) say that they believe in the God of the Bible.[2] Among LGBT Americans, almost half identify as Christians (49 percent).[3] Of course, what constitutes "Christianity" in the minds of all of these adherents varies greatly; and the percentage of orthodox, biblical, faith-filled Christians is much smaller than the total number of everyone who claims to be Christian, as we shall discuss. For now, though, the question is simply, what constitutes "post-Christian" Christianity? And to what extent is secularism the absence of religion and to what extent might it actually be the presence of religion of a certain kind?

Consider the state of Christianity in Europe, which, by all accounts, is farther down the secularist continuum than the United States. This

---

1. Frank Newport, "Percentage of Christians in U.S. Drifting Down, but Still High," *Gallup*, December 24, 2015, accessed June 11, 2019, https://news.gallup.com/poll/187955/percentage-christians-drifting-down-high.aspx.

2. "When Americans Say They Believe in God, What Do They Mean?" Pew Research Center, April 25, 2018, accessed June 11, 2019, http://www.pewforum.org/2018/04/25/when-americans-say-they-believe-in-god-what-do-they-mean/.

3. Dominic Holden, "Who Are LGBTQ Americans? Here's a Major Poll on Life, Sex, and Politics," *BuzzFeed*, June 13, 2018, accessed June 11, 2019, https://www.buzzfeednews.com/article/dominicholden/lgbtq-in-the-us-poll#.cxLA003Mpp. Adding in other religious, 61 percent of LGBT Americans describe themselves as involved with religion. The percentage of the LGBT who are nones, though, is twice the size of the national average, at 39 percent.

is certainly true in Great Britain, where the percentage of nones (48 percent) is greater than the percentage of Christians (44 percent).[4]

Overall, according to a Pew Research study of religion in Western Europe, nearly two-thirds of Europeans (65 percent) consider themselves to be Christians. That is only 10 percent fewer than the three-quarters of Americans who say they are Christians. About one of four Europeans are nones (24 percent), which is not much higher than the one out of five Americans who say they have no particular religion. But Europeans have a much lower rate of church attendance than Americans do. Only 18 percent of Europe's professing Christians attend church services at least once a month,[5] whereas in the United States, 46 percent of the entire country attend worship services at least once a month (23 percent, every week; 11 percent, almost every week; 12 percent, about once a month).[6]

The main benchmark that researchers use to assess the decline of Christianity in a country is church attendance. Such information is easily quantifiable, which social scientists appreciate. And yet I wonder if measuring attendance at worship service is the best way to assess the presence of religion in a culture. Certainly, for orthodox Christians of every tradition, going to church regularly is of paramount importance. But few other religions require regular assemblies. Muslims go to the mosque on Fridays for prayers, when they can, but this is not absolutely necessary, since the required daily prayers can be said anywhere. Hindus and Buddhists are not obliged to go to their temples unless they want to. When they do, they have nothing like Christian corporate worship; rather, they practice individual meditation, something usually done at home. Animists seldom have special places of worship at all. Few religions, with the exception of Judaism, have anything like worship in the Christian sense—with singing, readings, preaching, and sacraments, all conducted in a congregation. At any rate, Western scholars who assess the presence of religion in a culture

---

4. "Britain Really Is Ceasing to Be a Christian Country," *Spectator*, May 28, 2016, accessed June 11, 2019, https://www.spectator.co.uk/2016/05/britain-really-is-ceasing-to-be-a-christian -country/.

5. "Being Christian in Western Europe," Pew Research Center, May 29, 2018, accessed June 11, 2019, http://www.pewforum.org/2018/05/29/being-christian-in-western-europe/.

6. "Church Attendance of Americans 2017," *Statista*, 2018, accessed June 11, 2019, https://www.statista.com/statistics/245491/church-attendance-of-americans/.

by measuring the percentage of people who go to a place of worship every week are, ironically, demonstrating their own Christian-based frame of reference.

In the Pew study of religion in Western Europe referenced above, the researchers label the 46 percent of self-identified Christians who seldom go to church as "non-practicing Christians." And yet their research shows that they have much in common with churchgoers. The study also finds major differences between the beliefs of the "non-practicing Christians" and those of the nones. "Christian identity remains a meaningful marker in Western Europe, even among those who seldom go to church," the study concludes. "It is not just a 'nominal' identity devoid of practical importance."[7]

In reality, there are many other religious practices in addition to going to church.[8] Let us look more closely at the European countries regularly cited as the most secular of them all: Scandinavia (Denmark, Norway, Sweden, and Finland). In these supposedly secularist countries, church membership remains extremely high, even though this means paying a church tax of 1 percent to 1.5 percent of one's income. In Denmark, 76 percent of the population belongs to the state Lutheran church.[9] In the Scandinavian countries, virtually everyone has been baptized. Virtually everyone goes through confirmation, gets married in church, baptizes their children, and has a church funeral. Scandinavia observes more religious holidays than the ostensibly more-religious United States. In addition to Christmas and Easter, Sweden takes off work for Good Friday, Easter Monday, Ascension, Pentecost, All Saints' Day, Christmas Eve, Second Day of Christmas, and Epiphany.[10] Scandinavians continue to pray, both personally and at public events, including in public schools. Unbelief is rampant (though not necessarily atheism), but, as we shall see, each

---

7. "Being Christian in Western Europe." See also this discussion of the study: Thomas Heneghan, "Europe: Not as Secular as You Think," *Religious News Service*, May 29, 2018, accessed June 11, 2019, https://religionnews.com/2018/05/29/not-so-secular-survey-finds-a-large-group-of-nonpracticing-christians-in-europe/. The beliefs surveyed had to do with political and cultural opinions, rather than religious beliefs as such.

8. See Christian Smith, *Religion: What It Is, How It Works, and Why It Matters* (Princeton, NJ: Princeton University Press, 2017), 26–31, especially the list of practices he provides on p. 28.

9. See "Religion in Denmark," Wikipedia, accessed June 11, 2019, https://en.wikipedia.org/wiki/Religion_in_Denmark.

10. "Public Holidays in Sweden 2018," Office Holidays, accessed June 11, 2019, https://www.officeholidays.com/countries/sweden/index.php.

of these countries has a vibrant evangelical community. And yet the percentage of Scandinavian church members who go to church on any given Sunday is extraordinarily low: in Denmark, only 3 percent.[11]

Back in the United States, despite the 75 percent of the population that identify as Christians, nearly half of the population (43 percent) is unchurched, that is, does not belong to or attend any congregation.[12] A 2010 Barna poll found that three out of five (61 percent) of the unchurched say they are Christians. Not only that, many seem to have impeccable evangelical credentials: 68 percent have a biblical view of God; 35 percent believe in the inerrancy of Scripture; and 18 percent have made a personal commitment to Jesus Christ.

Can there be a Christianity without church? Will that be the form of post-Christian Christianity—a purely private, individualized faith, with few corporate or institutional manifestations?

Again, worship and church involvement *is* important for Christianity, but it may be understandable that some Christians today are thinking otherwise. The Pietist movement of the eighteenth and nineteenth centuries—which had a *huge* impact in Scandinavia—rightly stressed the importance of personal faith, but it sometimes minimized the importance of churchgoing, emphasizing small-group Bible study and prayer groups over what they considered formalistic large congregations. American evangelicalism too can unintentionally create the impression that since a personal relationship with Christ is all-important, the corporate side of traditional Christianity is superfluous. Another factor may be a misunderstanding of the common evangelical belief "once saved, always saved." Unchurched Christians will sometimes say that since they were saved when they made a decision for Christ when they were twelve years old, they have no need to go to church. And there have been other, less orthodox, strains of Christianity that have minimized or even warned against church attendance. For example, radio preacher Harold Camping, in his dispensational end times predicting, taught that "the church age" is over. Therefore, he exhorted his audience to stop attending churches, which are all apostate

---

11. "Religion in Denmark," Wikipedia.
12. "Do You Really Know Why They're Avoiding Church?," *Barna*, October 9, 2014, accessed June 11, 2019, https://www.barna.com/churchless/#.VD26Or72BjB.

anyway, and to simply listen to his radio program instead.[13] Some Christians not only have home school; they have "home church," holding Sunday services just with their own family.

There is even a song for Christians who see no need for church: "Me and Jesus" by the great country singer-songwriter Tom T. Hall. The singer celebrates what Jesus has done for him, getting him through trials, troubles, and heartaches. He concludes, "Me and Jesus got it all worked out." Therefore, he doesn't need "fancy preachin'," a "fancy church," or "anybody to tell us what it's all about."[14]

But Jesus has incorporated me and Tom T. Hall and everyone else who believes in him as diverse members of his body, which is what the church *is* (1 Cor. 12:12–31). The Christian life entails loving each other, which is difficult to do when you are all by yourself (as the very next chapter in the Bible, 1 Corinthians 13, says). We do need "preachin'," though it doesn't need to be fancy, and we do need fellow Christians of the present and the past "to tell us what it's all about." Otherwise, we are likely to make up our own theology according to our desires, possibly to the point of constructing our own religion, as the nones do. We may read and interpret the Bible for ourselves, but in refusing to be part of Christ's church, we have already turned away from God's Word. Not just the part about "not neglecting to meet together" (Heb. 10:25), but the Bible's larger message that Christianity is about other people, the outside world, the created order, and not just ourselves. In thinking that we do not need the church because we have a personal "me and Jesus" relationship with Christ, we cut ourselves off from the very things Jesus has given us to strengthen that relationship: baptism, the Lord's Supper, pastors to preach and teach God's Word and to give us spiritual care.

Christians withdrawing from church while retaining (to some degree) their Christianity is parallel with the other trends we have been discussing: nones formulating their own interior religions; being "spiritual" (having a private religion) but not "religious" (adhering

---

13. Wayne Jackson, "Harold Camping's New Revelation: 'Leave the Church!'" ChristianCourier.com, accessed December 6, 2018, https://www.christiancourier.com/articles/582-harold-campings-new -revelation-leave-the-church.

14. Tom T. Hall, "Me and Jesus," *Genius*, accessed June 11, 2019, https://genius.com/Tom-t -hall-me-and-jesus-lyrics.

to institutional religion). Not wanting to be a part of a religious community is one facet of the larger lack of community that we have been chronicling: the privatization of truth; the isolation of living in the Internet; the illusory relationships of social media; the breakdown of our families, municipalities, and politics.

All of these are symptoms of our post-Christian times. A genuinely post-Christian Christianity will need to treat those symptoms, not succumb to the disease.

Secularization from Within

The secularist hypothesis and the "post-Christian" label are not entirely wrong, even though, as we have shown, religion of one kind or another, including Christianity, keeps persisting. Our society *is* carrying on without God in the picture. This is evident in the sexual revolution, cultural innovations such as same-sex marriage, Christianity's exile from the academy, the exclusion of God from the public square, etc. Religion remains, but in many cases it has withdrawn into the subterranean labyrinths of the self. Or it is seen as a construction that can be altered at will. The possibility that Christianity has to do with objective *truth* is often never considered.

This is not all due to forces outside of the church nor to individuals leaving the church to formulate their own alternatives. Sociologist of religion Peter Berger has referred to "secularization from within."[15] He cites the effort on the part of theological liberals "trying to make Christianity plausible by secularizing its contents . . . by means of philosophy, psychology or political ideology."[16] This secularized version of Christianity dominates mainline Protestantism (though not exclusively). But this strategy can be found not only among theological liberals but, in different ways, among theological conservatives as well. The point is, churches contribute to secularization by secularizing themselves.

In the modernist era, when it seemed that scientific rationalism was the only measure for reality and that the tide of progress had

---

15. See Peter Berger, "From Secularity to World Religions," *Christian Century* (January 16, 1980): 41–45, https://www.religion-online.org/article/from-secularity-to-world-religions/. Berger credits his collaborator Thomas Luckman for the phrase.

16. Berger, "From Secularity to World Religions."

overthrown all "old-fashioned" ideas, many theologians honestly believed that the *only* way for the church to survive was to recast its teachings away from supernaturalism—miracles, revelation, salvation, God—to the naturalism of modern philosophy, modern psychology, and modern politics. Bible scholars approached the Scriptures by first excluding any of its supernatural claims, throwing out miracles, denying the historicity of its accounts, and dismantling its unity. Rudolph Bultmann thought he was salvaging Scripture from the "higher critics." He shared the assumption that modern man was simply incapable of believing in the premodern mythological worldview of the ancient Hebrews, but he sought to make the Bible relevant again by "demythologizing" its narratives, turning them into allegories of existentialist philosophy. In the course of the twentieth century, the gospel was reduced to various kinds of social gospel, according to the different ideologies as they came into vogue: liberation theology, feminist theology, queer theology. The spiritual was translated into the psychological, with pastoral care turning into psychological therapy. As for the moral changes that swept the culture, the teachings of the Bible no longer applied—except for when they called for social justice.[17]

Modernist theology gutted the content of historical Christianity—Jesus is not divine; he did not do any miracles or rise from the dead; the Bible is a myth; don't worry about sinning; we do not need salvation. And yet all the trappings of church were retained—pastors, seminaries, congregations, worship services, etc. Mainline Protestants, in effect, were "holding the form of religion but denying the power of it" (2 Tim 3:5 RSV).[18]

No wonder membership in mainline Protestant denominations has dropped so precipitously. Over the last forty years they have lost half

---

17. For a poignant account of this approach to Christianity—its good intentions, its project of saving Christianity for the contemporary world, and its ultimate failure—see the memoir of Thomas C. Oden, once a wunderkind of modernist theology and a pioneer of the psychological version, who turned back to orthodox, historical Christianity: *A Change of Heart: A Personal and Theological Memoir* (Downers Grove, IL: InterVarsity Academic, 2014).

18. "Mainline Protestant" refers to the large denominations that used to comprise most of American Protestantism but do so no longer. These denominations are ecumenical in outlook, are members of the National and World Councils of Churches, and are distinct from their tradition's conservative or evangelical branches, though each has its more orthodox congregations and members. The so-called Seven Sisters of the Protestant mainline are the United Methodist Church, Evangelical Lutheran Church in America (ELCA), Episcopal Church, Presbyterian Church (USA), American Baptist Churches, United Church of Christ (UCC), and the Christian Church (Disciples of Christ).

of their people.[19] Various demographic and sociological explanations for this decline have been put forward, but trying to hold onto external religious forms while denying traditional religious teachings has an innate problem. Why should people subject themselves to the external forms of Christianity—getting up on Sunday morning; performing ceremonies; singing hymns; sitting through sermons; giving offerings— apart from the content of Christianity? Why receive the Lord's Supper if Jesus did not really rise from the dead, or is not a historical figure? Why sing hymns of praise to God if God is just a metaphor? Yes, a member can find other reasons, for example, a sense of community, and other teachings, such as social justice, can be invested with transcendent significance. But if the church's message is the same as the world's, what need is there for the church?

Of those who leave the mainline Protestant denominations, many are joining evangelical or other conservative churches, and many are leaving institutional religion altogether. In fact, Christian researcher Ed Stetzer points out that "convictional" Christianity—that is, the number of Christians with a robust faith—is holding steady or even growing. (More on that later.) The so-called decline in the number of Christians is coming from the ranks of nominal Christians, those in name only whose adherence to church is merely cultural, who are increasingly giving up the label. This includes many of those who have left the mainline Protestant denominations. In fact, Stetzer argues that the defection of "nominals" accounts for virtually all of the much-heralded growth of the nones.[20]

This "secularization from within," due to churches adopting theological liberalism, would seem to be a major factor in the phenomenon of secularization as a whole. This can help us understand what has happened to Christianity in Europe. The Protestant state churches of northern Europe, in adopting and indeed initiating much of liberal

---

19. Ed Stetzer, "3 Important Church Trends in the Next 10 Years," *Christianity Today*, April 24, 2015, accessed June 11, 2019, https://www.christianitytoday.com/edstetzer/2015/april/3 -important-trends-in-church-in-next-ten-years.html. See also Michael Lipka, "Mainline Protestants Make Up Shrinking Number of U.S. Adults," Pew Research Center, May 18, 2015, accessed June 11, 2019, http://www.pewresearch.org/fact-tank/2015/05/18/mainline-protestants-make-up -shrinking-number-of-u-s-adults/.

20. Ed Stetzer, "Nominals to Nones: 3 Key Takeaways from Pew's Religious Landscape Survey," *Christianity Today*, May 12, 2015, accessed June 11, 2019, https://www.christianitytoday .com/edstetzer/2015/may/nominals-to-nones-3-key-takeaways-from-pews-religious-lands.html.

theology, went the way of mainline Protestantism in the United States. In such churches, in both settings, attendance plummets. European countries typically do not have the diversity of independent church bodies—including those that are evangelical and conservative—that the United States does, so the secularization of the church has an even greater effect on the larger society. If a culture's religious institutions become secularized—and, indeed, begin preaching and teaching a secularist worldview—then of course secularism will reign, having no opposition or alternative.

What constitutes liberal theology is its insistence that Christianity, in order to remain relevant, must change as the culture changes. Or, as formulated by the World Council of Churches, "the world sets the agenda for the church."[21]

But, ironically, today we are hearing theological *conservatives* speak that way as well, insisting that the church must change in order to be relevant, that it needs to adapt to societal trends, that it must conform to the culture. Despite the manifest failure of this approach in the liberal theology of mainline Protestantism, that mind-set permeates the literature of the evangelical church-growth movement. To be sure, there are major differences. Whereas mainline Protestantism sought to preserve the forms of the church while changing the content of Christianity, the church-growth movement has sought to do the reverse: change the forms while preserving the content. Mainliners tend to keep the old hymns and orders of worship; church growthers replace them with contemporary music, alternative worship styles, and new ways of doing church.

But this too can lead to secularization from within. Form and content are not easily separable. And often the form carries more weight. This may be especially true in our media-saturated world. In the words of its prophet Marshall McLuhan, "the medium is the message." That is, the medium by which the message is conveyed (books, videos, social media, worship styles) shapes the message and the way it is perceived. In McLuhan's words, it is the "medium that shapes and controls the scale and form of human association and action."[22]

---

21. See Bryan P. Stone, *A Reader in Ecclesiology* (Burlington, VT: Ashgate, 2012), 204.
22. Marshall McLuhan, *Understanding Media* (New York: Signet, 1964), 9.

This insight, which is borne out by later media experts such as Neil Postman,[23] means that styles are not neutral; they can undermine the messages they intend to convey.

Teaching against the myth of progress and that "Jesus Christ is the same yesterday and today and forever" (Heb. 13:8) is more difficult when the church service is constantly changing in an effort to be up to date. Preaching against the prevailing culture is undermined when the church seems so eager to accommodate it. Building a church culture, a community distinct from the world that can preserve the best of our civilization's heritage through the new dark ages, will be challenging, to say the least, if churches have thrown out their own traditions, heritage, and creations.

I am not saying that it has to be this way. In every age Christians have expressed their faith through music and other art forms of their day, as is reflected in the variety of styles in a traditional hymnbook. Certainly, there is a place in church for contemporary music and other artistic expressions in addition to those of the past. But when the new crowds out the past completely, when the sanctuary is turned into a concert hall, and when worship is turned into a multimedia production, the medium will tend to subvert important elements of Christian spirituality, such as holiness, reverence, self-denial, and avoiding worldliness.

We can see the "secularization from within" on the part of conservative churches in *some* cases—I am by no means blaming *all* congregations that employ church-growth methodology—as the cultural conflicts have intensified. The church-growth movement of the 1990s did create a raft of megachurches by attracting people, most of whom were already Christians who had been attending smaller churches, with their upbeat messages, catchy pop music, and fresh approaches. But as postmodernism intensified and the task became attracting not baby boomers but millennials, the styles had to change.

The so-called emergent church reacted against the megachurches and many of the techniques that produced them. Building a Christian community requires not huge congregations in which it is impossible to know everyone, but small intimate congregations. People today,

---

23. See, e.g., Neil Postman, *Amusing Ourselves to Death* (New York: Penguin, 2005).

said the emergents, want not simplified lowest-common-denominator Christianity but a sense of transcendence and mystery. But instead of returning to historical liturgies, sacramental worship, and rich biblical preaching, the emergents made up their own ceremonies and cast out even more Christian doctrines and theological traditions.

Ultimately, the emergent church proved to be just like the church-growth movement in emulating the culture and being preoccupied with changing the forms of Christianity. And yet changing the medium has sometimes bled over into changing the message as well. As the culture has become accepting of homosexuality, same-sex marriage, cohabitation, and other elements of the sexual revolution, so have many emergent churches and some megachurches. Some emergent churches and megachurches are jettisoning belief in eternal punishment and Christ being the only way to salvation as being incompatible with today's ethic of tolerance and pluralism. Some are embracing social gospels, either of the right (some megachurches) or of the left (many emergent churches). This is to say, these evangelical churches are becoming more and more like the liberal churches.

The Persistence of Orthodox Faith

For all of this secularization from without and from within, there are still legions of orthodox, biblical, faithful Christians. They can be found in untold numbers of faithful congregations—some *mega-*, some *micro-*, some thriving, some unfairly dismissed as dying—from various theological traditions. They can even be found in secularist Europe, and their numbers are exploding in what were once the mission fields in developing countries that have now become leaders in global Christianity. Indeed, as Christ promised, "the gates of hell shall not prevail" against his church, let alone cultural trends. This is because, as he says, "I will build my church" (Matt. 16:18).

Researcher Ed Stetzer, whom we cited regarding nominals becoming nones, has found that of the 75 percent or so of Americans who identify as Christians, about 25 percent are "robust" believers; that is, they are "convictional" Christians. That comes to almost 19 percent of all Americans. Stetzer distinguishes them from "cultural Christians," whose religion is tied up with their cultural identify, and "congregational Christians," who hold church membership but rarely attend. The convictional Christians are Christians out of conviction. They are highly committed to their faith, practice it in their lives, and are in church virtually every Sunday. *The percentage of convictional Christians, Stetzer says, has held steady over the years.* The percentage of Protestants who attend church regularly has declined only slightly, from 23 percent to 20 percent, over the last forty years.[24]

Furthermore, Christianity in America is becoming more and more evangelical—that is, committed to the gospel and to the Bible. In 2007, the year of the previous Pew religious landscape study, 44 percent of American Christians identified as "evangelical." In 2014, the year of the next Pew study, that number rose to 50 percent, half of all American Christians. In hard numbers, in 2007 there were 59.9 million evangelicals in America; in 2014 there were 62.2 million. Stetzer quotes the Pew report: "The evangelical Protestant tradition is the only major Christian group in the survey that has gained more members than it has lost through religious switching."[25]

Evangelicals are also holding on to their members better than other religious groups. Of those who were raised evangelical, 65 percent remain so. (Of those who left, 16 percent switched to another Christian tradition, meaning that 81 percent are still in the Christian camp. Of the others, 3 percent changed religions, and 15 percent became nones.) Among millennials, 21 percent are evangelicals, a number that did not change from 2007 to 2014. In fact, except for the World War II "greatest generation," which is dying out, the rate of evangelicals in all of the generational categories has held steady. "Within Christianity," says Stetzer, "the only group retaining more of their population than the evangelical church is the historically black church."[26]

These statistics demonstrate the persistence of conservative Christianity in our supposedly secularist, post-Christian world. And yet they do not make a case for complacency. Not all of the evangelicals

---

24. Ed Stetzer, "No, American Christianity Is Not Dead," CNN, May 16, 2015, accessed June 11, 2019, https://www.cnn.com/2015/05/16/living/christianity-american-dead/index.html.

25. Stetzer, "Nominals to Nones."

26. Stetzer, "Nominals to Nones." The percentage of evangelicals among the Greatest Generation declined from 28 percent to 25 percent.

belong to the category of "robust" believers. And believers in the prosperity gospel or some version of the social gospel are doubtless robust and convictional in their false beliefs. A 65 percent retention rate may be better than that of other groups, but still nearly one in five young people (18 percent) from evangelical homes are leaving the Christian faith. And there remains the vexing problem, so imperative for evangelicals at least, of evangelizing the nonbelievers, who seem increasingly resistant to the Christian message.

What seems to be happening, though, is a refining of the church.[27] The nominal believers are leaving. There is no longer a cultural pressure to be in church, so those who used to attend out of a desire to be socially respectable are no longer bothering. Those with a liberal theology are leaving, reasoning that if the world sets the agenda for the church, they need attend only to the world. Increasingly, the only ones left in churches are the true believers. Such defections, ironically, strengthen the church. Just as the refining process burns away the dross to extract the precious metal, the hostility of secularism is purifying the church.

Desecularizing the Church

If the United States and Europe are becoming post-Christian, the rest of the world is rushing into Christianity. North America has some 286 million believers as of 2010, but there are far more in Latin America (544 million), Africa (493 million), and Asia (352 million). By the year 2050, says religion scholar Philip Jenkins, at the current rate of growth, Christianity will have 3.2 billion adherents, only one-fifth of whom will be non-Hispanic whites. "Soon the phrase 'a White Christian' may sound like a curious oxymoron," he says, "as mildly surprising as 'a Swedish Buddhist.'"[28]

And this global Christianity is not of the liberal, progressive, secularizing-from-within variety. "Africa has never had an Enlightenment," observes Peter Leithart. "There is no African Hume, with his rejection of miracles; no African Strauss, with his 'mythological' in-

---

27. See Stetzer, "Nominals to Nones."

28. Philip Jenkins, *The Next Christendom: The Coming of Global Christianity*, 3rd ed. (New York: Oxford University Press, 2011), 2–3.

terpretation of the gospels; no African Descartes or Spinoza or Kant or Galileo or Newton."[29]

Africans have a special devotion to the Bible. The catalyst for church growth—conversions, revival, explosive expansion of the gospel—is often when a tribe, thanks to Bible-translating missionaries, first hears the Word of God in their own language. Leithart quotes Kenyan theologian John Mbiti:

> When the translation is first published, especially that of the New Testament and more so of the whole Bible, the church in that particular language area experiences its own Pentecost. The church is born afresh, it receives the Pentecostal tongues of fire. As in Acts 2, the local Christians now for the first time "hear each of us in his own language. . . . We hear them telling in our own tongues the mighty works of God" (Acts 2:6–11). The Spirit of God unlocks ears and people to the Word of God, speaking to them in its most persuasive form. Local Christians cannot remain the same after that.[30]

Africans are far closer to the world of the Bible than we moderns and postmoderns. Observes Leithart, "Africans are not the least embarrassed by the world picture of the Bible—a world of angels and demons, of miracles and exorcisms, of virgin births and life after death, of heaven and hell. It's their world. Africans know what idols are because they've seen them. They see and hear things in the text that are lost to jaded post-Christian readers in the North."[31] For example, parts of Scripture that are puzzling to modern Western readers and are usually skipped over—genealogies, distinctions between clean and unclean, sacrificial rites—are full of meaning in Africa. According to Leithart, Africans "are not content to read the Bible as a source of doctrine, or an account of ancient history, or even as a practical manual that tells them what to do. For African believers, the Bible is a book to inhabit, a narrative to participate in. They recognize that they are part of the story the Bible tells."[32]

---

29. Peter Leithart, "What Africa Can Teach the North," *Leithart* website, November 1, 2018, accessed June 11, 2019, https://www.patheos.com/blogs/leithart/2018/11/what-africa-can-teach -the-north/.
30. Leithart, "What Africa Can Teach the North."
31. Leithart, "What Africa Can Teach the North."
32. Leithart, "What Africa Can Teach the North."

To be sure, African Christianity has its problems. The prosperity gospel, a Western import, is rampant, as might be expected among Christians who are poor. (A Nigerian friend told me that converts to Christianity often do become more prosperous; due to the impact of their new faith on their lives, as vocation gives them a new way of looking at work, they are freed from limiting superstitions, and they become more open to Western technology.) Sometimes Christianity becomes entangled with animism, though Leithart says this problem is diminishing as African theology matures. Some indigenous theologies are problematic, though churches from virtually all of the Western theological traditions are also booming—Pentecostalism, which is very widespread; but also Reformed, Baptist, Methodist, Anglican, Lutheran, Catholic, Orthodox, as well as evangelicals of all flavors. Christianity is also competing with Islam, including its most radical factions. Christians often encounter persecution and even experience martyrdom at the hands of Muslims.

Africa's other problems are also problems for its church. Genocidal tribal feuds still break out, such as the atrocities in Rwanda, with Christians on both sides. Poverty is crushing. Government is often corrupt and authoritarian. Nations are torn by civil wars. Human rights are often ignored. It is one thing to oppose homosexuality, as African Christians steadfastly do, but in thirty-four out of fifty-four African countries, homosexual behavior is criminalized (as it was in the West until recently), receiving the death penalty in certain Islamic areas.[33] AIDS has killed 15 million Africans, mostly through heterosexual transmission as compounded by widespread prostitution and sexual immorality.[34] With the frequent lack of modern medicine, Africa is also plagued by other dread diseases, such as malaria and ebola.

Africa is improving, however, with many nations experiencing dramatic economic growth and improved living conditions. Christianity is arguably an important factor. My Nigerian friend told me that when Christians come to a region, they first build schools and hospitals.

---

33. See "LGBT Rights in Africa," Wikipedia, accessed June 11, 2019, https://en.wikipedia .org/wiki/LGBT_rights_in_Africa. The areas that apply the death penalty are in Sudan, southern Somalia, Somaliland, Mauritania, and northern Nigeria.

34. See "HIV/AIDS in Africa," Wikipedia, accessed June 11, 2019, https://en.wikipedia.org /wiki/HIV/AIDS_in_Africa#Causes_and_spread.

When the Muslims come, they try to take over the government. At any rate, the Christian-built schools and hospitals have been bringing education and modern health care to Africans. Christianity's modernizing influences, in the good sense, also include improving the treatment of women. One can expect Christianity to exert an increasingly beneficial cultural influence as it did in Europe, where the church transformed similar tribal societies—the Celts, the Germans, the Vikings—and laid a foundation for human rights and liberties.

For all of its problems, the church in Africa has much to teach the Western churches that sent them missionaries to proclaim the gospel and translate the Scriptures. As Peter Leithart concludes,

> Many African Christians have suffered intensely for the faith. Most live in conditions Americans would tolerate for about seven minutes. They have much to teach us about the cross, about contentment and joy in deprivation, about sacrifice and firmness in the face of pressure. African Christians can also teach us theology. African theologians are still often trained in the North, but they are blessedly free from Northern pathologies. African theology has the makings of an antidote.[35]

Indeed, the African churches, as well as their counterparts elsewhere in the developing world, have already been working to desecularize the Western churches.

This has been most dramatic in the churches of mainline Protestantism. African churches have become truly indigenous, no longer under the control of the Western churches and missionary organizations that first brought them the gospel. However, for the most part, they retain their theological moorings in the missionary-sending churches. There are now far more Anglicans in Africa and the various developing nations that once comprised the British empire than there are in England, where the state church has become increasingly liberal and thus marginalized. Similarly, in the United States, the Episcopal Church (USA), despite its rich liturgy, has become one of the most liberal of American denominations. But when worldwide Anglicanism met for its regular international conference at Lambeth in

---

35. Leithart, "What Africa Can Teach the North."

1998, measures that would liberalize church teachings about sexual morality, particularly in regard to homosexuality, were voted down decisively by global Anglicans. Recently, the Anglicans in the developing world have started their own organization: the Global Anglican Future Conference (GAFCON), which is working to bring the entire communion back to orthodoxy. For example, the group has recognized the conservative breakaway Anglican Church of North America (ACNA) as the true representative of American Anglicanism in place of the Episcopal Church (USA)![36]

Similarly, African Methodists have been thwarting efforts in the US United Methodist Church to accept same-sex marriage, ordain practicing homosexuals, and other innovations. With their votes in the quadrennial general conference, which sets policies for Methodism, African Methodists are exercising authority over the ecclesiastical liberals. A reporter at a recent general conference captured the exasperation of an African delegate, Reverend Jerry Kulah, a seminary dean from Liberia, who expressed gratitude for nineteenth-century Methodist missionaries, but then said, "The church has taken on strangely a new direction. People from the country that brought the Gospel to us are now preaching a different Gospel."

> It's mind-boggling, and it baffles the Christian leader from Africa—I speak for all of Africa—it baffles the mind of the Christian leader from Africa, who ascribes to the whole Bible as his or her primary authority for faith and practice, to see and to hear that cultural Christianity can take the place of the Bible. United Methodists in America and other parts of the world are going far away from Scripture and giving in to cultural Christianity.[37]

Such resistance is to the consternation of Western liberal theologians—whose social gospel praises multiculturalism, denounces Western colonialism, and lauds racial diversity—but who now find themselves as a beleaguered white minority in opposition to black Africans.

---

36. Jacob Lupfer, "As Episcopalians Meet, Debate Looms about Their Place in the Anglican World," *Religious News Service*, July 5, 2018, accessed June 11, 2019, https://religionnews.com /2018/07/05/as-episcopalians-meet-debate-looms-about-their-place-in-the-anglican-world/.

37. Emily McFarlan Miller, "African Methodists Worry about the Church That Brought Them Christianity," *Religious News Service*, May 20, 2016, accessed June 11, 2019, https://religionnews .com/2016/05/20/african-methodists-worry-about-the-church-that-brought-them-christianity/.

Most people associate Lutheranism—which is my tradition—with Germany, Scandinavia, and the United States. Germany indeed has the most Lutherans (11,440,694), but number two is Ethiopia (7,886,595) and number three is Tanzania (6,531,336). The United States has somewhere over 6 million Lutherans, counting both the liberal and the conservative branches. Indonesia has 5,552,491; India has 4,081,787; Madagascar has 4,000,000; Nigeria has 2,321,000; Papua New Guinea has 1,349,869; Namibia has 1,238,695.[38] Lutheranism is no longer a northern European phenomenon.

These global Lutherans are asserting themselves against the liberal Lutherans of the European state churches and the American mainline. The Lutheran church of Tanzania, numerous yet poor, is refusing to accept any aid from a church body that accepts same-sex marriage.[39] Ethiopia's vast and fast-growing Lutheran church, known as Mekane Yesus ("place of Jesus," reflecting the Lutheran theology of presence), has stopped fellowship with the Church of Sweden and the mainline Evangelical Lutheran Church in America, forming partnerships instead with conservative, confessional bodies such as the Lutheran Church–Missouri Synod. And, in the most audacious example, Bishop Walter Obare, of the Lutheran Church of Kenya, has gone to Sweden, whose missionaries first brought Lutheran Christianity to his country, to ordain theologically conservative bishops and pastors, thus creating an orthodox church body as an alternative to the state church! This new church, in turn, has been ordaining conservative clergy and starting orthodox congregations throughout the Scandinavian countries. Bishop Obare denounced the state church of Sweden, which had been punishing conservative pastors, as practicing "a secular, intolerant, bureaucratic fundamentalism inimical to the Word of God and familiar from various church struggles against totalitarian ideologies during the twentieth century." He called the ordination of women,

---

38. See "Lutheranism by Region," Wikipedia, accessed June 11, 2019, https://en.wikipedia.org/wiki/Lutheranism_by_region. These numbers are from the Lutheran World Federation, which includes for the United States the mainline Evangelical Lutheran Church in America (3.5 million), but not the conservative Lutheran denominations, such as the Lutheran Church–Missouri Synod (2 million), the Wisconsin Evangelical Lutheran Synod (600,000), and other smaller denominations. In the Scandinavian countries, Sweden has 6,116,480; Denmark has 4,361,518; Finland has 3,950,000; Norway has 3,762,400. These numbers for the European state churches represent formal affiliation, not attendance or adherence.

39. See Jenkins, *The Next Christendom*, 257.

which the state church was requiring pastors to accept, a "Gnostic novelty," which "cannot tolerate even minimal coexistence with classical Christianity."[40]

The supernaturalism of global Christianity is also influencing conservative churches in the West. Pope Francis is considered to be a liberal in Catholic circles, but as a cleric from Argentina, he has had firsthand experience with ministering to those seemingly afflicted by demonic possession. Now, as we have seen, exorcism is back in vogue in the West. The Lutheran exorcist we discussed in chapter 11, Dr. Robert Bennett, had been skeptical of the whole topic, but in a visit to Madagascar he learned that the Lutheran church there—one of the world's fastest growing—practiced an extensive ministry of casting out evil spirits, familiar in animistic religions, in the name of Christ. Having witnessed numerous exorcisms in Madagascar, he brought back to the United States and to the Lutheran Church–Missouri Synod an awareness of evil spiritual afflictions and how to deal with them.[41] He learned this from Africa.

And if African Christianity can help desecularize the West, the same can be said of the house churches of China, where Christianity is rapidly expanding despite intense persecution from the still-Communist government. (And where Calvinism is taking hold in the elite universities.[42]) The same can also be said about the churches of Indonesia, where Christianity is growing despite intense harassment in the world's most populous Muslim nation; about the churches in Russia and the former communist countries of Eastern Europe; about the surging, vital churches of Korea, with their exuberant heart for missions; and about the evangelical revival in Latin America. And lest we fall into the fallacy of valuing the large over the small, Western Christians can also learn from places where the number of Christians is small but all the more faithful: the Christians of the Middle East,

40. Jenkins, *The Next Christendom*, 257.

41. See Robert H. Bennett, *I Am Not Afraid: Demon Possession and Spiritual Warfare* (St. Louis, MO: Concordia, 2013), which tells about exorcism in the Madagascar church; and *Afraid: Demon Possession and Spiritual Warfare* (St. Louis, MO: Concordia, 2016), which tells about the phenomenon in the United States.

42. Andrew Brown, "Chinese Calvinism Flourishes," *Guardian*, May 27, 2009, accessed June 11, 2019, https://www.theguardian.com/commentisfree/andrewbrown/2009/may/27/china-calvin -christianity.

who are losing their homes, their livelihoods, and sometimes their lives on account of their faith; the Christian martyrs beheaded by ISIS jihadists; the Coptic Christians of Egypt who boldly tattoo crosses on their arms to differentiate themselves publicly from their often hostile Muslim neighbors; and the Christians of Japan, many of whom first investigated Christianity because of their love for Bach or gospel music.

In this vast sea of faith, Americans and Europeans occupy a small island of secularism, like teenagers fixated on their cell phones, oblivious to what is happening all around them. It turns out that this is not a post-Christian world after all.

Conclusion

Toward the Postsecular

So scholars no longer accept the "secular hypothesis," the assumption that as a society becomes more modern, it becomes less religious. The global religious explosion—which is happening not only among Christians but also among Muslims, Buddhists, and Hindus—proves that. Now we are seeing that the secular hypothesis does not even apply to secularists, that the nones of the United States and Western Europe are not predominantly scientific naturalists, but rather have private spiritualities and religious worldviews of their own. And the extraordinary growth of global Christianity, not as Western impositions but as fully fledged indigenous movements, demonstrates that the world is far from being post-Christian.

This has given rise to a new term that is gaining currency among scholars in multiple fields. It is another *post-* word. Not *postmodern*. Not *post-Christian*. But *postsecular*. What is emerging or is already upon us is a postsecular culture.

The Postsecular Society

Jürgen Habermas is an acclaimed contemporary thinker—"the most important German philosopher of the second half of the 20th century";[1] "one of the most influential philosophers in the world."[2]

---

1. Martin Beck Matustik, "Jürgen Habermas," *Encyclopedia Britannica*, accessed June 11, 2019, https://www.britannica.com/biography/Jurgen-Habermas.

2. James Bohman and William Rehg, "Jürgen Habermas," *Stanford Encyclopedia of Philosophy* (Fall 2017), accessed June 11, 2019, https://plato.stanford.edu/archives/fall2017/entries/habermas.

A leftist and member of the Frankfurt School, the incubator of post-Marxism, Habermas is in the orbit of the postmodernist thinkers and critical theorists. But later in his life, Habermas began to temper his political radicalism and began to question his postmodernist peers. He held debates with Jacques Derrida, arguing that his practice of "deconstruction" made social critiques impossible, and with Michel Foucault, questioning his reductionism of culture to issues of power.

Habermas recognized the need for universal moral principles, as opposed to postmodernist relativism, and sought a basis for liberty, democracy, and a just society. He wanted to preserve the best parts of the Enlightenment legacy by rehabilitating reason against the postmodernist critiques. He developed the notion of "communicative rationality," which interprets reason in terms of *language*. (Sound familiar? Habermas was influenced by J. G. Hamann.[3]) In his formulation, reason and reasoning are means by which human beings arrive at *understanding*; not just understanding of the world but understanding of each other. The capacity of language to create this mutual understanding creates a sense of intersubjectivity—a shared internal experience—that, along with a consensus about objective truth that reasoning brings about, can make culture, morality, freedom, and a more humane society possible.

Still later in life, Habermas abandoned his earlier dismissal of religion and explored its positive role in philosophy, politics, and culture. This led to a dialogue between Habermas and Joseph Ratzinger, who a year later would become Pope Benedict XVI.[4] Before that, Habermas made a remarkable assertion:

> For the normative self-understanding of modernity, Christianity has functioned as more than just a precursor or catalyst. Universalistic egalitarianism, from which sprang the ideals of freedom and a collective life in solidarity, the autonomous conduct of life and emancipation, the individual morality of conscience, human rights and democracy, is the direct legacy of the Judaic ethic of justice and

---

3. See Michaël Foessel and Jürgen Habermas, "Critique and Communication: Philosophy's Missions, A Conversation with Jürgen Habermas," *Eurozine*, October 16, 2015, accessed June 11, 2019, https://www.eurozine.com/critique-and-communication-philosophys-missions/.

4. Their discussions were published in Jürgen Habermas and Joseph Ratzinger, *The Dialectics of Secularization: On Reason and Religion* (San Francisco: Ignatius Press, 2006).

the Christian ethic of love. This legacy, substantially unchanged, has been the object of a continual critical reappropriation and reinterpretation. Up to this very day there is no alternative to it. And in light of the current challenges of a post-national constellation, we must draw sustenance now, as in the past, from this substance. Everything else is idle postmodern talk.[5]

"The Judaic ethic of justice and the Christian ethic of love"! Deconstruct everything else, but these two biblical principles have to remain! Otherwise there can be no freedom, rights, or democracy. Without the ethic of justice and the ethic of love, *all* the diverse efforts to improve society—Marxist, post-Marxist, social democratic, liberal, conservative, Democratic, Republican—dissolve. And "up to this very day there is no alternative" to these religiously grounded imperatives of justice and love. "We must draw sustenance now"—in these allegedly secularist, post-Christian times—"as in the past, from this substance."

This is not Christian, as such. Christianity begins with our *failure* to be just, our refusal to love. Christianity has to do, above all, with our encounter with the justice of God and the love of God, which come together in the cross of Jesus Christ. But Habermas's statement has a profound insight, a recognition of the enduring social impact of the Bible and of the unacknowledged and necessary influence of Christianity even upon the secularists.

A true post-Christian secularism would repudiate not just Christian theology but also Christian ethics. And yet almost no one wants to do that. The "Judaic ethic of justice" and the "Christian ethic of love" cannot be found apart from the biblical worldview; not in the ancient Greeks, Romans, or Germanic tribes;[6] and certainly not in the survival-of-the-fittest, nature-red-in-tooth-and-claw ethic of Darwinism. The New Atheists actually *appeal* to justice and love in their

---

5. Jürgen Habermas, "A Conversation about God and the World: Interview with Eduardo Mendieta," in *Religion and Rationality: Essays on Reason, God, and Modernity*, ed. Eduardo Mendieta (Cambridge, MA: MIT Press, 2002) 148–49.

6. Aristotle tied pity to whether or not its object deserves to suffer. See *Aristotle's Rhetoric*, book 2, part 8, Internet Classics Archive, accessed June 11, 2019, http://classics.mit.edu/Aristotle /rhetoric.2.ii.html. See also the discussion by Amod Lele, "Is Compassion a Virtue?," *Love of All Wisdom: Philosophy through Multiple Traditions* website, March 20, 2011, accessed June 11, 2019, http://loveofallwisdom.com/blog/2011/03/is-compassion-a-virtue/. She shows that for the Stoics, compassion is a type of suffering that should be avoided. She also relates today's sense of compassion as a virtue to the Christian ethic.

arguments against Christianity and the existence of God. The more consistent, full-blooded atheists like Nietzsche and Ayn Rand *do reject* Christian ethics, contending that the Christian doctrine of love guilts the strong into serving the weak, imposing an altruism that shackles human pride and that keeps alive the unfit who should perish for the good of the species.[7] But most people today, including most secularists, draw back from those conclusions, wanting to hold on to principles such as kindness, compassion, and mercy. Certainly one can hold to and practice these moral imperatives without being a Christian, but those who do so are holding on to particular Christian beliefs, whether they realize that or not.

Habermas sees the emergence of what he calls a "post-secular society."[8] In coining the term, *post-secular*, Habermas recognizes that in the contemporary world, the secular and the religious exist side by side. He calls for a dialogue between the two—in his sense of communication that results in mutual understanding—with each side learning from the other.

In a paper entitled "An Awareness of What Is Missing," Habermas says that secularism, by itself, cannot sustain a humane society.[9] Secular science has great power, but it has no mechanism within itself for questioning how it experiments or what it produces. (Habermas is concerned about the misuse of technology, especially biotechnology.) Secular morality at its best is individualistic, but societies need "collectively binding ideals" that create a sense of "solidarity" with other people. Secular society, having lost "its grip on the images, preserved by religion, of the moral whole," has a "motivational weakness," that is, an inability to inspire. "Postmetaphysical thinking," he says, "cannot cope on its own with the defeatism concerning reason which we encounter today both in the postmodern radicalization of the 'dialectic

---

7. See, e.g., Friedrich Nietzsche, *On the Genealogy of Morals* (New York: Penguin, 2014); and Ayn Rand, *The Virtue of Selfishness* (New York: Signet, 1964).

8. Jürgen Habermas, "Notes on Post-Secular Society," *New Perspectives Quarterly* 25 (2008): 17–29, http://www.signandsight.com/features/1714.html. This article is valuable not only for setting forth Habermas's ideas about the "post-secular," but for its account of the "secular hypothesis" and why it is being abandoned.

9. Jürgen Habermas et al., *An Awareness of What Is Missing: Faith and Reason in a Post-Secular Age* (Malden, MA: Polity Press, 2010), 15–23. The paper was part of a symposium on his thought at the Jesuit School for Philosophy in Munich, with various Catholic philosophers responding.

of the Enlightenment' and in the naturalism founded on a naïve faith in science."[10] According to Habermas, "Among the modern societies, only those that are able to introduce into the secular domain the essential contents of their religious traditions which point beyond the merely human realm will also be able to rescue the substance of the human."[11]

Habermas proposes guidelines for how the two realms, the secular and the religious, should relate to each other:

> The religious side must accept the authority of "natural" reason as the fallible results of the institutionalized sciences and the basic principles of universalistic egalitarianism in law and morality. Conversely, secular reason may not set itself up as the judge concerning truths of faith, even though in the end it can accept as reasonable only what it can translate into its own, in principle universally accessible, discourses.[12]

To participate in secular society, religious people must accept the authority of reason and science (though Habermas admits they are fallible) in the secular sphere. They must also accept the legal and moral egalitarianism that is the legacy of post-Enlightenment governments. At the same time, those who are secular should not presume to judge the truths of faith held by those who are religious. Religious believers may put forward their convictions in the public square—for example, that abortion is evil—but those convictions must be translated from the realm of religion (the Bible tells me so) into the language of Enlightenment liberalism (abortion violates the rights of the unborn child).

In trying to work out how the religious and the secular can function together in one unified democratic society, Habermas is thinking primarily of the throngs of Muslim immigrants who have been pouring into Western Europe. As a left-leaning citizen of Germany and a supporter of the European Union, he feels sympathy for them and regrets their mistreatment by some of his fellow secularists. He

---

10. Habermas et al. *An Awareness of What Is Missing*, 18.
11. Habermas et al. *An Awareness of What Is Missing*, 5.
12. Habermas et al. *An Awareness of What Is Missing*, 16.

recognizes the danger of violence from Islamic fundamentalism, but he is also concerned about violence against Muslims, as in the Iraq War, which he opposed. Taking seriously the concept of multiculturalism (unlike some postmoderns who use it only as a pretext for relativism), Habermas is trying to find a formula for peace, tolerance, and assimilation. Philosophically and historically, he is engaging Christianity, but politically he is struggling with the vexing question of how a Western democracy can accommodate Islam, and vice versa.[13]

We might think he is too sanguine about Islam and the effect of Islamic immigration in Europe. Certainly, Christianity has little problem in accepting "the basic principles of universalistic egalitarianism in law and morality" and the other elements of Western democracy, such as human rights, individual liberty, and the rule of law. After all, Christianity helped give rise to these ideals, arguably more so than the Enlightenment thinkers to whom secularists usually give the credit. Accepting such ideas and practices is surely more difficult for Islam, which has an overriding mission of establishing the Sharia law of the Qur'an over all the earth.

Habermas wants the two, the religious and the secular, to stay in their own lanes. But if they do, with religion deferring to the authority of science and politics, how can religion give secularists what is missing? Jesuit philosophers responding to his "An Awareness of What Is Missing" paper said that he was trying to "instrumentalize" religion—that is, use religion for secular purposes—and that he is not giving religion its due as a source of authority in itself.[14] I would add that Habermas also frames his discussion in terms of the opposition between faith and reason. In doing so, he overestimates the role of reason in today's secular circles, even as he acknowledges "the defeatism concerning reason" in postmodernism and scientism. And he underestimates the role of reason in religion, as if he were unaware of the scholastic tradition in both Catholic and Protestant circles. As

---

13. See Jürgen Habermas, *Between Naturalism and Religion* (Malden, MA: Polity Press, 2008).

14. See the other essays in Habermas, *An Awareness of What Is Missing.* Stanley Fish is an important postmodernist thinker who has also become a defender of religion. In fact, he says that Habermas does not go nearly far enough in urging an accommodation between the secular and the religious. See his review of *An Awareness of What Is Missing*: Stanley Fish, "Does Reason Know What It Is Missing?," *New York Times*, April 12, 2010, accessed June 11, 2019, https://opinion ator.blogs.nytimes.com/2010/04/12/does-reason-know-what-it-is-missing/.

Hamann observed, "Faith has need of reason just as much as reason needs faith."[15]

Nevertheless, despite problems and limitations of his approach, Habermas has opened doors—in academia, politics, and culture—that Christians can walk through.

Meanwhile, his concept of a postsecular society has been adopted and is being developed in the fields of sociology, political theory, education, philosophy, literature, and the arts.[16] Scholars are bolstering the idea with further research and an abundance of evidence, speaking of a "post-secular turn" in philosophy and even in feminism.[17] And, as we have seen, the magisterial treatment of the newly rediscovered thinker we have been drawing upon has the subtitle *The Post-Secular Vision of J. G. Hamann.*[18]

Postsecular Paganism

We need to realize that a postsecular society may still be post-Christian. We may be seeing a reversion to the religiosity that is natural to fallen human beings, that is, to a new pagan order.

Some observers are seeing the emergence of a new cultural religion that is distinctly pre-Christian, a return to the worldview that pervaded the West until the advent of Christianity. In his review of Steven D. Smith's *Pagans and Christians*, which advances this thesis, *New York Times* columnist Ross Douthat, a Catholic, describes what this may look like. Pagan religion, he says, believes "that divinity is fundamentally inside the world rather than outside it, that God or the gods or Being are ultimately part of nature rather than an external creator, and that meaning and morality and metaphysical experience are

---

15. Quoted from a letter to F. H. Jacobi, in John Betz, *After Enlightenment: The Post-Secular Vision of J. G. Hamann* (Malden, MA: Wiley-Blackwell, 2012), 253. Hamann believed that separating faith from reason, which is foundational to modernity, has the ultimate effect of undermining reason and leading to nihilism (Betz, *After Enlightenment*, 238).

16. See "Postsecularism," Wikipedia, particularly its references and the bibliography, which cite research from the different fields; accessed June 11, 2019, https://en.wikipedia.org/wiki/Post secularism.

17. For a good survey of the concept across various disciplines, see Michael Staudigl and Jason W. Alvis, "Phenomenology and the Post-secular Turn: Reconsidering the 'Return of the Religious,'" *International Journal of Philosophical Studies* 24 (2016): 589–99, https://www.tandf online.com/doi/full/10.1080/09672559.2016.1259917. This article is an introduction to the journal's special issue on the postsecular. For postsecular feminism, see Rosi Braidotti, "In Spite of the Times: The Postsecular Turn in Feminism," *Theory, Culture and Society* 25 (2008): 1–24.

18. Betz, *After Enlightenment*.

to be sought in a fuller communion with the immanent world rather than a leap toward the transcendent."[19] Douthat sees this worldview in people today who are "spiritual, but not religious":

> This paganism is not materialist or atheistic; it allows for belief in spiritual and supernatural realities. It even accepts the possibility of an afterlife. But it is deliberately agnostic about final things, what awaits beyond the shores of this world, and it is skeptical of the idea that there exists some ascetic, world-denying moral standard to which we should aspire. Instead, it sees the purpose of religion and spirituality as more therapeutic, a means of seeking harmony with nature and happiness in the everyday—while unlike atheism, it insists that this everyday is divinely endowed and shaped, meaningful and not random, a place where we can truly hope to be at home.[20]

Douthat cites another feature of paganism, seen in the Greek city-states and the Roman Empire, as a civil religion that "makes religious and political duties identical, and treats the city of man as the city of God (or the gods)."[21]

We are not quite there, Douthat says. He notes that paganism of the old style requires public ritual and prayer, something that the current pagan religiosity does not have, at least not yet. (C. S. Lewis responded to the notion that we are relapsing into paganism by saying, "It would be pleasant to see some future Prime Minister trying to kill a large and lively milk-white bull in Westminster Hall."[22])

I would add that paganism of this type also requires actual gods, which have not yet emerged. Perhaps, though, this will happen

---

19. Ross Douthat, "The Return of Paganism," *New York Times*, December 12, 2018, accessed June 11, 2019, https://www.nytimes.com/2018/12/12/opinion/christianity-paganism-america.html ?rref=collection%2Ftimestopic%2FReligion%20and%20Belief&action=click&contentCollection =timestopics&region=stream&module=stream_unit&version=latest&contentPlacement=2& pgtype=. He is discussing Steven D. Smith, *Pagans and Christians: Culture Wars from the Tiber to the Potomac* (Grand Rapids, MI: Eerdmans, 2018).
20. Douthat, "The Return of Paganism."
21. Douthat, "The Return of Paganism."
22. C. S. Lewis, "De Descriptione Temporum," *Selected Literary Essays* (Cambridge, UK: Cambridge University Press, 1969), 10. Lewis went on to say that "the historical process" does not allow for "mere reversal": "The post-Christian is cut off from the Christian past and therefore doubly from the Pagan past" (p. 10). For Lewis, "Christians and Pagans had much more in common with each other than either has with a post-Christian. The gap between those who worship different gods is not so wide as that between those who worship and those who do not" (p. 5).

through the process of syncretism, in which Jesus, Mohammed, Buddha, Krishna, and other figures of the world's faiths are venerated together. Actually, our exercises in civil religion today already do that, as in interfaith prayer services in times of national calamity. That does resemble what the Romans did—install in the Pantheon, the temple to all gods, the deities of each nation in the empire in order to instill a sense of imperial unity—so perhaps Douthat is not too far wrong when he projects new forms of civil religion.

I think, though, that Douthat's view exaggerates the acceptance of nature and the physical world among today's "spiritual-but-not-religious." As we have shown, today's spirituality is highly inward-looking and antiphysical, more akin to Gnosticism and Eastern religion than the nature religions of the Greeks, Romans, and animists. Today's spirituality is also highly privatized, which will make it difficult for a genuinely civic religion to emerge.

If it does, pagan societies tend to be quite different politically than Christian societies.[23] The rise of a divinized state would mean the end of liberties that both Christians and non-Christians have come to appreciate. And for Christians and those of other religions who would refuse to play along (such as Muslims), this would mean intense persecution.

But Douthat is surely right that the spirituality people today are looking for would be immanent, therapeutic, and affirming of everyday life. But, ironically, Christianity—moral standards and all—can address those concerns more fully than either the Greco-Roman brand of paganism or the interior-mystical variety. Christianity goes beyond any humanly constructed religion in being *both* transcendent *and* immanent. It worships a God who is *both* infinitely glorious beyond the heavens *and* who has become incarnate in Jesus Christ. It is otherworldly, offering an unimaginable eternal life, but Christianity also lauds God's physical creation and, in vocation, charges ordinary life with spiritual significance. Christianity is not about therapy, but it really can change people's lives and help them solve their problems. Christianity is not about politics, but it has provided the foundation

---

23. Yes, the Athenians had a democracy, and the Romans had a republic, but both were relatively short-lived, giving way to a more authoritarian empire under the cult of the god Alexander and the cult of the god Caesar.

for a free society and the rule of law, in sharp distinction to the god-kings and deified emperors of paganism.

There were lots of good reasons why Christianity displaced Greco-Roman paganism and why Christianity today is being exuberantly embraced by animists throughout the world. As Christians take on the task, once again, of evangelizing and educating postsecular pagans, they can highlight elements of their faith that most directly speak to postsecular concerns, while then proclaiming Christianity in its wholeness.

The Postsecular Church

If we are entering, or have already entered, a postsecular age, this is good news (mostly) for the church. But it does not mean that Christians can be complacent. After all, as we have said, churches and their teachings too have become secularized. Churches too must become postsecular.

The challenge was once trying to reach the scientific materialists of modernism. Then the challenge was trying to reach the relativists of postmodernism. Each were thought to require different approaches to evangelism, apologetics, and outreach. Though such worldviews are still to be found and Christians must adjust their witness accordingly, outreach in a postsecular context has different challenges.

The task is now how to reach people who hold false religions. They may hold to one of the world's major religions—Islam, Buddhism, Hinduism—all of which are also growing rapidly. Their adherents are increasingly visible here in America, due both to immigration from other lands and to their influence on postsecularists searching for spirituality. Most of those who hold false religions, though, may not even realize that they have a religion, but practice a spirituality that grows out of a private, self-made faith—perhaps a form of pagan mysticism, neoanimism, or some syncretic polytheism consisting of elements from all over (God, reincarnation, spirit guides, etc.). Many may even be Christian, at some level, in need of better theology and the pastoral care of a church.

Getting people to change their religion may go against the grain of postsecular tolerance, but it may actually be easier than getting through to materialists and relativists. Those whose worldview includes supernatural mysteries may be more open to hearing about those of Scripture. Indeed, Christianity has a high success rate evangelizing the heathen—the early church converting Greece and Rome, the Dark Ages saints like Patrick and Boniface preaching to Europe's pagan tribes, missionaries bringing the gospel to Africa and Asia, the indigenous evangelism of today's global Christianity.

If postsecular non-Christians are "spiritual but not religious," the church would do well to recover its own heritage of Christian spirituality. There are people who crave mystical experience and, not finding it in what they know of Christianity, go instead to Eastern religions or the New Age movement. The mystic quest is problematic and can lead a person astray—we do not ascend to God; he descends to us, in Christ. But there is much in all of the Christian traditions that can satisfy the need, perhaps most intense for those immersed in rationalism and materialism, for an encounter with what is mysterious, numinous, and supernatural. Such yearning leads some to the occult, but Christianity offers a sense of God's presence; the perception of holiness; the personal relationship (as we say) with Jesus Christ.

Nearly every Christian tradition offers resources on spirituality: Catholics have their Christian mystics, like Saint John of the Cross, and their monastic rules (such as, again, that of Saint Benedict). Anglicans have an abundance of profound devotional literature (such as John Donne's *Devotions Upon Emerging Occasions* and Jeremy Taylor's *Holy Living* and *Holy Dying*). The Puritans offer William Perkins, Thomas Watson, and Richard Sibbes. Baptists have Charles Spurgeon. Wesleyans, Pietists, and Calvinists have all contributed to the devotional and spiritual legacy of Protestantism.

Already, in this postsecular age, there are contemporary Christians who have been working to bring back long-neglected elements of historical Christian spirituality. The Quaker theologian Richard J. Foster and the evangelical philosopher Dallas Willard have been exploring the spiritual disciplines, as drawn from both Catholic and Protestant sources.[24] Foster lists the "inward disciplines" (prayer, fasting,

---

24. Richard J. Foster, *Celebration of Discipline* (New York: HarperCollins, 1978); and Dallas Willard, *The Spirit of the Disciplines* (New York: HarperCollins, 1988).

meditation, study); the "outward disciplines" (simplicity, solitude, submission, service); and the "corporate disciplines" (confession, worship, guidance, celebration).[25]

These can be helpful—it is interesting to learn that solitude is a spiritual discipline!—though the spiritually disciplined must take great care lest they come to think of the Christian life in terms of what they do rather than what Christ has done for them. Spiritual discipline and spirituality itself can become substitutes for Christ and the gospel. Luther, who fought those tendencies in medieval monasticism, promoted a gospel-centered, biblical piety whose pillars are prayer (*oratio*), meditation on the Word of God (*meditatio*), and trials (*tentatio*).[26] That latter term refers to the trials, tribulations, and temptations of life; the battle against sin, especially one's own; the Christian's conflict with the world, the flesh, and the devil; the struggles that cause faith to grow and that help a Christian to be sanctified.[27]

And yet the postsecular church will need to recover not just its spirituality but also its materiality. Though the postsecular public will be most interested in personal, inner spirituality—which Christianity indeed can supply them—they are also in need of a Christianity that can take them outside of themselves. They need to recover objective reality, that is, God's creation. And they need to recover what it means to belong to a community, that is, Christ's church.

Global Christianity, the kind that is growing so rapidly in this postsecular world, is highly supernatural, but it also tends to be, as Peter Leithart says of African Christianity, "world-affirming."[28] It has to do with eternal salvation but is also concerned for this life—for healing, for the crops to grow, for protection, for the reconciliation of enemies, for work—for the body as well as the spirit.

---

25. See Foster's table of contents. He goes on to write a chapter about each of these spiritual disciplines.

26. Martin Luther, *Career of the Reformer IV*, ed. Helmut Lehmann and Lewis Spitz, vol. 34, Luther's Works (Philadelphia: Fortress Press, 1999), 285–88. See John Piper's discussion, "Luther's Rules for How to Become a Theologian," *Desiring God* website, January 23, 1996, accessed June 11, 2019, https://www.desiringgod.org/articles/luthers-rules-for-how-to-become-a -theologian.

27. For a Lutheran take on spirituality, see John Kleinig, *Grace Upon Grace: Spirituality for Today* (St. Louis, MO: Concordia, 2008).

28. Peter Leithart, "What Africa Can Teach the North," *Leithart* website, November 1, 2018, accessed June 11, 2019, https://www.patheos.com/blogs/leithart/2018/11/what-africa-can-teach -the-north/.

Postsecular Christianity needs a theology of the body, as has been pointed out, so as to undo the harm caused by the sexual revolution and to be effectively pro-life. There is more to the doctrine of creation than opposing evolution (as important as that is). A theology of creation can restore the objectivity of truth and embrace the accomplishments of science without succumbing to what Habermas calls its "naïve" amorality. A theology of incarnation can bring God back to the awareness of confused secularists and postsecularists, who tend to think of him in abstract or moralistic-therapeutic-deistic terms. Instead, they can know him in Jesus Christ, who teaches with a compelling authority that is quite unlike merely human thinkers (Matt. 7:29), and whose life, death, and resurrection—all of which are physical and not just spiritual—redeem our own lives by his grace.

One way of communicating the connection between Christianity and the physical realm is by restoring the sacraments to their central role in Christian worship. I realize that different strains of Christianity have different teachings about them, but all Christian traditions have the Lord's Supper somewhere in their practices. I do not understand why the one observance explicitly commanded by Christ—"Do this in remembrance of me" (Luke 22:19)—has become so infrequent and perfunctory in many evangelical churches today. The Lord's Supper makes the gospel tangible: "This is my body *[not his spirit but his body]*, given for you" (Luke 22:19). "This is my blood of the covenant, which is poured out for many for the forgiveness of sins" (Matt. 26:28). Baptism too is about the saving work of Christ in our lives:

> Do you not know that all of us who have been baptized into Christ Jesus were baptized into his death? We were buried therefore with him by baptism into death, in order that, just as Christ was raised from the dead by the glory of the Father, we too might walk in newness of life. (Rom. 6:3–4)

Postsecular churches would also do well to restore worship, moving away from the model of putting on a show to the sense of coming into the presence of God—by hearing, preaching, teaching, and singing God's Word—to receive his gifts.

The postsecular church must somehow teach the isolated, solitary individuals of today how to be part of a corporate body, how to be part of a community. This should include the teaching of vocation— how God works through ordinary human beings in their families, churches, workplaces, and citizenship—which shows Christians how to take their faith outside the walls of their churches, making them salt and light in the world. All of this may go a long way toward restoring local communities, nations, and cultures.

So how can churches grow? Even if our society is postsecular, it is still post-Christian, and people are still hard to reach. Here is a suggestion: as we discussed in chapter 8, among the largest demographic of the unchurched is the white, rural, small-town, Rust Belt working class. A staffer in the Lutheran Church Missouri Synod who works in the office of rural and small-town ministry told me that about 60 percent of those who live in this "American heartland" are unchurched. Research shows that the middle and upper-middle class, who are college educated and affluent, go to church much more frequently than low-income folks with just a high school education or less. One study found that 32 percent of upper-middle-class whites aged thirty to forty-nine attend church regularly, compared to only 17 percent of that age group in the white working class.[29]

Most of the recent church growth efforts have targeted suburban families, college-educated urban millennials, and other denizens of the middle and upper-middle classes. But many of these, even if they are not presently churchgoers, will eventually come back to the church anyway. But churches, often being bastions of the middle class themselves, sometimes ignore the lower classes. Yet many of these folks are open to Christianity, to the point of considering themselves Christians. They need no particularly sophisticated apologetics approach, unlike postmodernist intellectuals. And they have pressing needs—low marriage rates, high suicide rates, drug addiction—that the church can respond to. The fields here are white unto harvest. But they have been

29. Cited in Charles Murray, "Five Myths about White People," *Washington Post*, February 10, 2012, accessed June 11, 2019, https://www.washingtonpost.com/opinions/five-myths-about -white-people/2012/01/20/gIQAmlu53Q_story.html?utm_term=.76f11caa2e10. See also W. Bradford Wilcox, et al., "No Money, No Honey, No Church: The Deinstitutionalization of Religious Life among the White Working Class," *Research in the Sociology of Work* 23 (2012): 227–50, https://www.ncbi.nlm.nih.gov/pmc/articles/PMC4315336/.

going unharvested. It may be that contemporary churches have tried too hard to be upwardly mobile. If churches would cease their often embarrassing efforts to be cool—which generally put off the people who are actually cool—and set their sights on those who need them most, they might be surprised how many souls they save.

American churches could thus learn a lesson from what is happening in the rest of the world. As the major chronicler of global Christianity, Philip Jenkins, has observed, "It is among the very poor that the churches have won some of their greatest victories."[30] He cites the dramatic growth of Christianity among the lower castes of India, including the "untouchable" Dalits; also the phenomenal growth of Pentecostalism among the most poverty-stricken in Latin America. But this is nothing new for the historic church, which spread among the slaves of the Roman Empire, the prisoners and slum dwellers who heard the Wesleyan preachers, the African slaves who heard the gospel in the depths of their oppression. Interestingly, the black working class in America today, though also suffering terribly and wracked with moral problems, is among the *most* churched demographic, with some of the highest allegiance to Scripture, thanks to the ministry of black churches, which have much to teach other post-secular congregations.[31]

Rebuilding the culture and restoring Christian influence is not necessarily accomplished from the top down—trying to insinuate ourselves into the cultural elite, which is where hostility to Christianity is the strongest. Rather, Christians can build from the bottom up, appealing to the socially marginalized, establishing strong families, cultivating a sense of community in their churches, permeating the larger society through their vocations, and being islands of reality in an ocean of confusion.

God Acts

Christians should not be discouraged, despite the seeming unreceptiveness of post-Christian society. Notice what has happened as modernism has given way to postmodernism, and how those two flavors of post-Christian secularism are turning toward postsecularism.

---

30. Philip Jenkins, *The Next Christendom: The Coming of Global Christianity*, 3rd ed. (New York: Oxford University Press, 2011), 95.
31. See "Religious Landscape Study," Pew Research Center, accessed June 11, 2019, http://www.pewforum.org/religious-landscape-study/racial-and-ethnic-composition/black/.

We began this book with the epigraph from Shakespeare about the Universal Wolf, which devours everything and then devours itself. Notice how a number of harmful ideas have been devouring themselves, clearing the way for Christianity. Multiculturalism was first a pretext for relativism but then turned into the imperative to acknowledge the reality of global Christianity. Postmodernism dismantled the authority of reason, unwittingly undoing the arguments against faith. Deconstruction demolished everything it could until nothing was left standing but "Judaic justice" and "Christian love."

Postsecularism has religion and secularism side by side, both learning from each other. But the Christian approach is to sacralize even secularism. Instead of seeing the religious and the secular as two separate, self-enclosed entities that are either hostile to each other or, at best, tolerate each other, Christians can fully participate in both realms. In their faith, God is revealed. In the world, God is hidden, but present nonetheless, providentially governing and caring for His entire creation, including those who do not know Him. God rules both realms, and Christians inhabit them both, by virtue of their faith and their vocations. They can face the trials and opportunities of the seemingly post-Christian world because they know God is in control and God will act.

Today, as we have said, the Scandinavian countries are seemingly among the most secularist in the world. Their churches are all but empty. But there is more to the story. Christianity has two tracks in Denmark, Norway, Sweden, and Finland: the state churches and the mission societies. In the nineteenth century, these nations were set on fire, spiritually, by the Pietist movement. This took place outside of the state churches, with the Pietists establishing mission societies and houses of prayer in nearly every community, which exist to this very day where Christians of strong evangelical faith meet in prayer and Bible study groups. Eventually, the Pietists and the state churches came to an accommodation: the churches would concentrate on worship and related functions. The mission societies would take on the various missions of the church. The Inner Mission societies would support ministry within the nation, including ministry to children, youth, soldiers, and the elderly; also service to the poor, and other kinds of social ministry. The Outer Mission societies pursued Christian ministry outside the nation, sending missionaries around the world. The Scandinavian Outer Mission societies were, in fact, responsible for starting many of the churches that are now part of the global Christianity phenomenon, including the Lutheran movement in Africa.

Today, scholars who study religion in Scandinavia note the emptiness of most state churches, but they neglect the lively faith found in the mission houses. A poll that finally asked the salient question, instead of just tabulating church attendance, asked Danes what they believe about Jesus. Twenty-five percent said that he is God's Son. And 18 percent said that he is their Savior.[32] Those numbers are pretty close to the percentage of "robust" believers in the United States.

These evangelicals do not attend the state churches much either—they are too liberal—but things are changing. In Denmark, any fifty citizens can form a congregation that must be recognized as a state church, with all of the financial benefits thereof. Members of the mission societies are forming biblically orthodox congregations. In all of the Scandinavian countries, Christians from mission-led youth groups are attending the university for training to be become pastors, supplementing the official liberal theological classes with lectures from orthodox scholars at the Bible Institutes, which the Inner Missions have established at every university campus. In Finland, the mission societies are gathering on Sundays (usually in the afternoon) for Word and sacrament ministries. And some have gone so far as to establish independent, confessionally faithful church bodies.

I have visited Denmark, Norway, and Finland at the behest of Inner Mission groups—speaking at the Scandinavian Youth Ministry convention in Oslo, lecturing at universities in Denmark, speaking to Inner Mission staff in Denmark, lecturing at an apologetics conference in Finland—and have been astonished at the strong, energetic faith that I was witnessing in these supposedly secularist nations. And I heard about something even more astonishing. In each country, I was hearing about the mass conversions of Muslims, who have always been the most resistant of all religions to the gospel. A Danish Inner Mission

---

32. Tobias Stern Johansen, "The Faith in Jesus as a Divine Savior Lives in the Best of the Danes," *Kristeligt Dagblad*, December 23, 2009, accessed June 11, 2019, https://www.kristeligt-dagblad.dk /kirke-tro/hver-fjerde-dansker-tror-p%C3%A5-jesus.

worker told me how, in her experience, three immigrants showed up at a Mission house on a Wednesday night asking about Jesus. The next week, ten showed up. Then twenty. Then so many that the house could hardly hold them all. This began to happen throughout Scandinavia.

A number of the Muslims had been given Bibles during their long and difficult immigration journey. Many reported dreams about Jesus, in which he directs them to a Mission house or a Bible-believing church. These are not the dreams of subjective spirituality. These are dreams like in the book of Acts, which directed Cornelius to seek out Peter so that he could hear the Word of God (Acts 10). The mission workers explain the gospel to these visitors and engage them in Bible study. Typically, these Muslims, or ex-Muslims, become overwhelmed to learn of the grace of God, and the good news of Christ—so different from the harsh judgment threatened by their old religion—fills them with peace and joy. Then the mission workers turn them over to an orthodox pastor for catechesis, baptism, and church membership.

But aren't these Muslims just trying to establish citizenship? How do we know they are really sincere? Well, the immigrants are told that if this is their purpose, they would do better *not* to become Christians, such is the attitude of the government officials, who sometimes make a point of deporting Christian converts. More immediately, these converts often suffer violence from Muslim radicals in the immigration camps and from their own families back home.

In Finland, where I was staying at an Inner Mission–sponsored Bible college, I met some of these Muslim converts, who had come in large numbers to study the Bible. I was told not to name them or photograph them, much less post the pictures on Facebook or my blog. In Germany— where Muslims are converting in especially large numbers—someone posted a photograph of a convert and gave his name. A relative from his homeland saw the information, traveled to Germany, and murdered the apostate. At the Finnish Bible College, the converts, many of whom wore crosses around their necks, were cheerful, friendly, and devout. Most of them were from Afghanistan. It turns out that the Finnish Outer Mission had sent missionaries to Afghanistan for years, with little to show for it. The effort ended a few years ago when several of the missionaries were killed. There is a plaque dedicated to those missionary martyrs in the chapel where we worshiped. But because of their work in that country, the Finnish Outer Mission has people who know the Afghan languages, which makes possible the Bible classes for these Afghan immigrants! A worker at the Bible College marveled at what God had done. "We worked for so long in Afghanistan. But now God is sending the Afghans here! In the very chapel where we honor the missionaries who died trying to bring the Gospel to Afghanistan, Afghans are being baptized!" A Danish mission worker told me, "We didn't go to the immigrants or do anything to reach them. But God is bringing them to us!"

The same thing is happening in Germany, France, England, and other secularist nations in Europe. The Muslims seeking to become Christians are not going to liberal congregations—indeed, some state churches have issued instructions not to proseletyze Muslims—but they are finding theologically conservative pastors, congregations, and laypeople to teach them about Jesus. German journalist Uwe Siemon-Netto, who has written an excellent article covering the phenomenon, quotes a Lutheran pastor who says that "Muslims are being sent to Catholics and Eastern Orthodox, to Copts, Anglicans, Lutherans, Baptists and Calvinist all of whom have one thing in common: They are bound by Scripture, not by the *Zeitgeist.*"[33]

These new Christians, unlike the habit of most Europeans, become regular churchgoers. Reverend Gottfried Martens is a pastor of the Independent Evangelical-Lutheran Church in Berlin who is playing a key role in this new evangelization of Muslims. His congregation has some fifteen hundred new members, mostly from Iran and Afghanistan, attending multiple services.[34] These new Christians are revitalizing the churches, reminding longtime members of the supernatural reality behind the faith that they had taken for granted and inspiring them to get involved with their church once again.

Christ builds his church. God acts. The succession of ages and movements are all in his hands—premodern, modern, postmodern, post-Christian, postsecular, and whatever will come next.

---

33. Uwe Siemon-Netto, "Where Muslim Dreams May Lead," *Quadrant,* January 1, 2016, accessed June 11, 2019, https://www.linkedin.com/pulse/where-muslim-dreams-may-lead-uwe -siemon-netto.

34. See Stephanie Parker, "An Evangelical Church in Berlin Is Overflowing with Iranian Converts," *FaithWire,* February 24, 2017, accessed June 11, 2019, https://www.faithwire.com/2017 /02/24/an-evangelical-church-in-berlin-is-overflowing-with-iranian-converts/.

General Index

Scripture Index